SARAH BEENY'S
100
DIY JOBS

THE ESSENTIALS MADE SIMPLE

'To my father, Richard, for inspiring me in all the things that ended up with me writing this book. Thank you for being great.'

Publishing Director: Jane O'Shea
Creative Director: Helen Lewis
Editor and Project Manager: Charlotte Coleman-Smith
Design and Art Direction: Dave Brown, Apeinc.co.uk
Research: Jenny Jacoby
Production Director: Vincent Smith
Production Controller: Leonie Kellman

Illustrators
Technical: Roy Cooper and Ian Moores
Individual tools and toolbox: Sister Arrow
Endpapers, jacket wallpaper and section headers: Rob Hunter

First published in 2014 by
Quadrille Publishing Limited
Alhambra House
27-31 Charing Cross Road
London WC2H 0LS
www.quadrille.co.uk

Cataloguing-in-Publication data: a catalogue record for this book is available from the British Library.

ISBN 978 184949 371 0

Printed in China

Every effort has been made to ensure that all information is accurate. However, a book of this nature cannot replace specialist advice in certain cases and therefore no responsibility can be accepted by the publishers or author for any loss or damage caused by reliance upon the accuracy of such information. Bear in mind, especially if you live outside Britain, that your local conditions may mean that some of this information is not appropriate. If in doubt, always consult a qualified electrician, plumber or surveyor.

SARAH BEENY'S 100 DIY JOBS

THE ESSENTIALS MADE SIMPLE

SARAH BEENY

WITH ANGELA F. ROBINSON

Quadrille
PUBLISHING

CONTENTS

INTRODUCTION

Being successful at DIY
is all about three things –
knowledge, experience
and a good dollop
of determination.

Once you have the knowledge you can
gather experience. Then, with a little
determination, you'll soon find you're
able to take charge of maintaining and
improving your own home, perhaps
even saving yourself thousands of
pounds along the way.

I was lucky, as my father encouraged us
from a very early age to do DIY. He was
not only a very positive role model but
also expected us to get on with helping.
He generally had one project or another
on at home, whether it was building
a new shed or re-roofing an old one.
First thing in the morning during
holidays and weekends he'd come into
our bedrooms and strongly suggest
we'd get up and lend a hand – generally,
by removing our duvets and opening
the windows!

My father always encouraged us to
'have a go'. In fact, when I was about
13 he gave me a £200 budget to
redecorate my bedroom. He took me
to choose wallpaper, paint and fabric,
then explained how to do it and left
me to get on with it. I'm not sure it was
the best job in the world but it gave
me a massive amount of confidence
and certainly taught me how to make
curtains and wallpaper!

It was when I bought my first flat with my brother, Diccon, and Graham (now my husband) that I really needed to learn fast, though. My father gave us his old hand drill and a few screwdrivers but the flat had an outside loo, no bathroom and no kitchen. So, it was an enormous challenge. I think when you are young, though, you have so much more energy. It's amazing how quickly you learn how to do things when you have to, especially, in my case, with a drip-feed of advice from my endlessly supportive father.

When I look back at those early days of DIY I know that, with or without my father, there was one thing that really would have helped me – a plain-talking reference book that would simply spell out the most straightforward way of going about the jobs you are most likely to want to do. I hope that *100 DIY Jobs* is that book.

I didn't have such a book then. I remember not soaking the wallpaper long enough and ending up with bubbles. It was my father who suggested injecting them with wallpaper paste – it worked a treat. It was he who suggested adding washing-up liquid to the render to make it stay on the wall. Sadly, he didn't remind me to check where the water pipes were before nailing the floorboards down. But that's another story!

I've now had 20 years of experience working in house renovation and building work. I've learned a lot. Now, I'd love to share all the information I've gathered along the way. I'd like to demystify those jobs that you may keep putting off because they feel too intimidating. Above all, I want to help you regain confidence in your DIY skills.

I've laid out every job in this book in simple-to-follow steps, with clear advice on how to get everything ready before you start. I've also included some of my own insider tips on getting a great finish (*How to Nail It!*), with each job.

As you'll soon gather, I can't emphasise enough the importance of preparation. In fact, preparation really should take up a good 80 per cent of any of the time you spend doing DIY. Think, think, think again, then plan, plan, plan again – then *do.*

In the same way that you'd get all your ingredients ready before starting to cook, you should also lay out all your tools for the job, checking you have the right bits and essential component parts to complete it. There is nothing more annoying than getting half-way through a job and finding you have a screw missing, or the wrong drill bit. That's also why I decided to have a toolbox section in this book – if you make sure you keep all the essentials (*illustrated on page 10*) in your toolbox, you'll have a much more enjoyable and productive experience next time you decide to DIY.

As you build confidence, you will no doubt find your own way of approaching certain jobs. Hopefully, however, the jobs in this book – some of them basic, many requiring a little more skill and patience – will give you a firm foundation, and a great starting point. With the knowledge you'll gain, you should never again feel that you don't know where to begin.

Whether you become a full-time DIY nut, or just a DIY dabbler, what's certain is that you'll have found a money-saving and creative hobby that you can enjoy for the rest of your life and that gives you far more satisfaction than you ever imagined.

Good luck!

Sarah Beeny

BACK TO BASICS

EVERYTHING YOU NEED TO GET THE JOB DONE

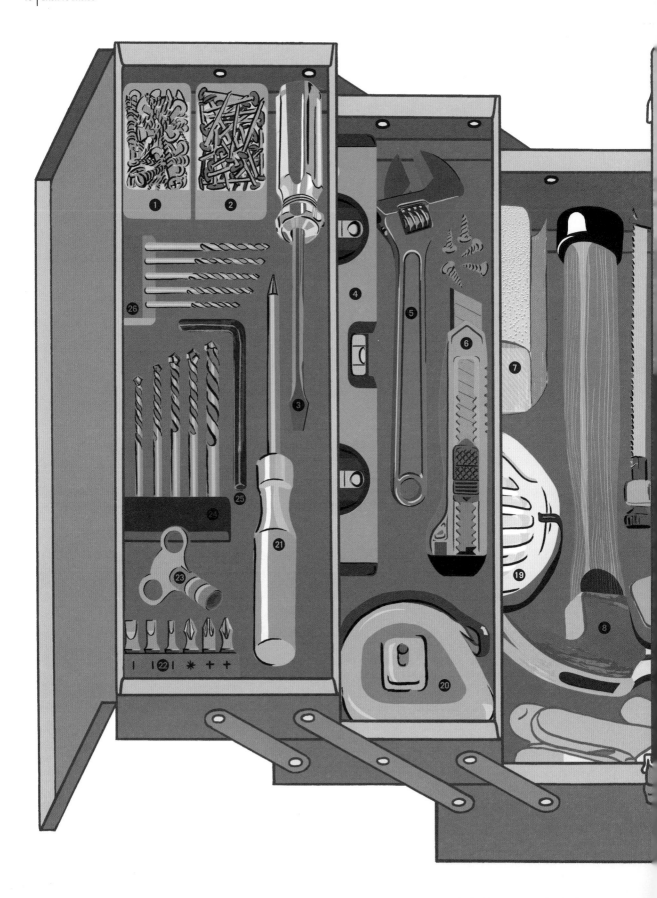

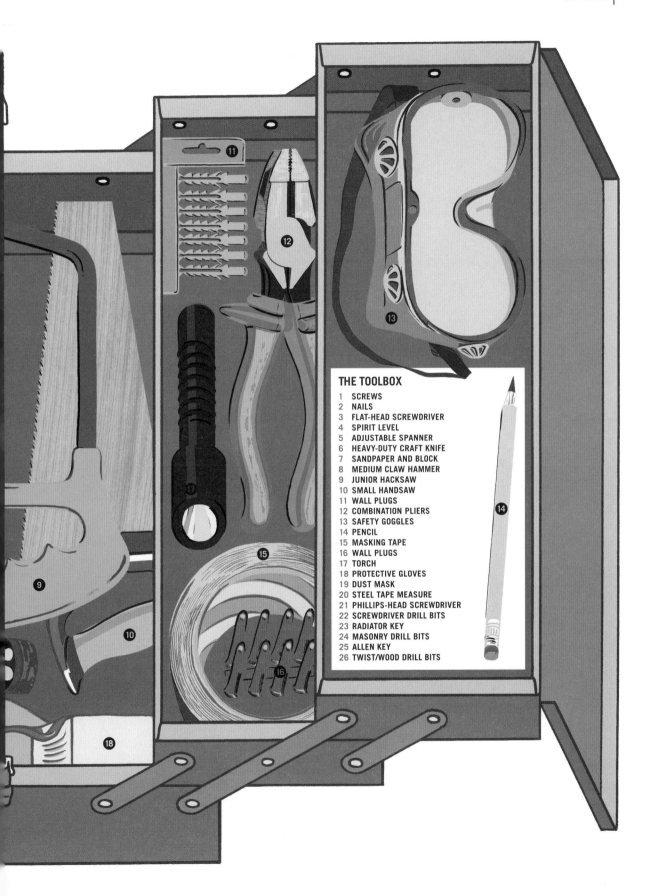

THE TOOLBOX

1 SCREWS
2 NAILS
3 FLAT-HEAD SCREWDRIVER
4 SPIRIT LEVEL
5 ADJUSTABLE SPANNER
6 HEAVY-DUTY CRAFT KNIFE
7 SANDPAPER AND BLOCK
8 MEDIUM CLAW HAMMER
9 JUNIOR HACKSAW
10 SMALL HANDSAW
11 WALL PLUGS
12 COMBINATION PLIERS
13 SAFETY GOGGLES
14 PENCIL
15 MASKING TAPE
16 WALL PLUGS
17 TORCH
18 PROTECTIVE GLOVES
19 DUST MASK
20 STEEL TAPE MEASURE
21 PHILLIPS-HEAD SCREWDRIVER
22 SCREWDRIVER DRILL BITS
23 RADIATOR KEY
24 MASONRY DRILL BITS
25 ALLEN KEY
26 TWIST/WOOD DRILL BITS

THE TOOLBOX

This should have plenty of compartments, so that you can get at everything easily. Don't skimp and buy a small box – you will only ever add to your tool collection. Choose one strong enough to withstand knocks and bumps. It should have a robust handle – the weight of all the tools can be considerable.

Make sure your toolbox has:

- A LARGE SPACE FOR LONG ITEMS, SUCH AS HAMMER AND HACKSAW
- SMALL STORAGE AREAS FOR NAILS, SCREWS AND SMALL BITS
- ENOUGH SPACE TO KEEP SHARP TOOLS SEPARATE

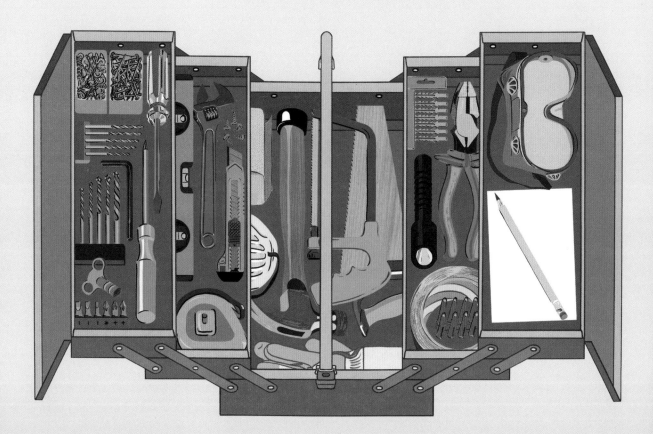

If you kit yourself out with these key tools, you'll be ready for a wide range of basic DIY jobs. Good-quality tools last a lifetime.

- **SCREWS:** multi-purpose wood screws, in a range of sizes. See also page 20.

- **NAILS:** a range of sizes for inside and outside. See also page 21.

- **SCREWDRIVERS:** flat- and Phillips-head/Pozidriv, to match screws. See also page 19.

- **SPIRIT LEVEL:** for checking true horizontal or vertical lines.

- **ADJUSTABLE SPANNER:** for loosening or tightening nuts and bolts.

- **CRAFT KNIFE:** a heavy-duty one can cut through multiple materials with precision. Keep a set of spare blades. Retractable are safest.

- **SANDPAPER AND BLOCK:** coarse-, medium- and fine-grade paper wraps around block and is held in place with fingers. See also page 23.

- **MEDIUM CLAW HAMMER:** for hammering in and taking out nails.

- **JUNIOR HACKSAW:** for cutting small pieces of metal, rigid plastic and wood. Has changeable blades. See also page 22.

- **SMALL HANDSAW:** for cutting wood. See also page 22.

- **WALL PLUGS:** give screws a fixing into masonry and cavity walls. In range of sizes and types. See also page 19.

- **COMBINATION PLIERS:** for gripping, twisting and wire-cutting.

- **SAFETY GOGGLES:** to protect eyes from dust and flying debris.

- **PENCIL:** for marking measurements.

- **MASKING TAPE:** essential for protecting surfaces when decorating. Great for marking and temporarily holding things in place.

- **TORCH:** for working in dark corners or without light or power.

- **PROTECTIVE GLOVES:** disposable rubber gloves for handling liquids, or reinforced gloves for work that's hard on your hands.

- **MASK:** to prevent inhalation of dust.

- **STEEL TAPE MEASURE:** retractable and robust.

- **RADIATOR KEY:** for bleeding radiators and to keep heating system efficient.

- **ALLEN KEYS:** for assembling flat-packs and tightening hex bolts (with six sides).

- **POWER DRILL:** for drilling into different materials and for using as a screwdriver. Cordless or mains-powered. Store in separate box and keep close to toolbox. See also page 18.

- **DRILL BITS:** store a selection with drill, including twist/wood and masonry, for a variety of materials and hole sizes, and a selection of screwdriver bits. See also page 18.

OTHER REALLY USEFUL STUFF

- **BRADAWL:** for making small indentation to mark fixing point for where screw will go. A long, thin nail will also do the trick.

- **CHISEL:** use carefully with hammer or mallet to cut out notches from wood.

- **MITRE BOX:** simple device for cutting 45-degree and 90-degree mitres. Use with tenon saw.

- **TENON SAW:** for fine woodworking and cutting mitres.

- **JIGSAW:** power tool for cutting difficult holes out of wood or cutting in restricted spaces.

- **PADSAW:** for cutting curves and enlarging holes in wood.

- **NAIL PUNCH:** for 'punching' nails flush with, or below, surface.

- **SPANNER SET:** a set of spanners in fixed sizes can work more reliably than an adjustable spanner.

- **DUCT TAPE:** heavy-duty, cloth-backed sticking tape for protecting or securing surfaces. Use only heat-resistant tape around heating and ventilation pipes.

- **GAFFER TAPE:** as duct tape, but designed not to leave sticky residue.

- **STAPLE GUN:** very useful for simple upholstery.

- **STRAIGHTEDGE:** a long metal ruler for aligning and marking.

- **CHALK LINE:** for marking long, straight lines on most surfaces.

- **PIPE-AND-CABLE-DETECTOR OR STUD DETECTOR:** the former indicates if any pipes or cables are hidden behind the surface where you intend to drill. Stud detectors locate studs in partition walls. Multi-purpose or triple detectors can locate pipes, cables and studs. It's a good idea to use a detector before drilling.

- **DECORATOR'S CAULK:** a flexible filler for smoothing over small holes, gaps and imperfections.

- **SILICONE SEALANT:** a flexible and waterproof sealant for use around sinks, baths and shower cubicles.

- **APPLICATOR GUN:** caulk/sealant canisters slot inside for easy application.

- **DECORATING BRUSHES:** good-quality bristle brushes are the best, but decent synthetic bristles can also give a good finish. The cheaper the brush, the more bristles it will lose.

- **DECORATING ROLLER AND TRAY:** painting with a roller gives a quicker, more even finish over walls and ceilings.

- **PALETTE KNIFE, FILLING KNIFE AND PUTTY KNIFE:** all useful for applying and smoothing putty and filler.

- **AEROSOL LUBRICANT, SUCH AS WD40:** useful for loosening stiff doors and locks; anti-rust.

- **WORKBENCH:** a secure surface for working on so you don't damage household furniture. Portable workbenches can pack away – useful if you're working in different areas around the house.

BEFORE YOU START

CHECK YOUR TOOLS

Having the right tools is the first step to completing a job to be proud of. Don't ruin your hard work with a bad paint job because you didn't have a brush the right size, or with wonky tiling because you didn't have the right spacers. Make sure you have all the fixings you need. See *Tools and Techniques* (page 18).

DO YOUR PREP

It can be very tempting to rush into a project, but time spent on preparation is essential. Each of the jobs described in this book gives clear details of any preparation needed in the *Getting Started* section. Think of each job as consisting of three stages: preparation, the main job, and finishing. Without proper preparation, your work will be harder to do, won't look as good and may not be as long-lasting.

MEASURE UP

Cutting timber, tiles, plasterboard or other hardware is final, and drilling holes in the wrong place can ruin a project, so always measure twice and measure right. Fixing errors will take up more time than that saved by not checking your measurements.

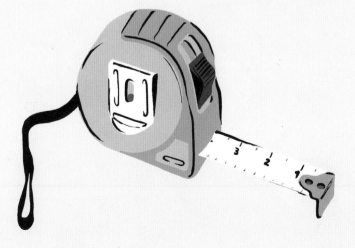

TOOLS AND TECHNIQUES

Before you buy any new tools, it's important to do a little research to make sure you buy the most suitable ones for your job. Once you have them safely home, take some time to think about technique and read any instructions carefully.

POWER DRILLS

DRILL TYPES

- **Cordless:** easier to use where there is no mains power, but can lack oomph.
- **Battery-powered:** 400-450 watts/12-volt should be enough for basic jobs. The stronger the battery, the faster and more powerful the drill action.
- **Mains-powered:** much more powerful but will need extension lead(s).

DRILL FEATURES

- **Hammer action:** for masonry drilling.
- **Speeds:** having variable speeds enables better control when drilling.
- **Reverse gears:** for removing screws.

DRILL BITS

Use the right bit for the material or wall type and size of hole required. Pointed ends give greater accuracy than flat ends. The most common types are:

- **Twist/wood:** in range of sizes from 1mm to 13mm; for wood, metal and plastic.
- **Masonry:** hardened bits to drill holes in masonry with hammer action.
- **Screwdriver:** for using drill as screwdriver.
- **Countersink:** for drilling small recess in wood to allow flat head of screw to sit flush with or below surface of wood.
- **Ceramic tile and glass:** sharp and curved, to cut through tile and glass safely.
- **Flat wood or spade:** for holes in wood larger than 13mm and up to 40mm.

HOLE TYPES

- **Pilot hole:** either a small hole that ensures screws go in easily and are positioned correctly, or a guide hole smaller than the size required that you then expand when drilling the final hole.
- **Countersink:** a wide, shallow hole drilled into the pilot hole, big enough so that the screw head sits just below the surface. It can then be filled and the screw head hidden. You can buy a special countersink bit, or just use a large bit, big enough to make a dip.

DRILL SAFETY

As a rule, it's a good idea to wear safety goggles when drilling – dust particles or chips can fly into your eyes. Always use goggles when drilling into masonry or hard materials. Remember to check for pipes and cables before drilling and be very careful when drilling above or below power sockets.

WALL PLUGS

Screws will only hold in masonry walls if used with wall plugs. As you screw into it, the plug expands to grip the sides of the hole, holding it in place.

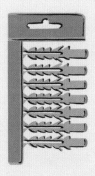

Choose wall plugs based on material being fixed to and weight of object being attached. Solid masonry wall plugs are usually yellow, red, brown or blue, with colour indicating size. Hollow wall fixings are usually grey, white or metal. Ensure the plug is long enough to receive the screw. For guide to choosing correct wall plug for screw size, see page 20.

FOR SOLID MASONRY

- **Plastic wall plugs:** available in various sizes to hold various weights. Lightly tap into drilled hole, then drive in screw to secure.
- **Hammer-in wall plugs:** hammer to insert wall plug into drilled hole, then fix with pre-supplied screw or nail.

FOR PLASTERBOARD/HARDBOARD/CAVITY WALL

- **Plastic wall plugs:** come with small wings that open up on the other side of the cavity to hold screw in place. These can be light- to medium-duty.
- **Self-tapping plugs:** screw straight into the plasterboard with no pre-drilling required.
- **Heavy-duty metal cavity wall fixings:** umbrella or wing fixings open up on the other side of the cavity to disperse weight and hold screw in place. Can be unscrewed but the fixing will be lost in the cavity.

CHOOSING THE RIGHT PLUG FOR YOUR OBJECT

- Use light-weight fixings for items such as curtain rails, tie-backs, pictures and small mirrors.
- Use medium-weight fixings or bathroom accessories, light-weight shelves, pictures, mirrors, wall lights and cabinets.
- Use heavy-weight plugs for bookshelves, cupboards, shower screens, TV brackets.

SCREWS AND SCREWDRIVERS

SCREWDRIVER TYPES

Ensure you match the screwdriver head to the screw and get a good fit or you'll risk damaging the screw and making it impossible to remove. The main screwdriver heads are:

- **Phillips-head:** fits cross-type screws.
- **Flat-head:** fits single-line-type (slotted) screws. Less common.
- **Pozidriv:** fits star-type screws. Taking over from Phillips-head screwdrivers as they are easier to use.

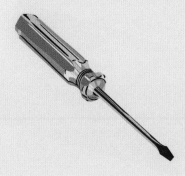

It is best to have at least one of each type of screwdriver in your toolbox, in large and small sizes. You can choose from hand-held or electric, or you could opt for a power drill with screwdriver bits. Hand-held screwdrivers with rubber grips are easiest to handle; electric screwdrivers can save time, but if you have a power drill, invest in some screwdriver bits to save time and effort. See *Drill Types* (opposite).

SCREW SIZES

Screws are still labelled in one of two ways, imperial or metric.

- **In imperial,** a screw labelled No. 8 x 2.5in, has a thickness/gauge number 8 and a length of 2.5 inches.
- **In metric,** a screw labelled 4.0 x 60mm has a thickness/gauge of 4mm and a length of 60mm.

The most useful screws to have in your toolbox are multi-purpose 4mm and 5mm (or imperial No. 8 and No. 10) in various lengths.

SCREW TYPES

- **Multi-purpose screw:** for use in wood. Screw head will sit above wood surface unless countersink holes are drilled before screwing in.
- **Masonry screw:** strong enough to be driven into masonry without a wall plug.
- **Chipboard screw:** for use in chipboard or wood. Deep threads extend right up screw head.
- **Carcass screw:** for securing chipboard. With thick shank and coarse thread.
- **Raised-head woodscrew:** good alternative to multi-purpose screw, if you don't mind screw head being visible.
- **Round-head wood screw:** sits above wood surface. Flat underside sits on surface. More decorative, for when you want screw head to be a feature.
- **Dry-wall screw:** for fixing plasterboard to timber studs. Has twin threads.
- **Hardened-steel woodscrew:** no pilot hole needed before screwing into soft wood. Has double thread.
- **Security screw/clutch-head screw:** for fixing locks and security devices. Head shape allows screw to go in, but not come out.
- **Self-tapping screw:** for fixing hard materials like metal and plastic. You can drill pilot hole the size of shank first; screw then cuts its own thread as it is tightened.

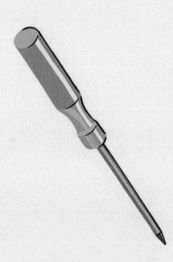

FIXING TO WOOD, INCLUDING WALL STUDS

Use a 4mm (No. 8) screw, with 2mm drill bit for the pilot hole, or a 5mm (No. 10) screw, with a 2.5mm drill bit for pilot hole. No wall plugs needed. Ensure length is appropriate to give a secure fixing.

FIXING TO MASONRY

- **For light fixings:** use 3.5mm (No. 6) or 4mm (No. 8) screws, with 5mm masonry drill bit and yellow wall plugs.
- **For general fixing:** use 4mm (No. 8) or 5mm (No. 10) screws, with 6mm masonry drill bit and red wall plugs.
- **Medium to heavy fixings:** use 5mm (No. 0) or (No. 12) 5.5mm screws, with 7mm masonry bit with brown or blue wall plugs.

The minimum depth for your hole should be the length of the plug used, but common sense is needed. Older walls with softer brick or thicker plaster need to be drilled a little deeper. Choose a length of screw that will go through the item to be fixed and well into the plastic plug. Remember the plaster will provide NO fixing – it is the brick, cement or concrete that provides the anchor. If the hole ends up too big, you can pack around the plug with matches. See *Wall Plugs* (page 19).

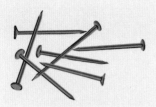

HOW TO FIND A WALL STUD

Either use a hand-held, battery-operated stud detector and follow manufacturer's instructions, or use the hammer-and-nail method. Tap firmly all along your wall with your knuckles and listen for a change in the sound. In areas where the wall sounds denser and more solid, try gently tapping in a thin nail in an inconspicuous area near the base of the wall. If there is resistance, you have found a stud. Most houses have studs 40mm wide, positioned 400mm apart.

HAMMERS

HAMMER TYPES

- **Claw hammer:** the basic hammer for all toolboxes. Remove nails with claw.
- **Cross-pein/Warrington hammer:** for hammering in fine or small nails, such as those used for securing hardboard or carpet to floor.
- **Club hammer:** big metal hammer for heavier work.
- **Mallet:** made of rubber or wood. Wide area gives a soft blow. Use for tapping items gently and firmly into place. Use with chisel.

HAMMERING TECHNIQUES

A simple rule for hammering is that the smaller the hitting area of the hammer, the greater the force; the larger the area, the gentler the force.

- For accuracy, hold handle nearer the head; for greater power, hold it near base.
- Aim to hit the target square-on, not at an angle.
- Try to use your whole arm and elbow when swinging hammer, keeping wrist straight. Allow hammer to do the work, not your arm.
- Use a hard surface. Soft surfaces such as carpets will absorb some of your effort.

SAFETY AND PROTECTION

- Check the head is firmly attached to the handle, and the handle is in good condition with no splits or splinters. If not – do not use!
- Look out behind and around you before swinging the hammer – don't catch it on anything or anyone.
- Protect delicate surfaces (such as tiles, which can be tapped into place) by hammering gently onto thin board held on top of surface.

NAILS

NAIL TYPES

- **Plain-head wire nail:** general-purpose nail. Can cause wood to split, though.
- **Oval wire nail:** oval shape helps stop the wood from splitting.
- **Ring-shanked nail:** ringed shank makes fixing more secure.
- **Lost-head nail:** can be punched under the surface with a nail punch or pin punch.
- **Masonry nail:** for fixing into masonry.
- **Panel pin:** slim nail for mouldings, joinery and carpentry.
- **Picture hooks:** use small nail to fix light- to medium-weight pictures to most surfaces.

SAWS

SAW TYPES

The fewer teeth-per-inch (TPI), the coarser the cut; the greater the TPI, the smoother the cut.

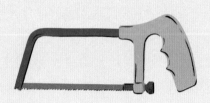

- **Hacksaw/junior hacksaw:** for small metal-cutting jobs; inexpensive.
- **Tenon saw:** a stiffened top edge and fine teeth, giving good control for fine woodworking. Best saw to use with mitre box.
- **Handsaw:** classic saw for cutting long pieces of wood in straight lines. Use when cut is too long for a tenon saw.
- **Circular saw:** a circular-bladed power saw, best suited for making long, straight cuts in wood quickly and easily.
- **Jigsaw:** a power saw best for cutting difficult holes, curves or patterns out of wood. Small size makes jigsaws good for working in restricted space, and finishing cuts that regular saws can't complete. Not suitable for fast, long or straight cuts.
- **Padsaw/keyhole saw:** shape allows for cutting curves, small or awkward holes and enlarging holes in wood.
- **Mitre box:** choose box size to fit wood. Use tenon saw and the guide slots to cut precise 45-degree or 90-degree angles in wood for mitred corners.

SAWING TECHNIQUES

Workbenches are the best place to do sawing work. You can fix wood securely in place and work in a clear area where you won't damage anything. If you don't have a workbench, other surfaces can act as one. Rest the wood on top of a low surface (such as an old coffee table) with excess extending off the 'bench'. Use your knee and body weight to secure wood and saw along marking. Catch excess before it snaps off.

To get a clean cut

- Ensure your blade is sharp; a dull blade will never make a perfect cut.
- Choose a blade with the right TPI grade for your needs (see above).
- Avoid letting the wood snap off before you complete the cut. Support both ends of the wood so that the end you're not holding doesn't have far to fall and won't snap off. You can balance this 'free' end on scrap support wood, or ask a helper to hold it.
- If you are supporting the fall-off section of wood, don't pull it towards you or the wood will bend in towards the saw as the cut progresses. This will pinch the saw and cause the wood and/or saw to buck, which will interrupt the clean cut.
- If possible, use a vice to clamp one end of wood, freeing your hand to control the saw.
- Start with the good side of the piece of wood facing up and saw at a 45-degree angle.
- Always cut into the wood so that the blades pull into the wood from the finished/right side. Ensure you engage the teeth on your forward stroke.
- You can use masking tape on both sides of edge to be cut, to hold wood fibres in place.

Using a jigsaw

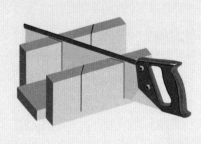

- Choose the right blade. Use a wood-cutting blade for wood, a metal-cutting blade for metal, a laminate-cutting blade for laminate and a ceramic-cutting blade for tiles.
- Check your blade is sharp. Maximum cutting depth is about 50-75mm thickness, depending on blade.
- To start sawing in the middle of a piece of wood, drill a large pilot hole first.

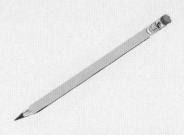

Using a circular saw

- Set the blade depth so that the blade extends around 6-12mm, at most, out of the wood. Too deep and the blade will be less effective and much more dangerous. Measure the blade depth alongside edge of wood before you turn the saw on.

- Support the fall-off wood to ensure a clean cut all the way through.

- If the saw wanders from the marked cut line, stop and start again on the right track, rather than trying to steer the saw back.

Caution: circular saws can be very dangerous if not used as per manufacturer's instructions.

SANDPAPER

Sandpaper is graded by the number of abrasive particles per square inch. The lower the number, the coarser the grit and the rougher the finish.

SANDPAPER GRADES

- **Coarse** (40-60 grit)
- **Very fine** (220-240 grit)
- **Medium** (80-120 grit)
- **Extra fine** (280-320 grit)
- **Fine** (150-180 grit)
- **Super fine** (360 and above)

Coarse, medium and fine grades are really all you need for general DIY. You will use fine grades for finishing but coarser grades for smoothing cut ends. Coarser grades remove more material but leave a rougher finish; finer grades remove less but give a smoother finish. Sand using progressively finer grades for best results.

SANDING BY HAND

Sandpaper usually comes in 230 x 280mm sheets. Cut them into quarters and wrap around a sanding block. Blocks are usually made of cork but you could also use a bit of wood measuring roughly 90 x 65 x 25mm – about the size of a washing-up sponge. Always sand with the grain – in other words, along the line of the wood.

POWER-SANDING

Some power sanders have bag attachments for collecting dust and some can even connect to your vacuum cleaner – this is a great feature, as sanding causes a huge amount of dust and if you have to do it indoors you'll be cleaning the dust from every room for weeks as it settles! Always use a dust mask when doing any sort of sanding. Some particles, especially old paint, can be really nasty if you inhale them.

- **Belt sander:** great if you want to remove a lot of material quickly. Works with a belt of sandpaper stretched over rollers, so only sands in one direction.

- **Orbital sander:** good for achieving smooth finishes on large, flat areas, but can leave circular marks because of the way it rotates.

- **Random-orbit:** this is the best all-rounder, combining the speed of a belt sander with the smoothness of an orbital sander, with less risk of surface-marking.

- **Detail- or delta-sander:** shaped a bit like an iron, this type of random-orbit sander is great for sanding tricky corners as well as flat surfaces. It doesn't usually come with a dust bag, so you won't want to do huge areas. Often comes palm- or hand-sized.

HOW TO USE A POWER SANDER

- Select grade of abrasive paper you need and attach to sander – this can vary, depending on type, so refer to manufacturer's instructions.

- If it has a vacuum cleaner attachment or dust bag, attach and turn on.

- Hold sander against the surface you want to sand and switch on.

- Keep the sander moving over the surface, until you have a smooth finish.

PAINTING

PAINT

VOCs are chemicals found in most paints that help the paint perform as you would expect. There are natural, eco-friendly alternatives that are improving all the time.

- **Oil-based:** dries slowly, allowing brush marks to even out and giving a glossy, durable finish. Dispose of waste paint carefully to minimise impact on the environment. Best suited to smaller, hard-wearing areas like furniture, trims and outside.
- **Water-based:** there are many different types for all surfaces. Quick-drying, easy to use, easy to clean and has a lower odour than oil-based.

PAINT FINISHES

- **Matt/flat:** has no shine, so is helpful in disguising uneven surfaces, as it doesn't reflect light. Not terribly durable and difficult to keep clean. Generally used on walls and ceilings.
- **Eggshell/satin:** between satin and matt in sheen and durability. Essentially matt with a little lustre, like eggshell. Covers imperfections well. Better than matt in high-traffic areas. Generally used on walls and ceilings.
- **Silk/semi-gloss:** shiny and reflective, and can be washed, so suitable for bathrooms, kitchens, children's rooms, halls and stairways. Can be used for trims, doors and furniture. Doesn't cover wall imperfections very well.
- **Gloss:** high-shine, washable and more durable than other finishes – reserve for windows, doors and furniture. Oil-based glosses are most durable for exterior use, but are toxic and difficult to apply well.

PAINT TYPES

- **Emulsion:** water-based, and dries quickly. Two coats usually needed. Essentially used on walls and ceilings. Doesn't generally need an undercoat or primer but you would need a wash coat (diluted coat) on bare plaster. There are many different types. For example: one-coat emulsion is thicker and with better coverage, so you only need one coat; kitchen and bathroom emulsion is moisture- and grease-resistant, and washable.
- **Resin-blocking primer:** always use this on new hardwood. Blocks resinous stains that would otherwise show through the paint. No need for extra primer. Knotting solution stops the bleed-through of resins but without the primer.
- **Primer:** if you are using oil-based paint on unpainted wood you will need to add a coat of primer, or the paint won't stick properly. If you're using emulsion paint, the emulsion soaks into the wood to act as its own primer. You will need more than one coat, though.
- **Undercoat:** some paints are formulated not to need an undercoat but you will always get a better result using one. Don't think about not using one if you are painting over dark or strong colours.
- **Topcoat:** your final coat of paint in your desired finish.

PAINTBRUSHES

Give thorough results, but can be slower than using a roller and leave brush marks.

- **Natural fibres:** best suited for oil-based paints and not for emulsion, as the bristles soak up the water and go limp.
- **Synthetic fibres:** can be used for any paint type.
- **Chisel-edged brush:** ideal for cutting-in or painting straight edges.
- **Split-end brush:** holds more paint, and spreads paint smoothly and evenly.

The size of brush required will depend on what you are painting. Small brushes (12-25mm) are good for fiddly work; medium brushes (50mm) for doors and skirting boards and large brushes (100-150mm) for walls, floors and ceilings.

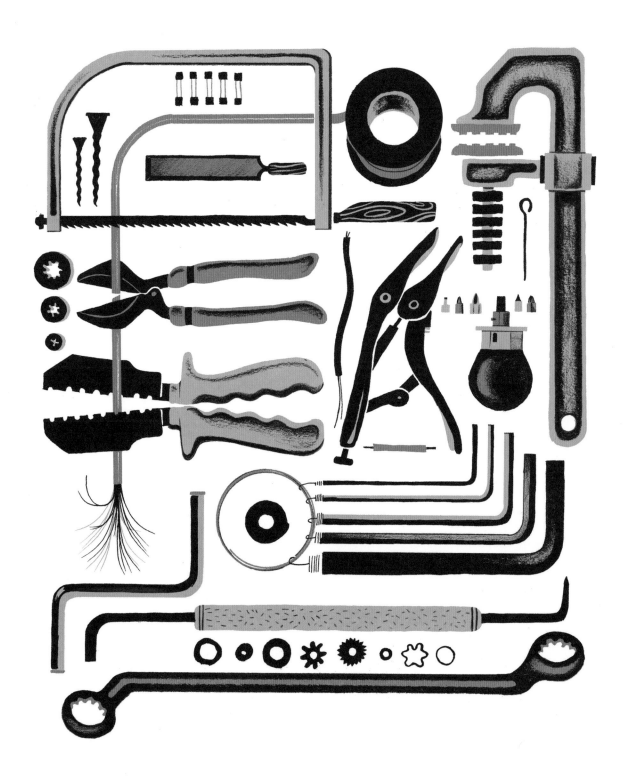

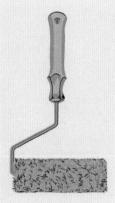

PAINT ROLLER

Covers walls quickly, but more coats needed as paint goes on thinly. Frame is made from durable wire cage with a sleeve of wool or synthetic material, which can be changed easily. Use with roller tray and pour paint into the deep end or reservoir. Dip roller into paint and run over ribbed surface to apply evenly. You'll still need to cut in around edges with a paintbrush.

- **Short-pile:** gives smooth results. Not for rough walls.
- **Shaggy-pile:** for textured results or rough walls. Finish edges with a brush.

SPRAY PAINT

Gives a professional-looking finish and is easy to apply. Great for improving the look of old furniture, or for objects with awkward surfaces. Use thin, multiple coats. Place small objects inside a cardboard box while spraying. For larger objects, work outside if possible, or use masking tape, scrap cardboard and dustsheets to protect surroundings.

TIPS FOR PAINTING INSIDE WALLS

- **Edges:** these blend in better if you paint them first. This is called 'cutting-in'. Paint overlapping parallel strips perpendicular to the edge, then one long sweeping line alongside the edge.
- **Walls:** start painting close to the light source (window), painting in bands, one at a time, as you move away from the light source.
- **Ceilings:** paint ceilings before walls, as paint will inevitably spray.
- **Roller:** angle roller at around 45 degrees, using even strokes in random directions. Start each freshly loaded roller in a new place, working back towards last painted place.
- **Brush:** paint panels of one square metre at a time, blending edges in while still wet.

TIPS FOR PAINTING OUTSIDE WALLS

- Paint when the weather is fine and dry.
- Try to paint in the shade where possible; direct sunlight can make it difficult to see how paint is going on, especially with white paint.
- Complete one section at a time, using windows and drainpipes to mark boundaries.
- Start at the top of the wall and work downwards as paint will splash on surfaces below.
- 'Stipple' the paintbrush on heavily-textured walls by holding brush at 90 degrees and dabbing paint on. Vary the direction of the brush as you go.
- Protect drainpipes by taping newspaper around them. Push brush carefully behind drainpipes.
- Start new brush-load of paint in unpainted area and work back to last painted section.
- Paint again in opposite direction to get an even coverage.
- Paint corners and edges in same way as internal painting.

PAINTING WOOD

When choosing paint and primer for wood, you'll find many modern paints that combine resin-blocker and primer (necessary for bare wood), primer and undercoat, or topcoats that require no undercoat. Water-based acrylic paint is flexible and can be a great time-saver. If using oil-based paints, however, it can be best to stick to the traditional method (see opposite). Talk to your local decorators' merchants for advice.

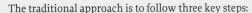

The traditional approach is to follow three key steps:

1 Primer: seals bare wood and provides a foundation for the paint which follows. Sand lightly after priming. You'll need to paint knotting solution over surface if wood is new.

2 Undercoat: main body of the paint. Provides good coverage and ensures a good bind between the topcoat and surface. Where there is a change of colour, two coats may be needed. No need to sand afterwards. Choose a colour that is close to your topcoat.

3 Topcoat: is the gloss (or satin, eggshell) that provides the finishing layer. For external wood, two coats will give a longer-lasting finish. For internal wood, one coat should be adequate, unless covering a strong colour. For oil paint, leave a few days between coats. If applying more than one coat, give a light sand in between, once fully dry.

GENERAL PAINTING RULES

- Follow these key steps: clean; sand; prime; undercoat; two coats of topcoat paint. Painting wood is a combination of these steps, so select as appropriate.

- Prepare thoroughly so surfaces are clean, grease- and dust-free and other surfaces are protected.

- Buy the best paint and brushes you can afford as quality does make a difference.

- It's much better to paint two thinner coats than try to apply too thick a coat at once. You don't want the paint to drip.

- For preparation, see individual jobs, *Painting and Decorating* (pages 142-170).

CLEANING UP PAINT

Water-based paints

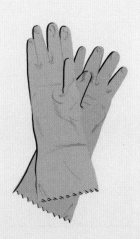

- Remove excess paint from brush or roller and roller tray by squeezing or pouring back into paint tin. Wipe with old cloth.

- Stir brush or roller in large bucket of warm water and washing-up liquid. Use at least three changes of water, fanning bristles out or massaging your fingers into roller to work out paint.

- Rinse brush, or roller and tray, under tap until water runs clear, then dry on old cloth.

- Store brushes, bristles-up, in old jars, with elastic band over bristles to keep together.

Oil-based paints

- Remove excess paint from brush by squeezing back into paint tin. Wipe with old cloth.

- Wearing rubber gloves, pour white spirit into an old jam jar, or glass or ceramic bowl. (NB, do not pour white spirits into plastic). Stir brush into the white spirit, working it into the bristles.

- Rub brush back and forth over your hand to rub the spirits into the bristles.

- Add washing-up liquid to the bristles and rub in using your fingers.

- Squeeze out as much of the paint/spirits/washing-up liquid as possible onto paper towels.

- Rinse brush under hot water, squeezing as much out as possible.

- Repeat above steps four or five times.

- Finish by rubbing in small amount of spirits and washing-up liquid and do not rinse.

- Wrap brush in paper towel, squeezing out as much moisture as possible.

- Store brushes, bristles-up, in old jam jars, with elastic band over bristles to keep them together.

SAFETY

No matter what job you are about to tackle, safety should always be your first consideration.

WORK SPACE

- **Clear your work space:** don't leave anything lying about. You could easily trip over, when carrying a freshly pasted sheet of wallpaper, for example; or you might drip paint or dust. Make sure power cables are kept well out of your way.

- **Ventilate your work space:** ensure you keep a supply of fresh air when working with oil-based paints, paint stripper and other chemicals. If you're creating lots of dust, open a window – but not an internal door or it will escape into the rest of your home.

- **Ensure your work space is well lit:** struggling to see can be tiring as well as dangerous.

CLOTHING

- **Avoid loose clothing, shoes, hair and accessories:** eliminate the chance of anything getting caught up in your work.

- **Wear comfortable, old clothes:** protect your body with trousers, long-sleeved T-shirt or sweatshirt and tough boots. Pockets are useful for holding tools. Avoid woolly clothes that can leave fibres on your work.

- **Wear protective clothing:** knee pads for working with flooring; rubber gloves to protect your hands from harsh liquids; reinforced gloves for anything hard or sharp on your hands; mask to protect your lungs from fine dust; safety goggles to save your eyes from dust and debris; ear defenders for even slightly noisy work over an extended time. Be cautious of chemicals that may be toxic. Always read manufacturer's guidelines. You may need added protection or even a respirator mask in some situations.

BEST PRACTICE

- **Put away sharp tools straight away after use.**

- **Be considerate where you place a ladder. Make sure anybody likely to be passing by is aware you may be up a ladder.**

- **Keep a mobile phone on your person in case of an accident.**

- **Don't work when you're tired.**

HOW TO USE THIS BOOK

The key features which accompany each of the jobs in this book will help you get the most out of your DIY projects. They've been designed with clarity in mind, but also with the idea that not everyone will approach each task in the same way. There are choices to make in terms of the tools you use, and how thorough you want to be, which will depend on experience, budget and confidence. Whatever your skill level, the job can be tailored to suit you.

 TOOL UP
TOOL DOWN It's often possible to make use of the basic toolbox kit you already own, rather than splashing out on new equipment. However, for some of the larger, or more time-intensive jobs, it really is worth investing in some specialised tools and materials – in the end, you may end up saving money as well as time. Where there is a choice, you'll see the Tool up/Tool down arrows, so you can make the decision yourself.

 Look for this symbol in the tools list. It will alert you to the fact that special care is needed when using this particular tool or material and that you may need to wear protective clothing such as goggles, mask or gloves. See *Clothing* (opposite). If in doubt, refer to manufacturer's instructions.

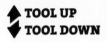 **GETTING STARTED** Nothing is more important to DIY success than preparation. Take time to read this section, which accompanies every job in this book, big or small – tempted as you may be to get stuck in. You'll save yourself a lot of time and hassle further down the line if you plan ahead properly.

⚠ **STAY SAFE!** Take extra care when you see this warning. The job may require you to turn off the mains electricity supply before starting, or may involve handling electrical wiring or hazardous materials. If in any doubt, consult a professional.

③ Whenever the step number of a job has an outline around it, you'll find an illustration to accompany it.

 **HOW TO NAIL IT!** Reading this section will give you the edge. You'll find tips and hints on how to go the extra mile and give your job the very best finish. This should mean your job or project will last longer and that the results will be more impressive.

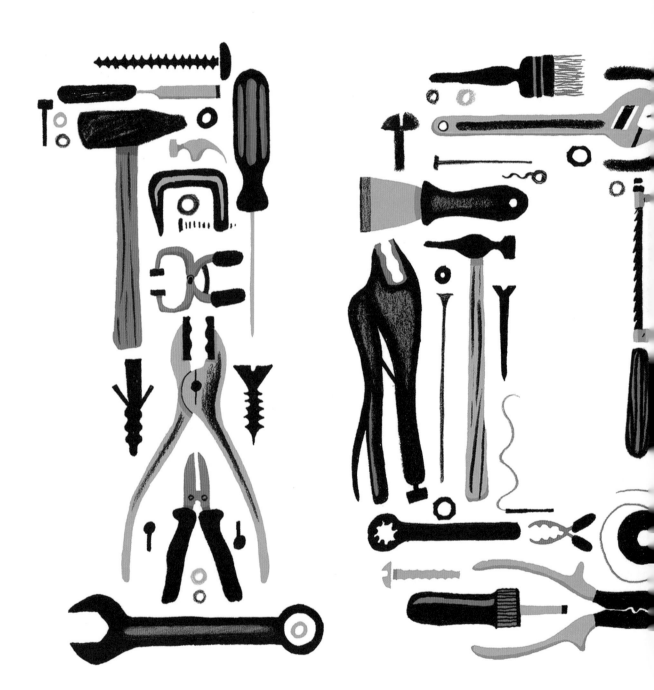

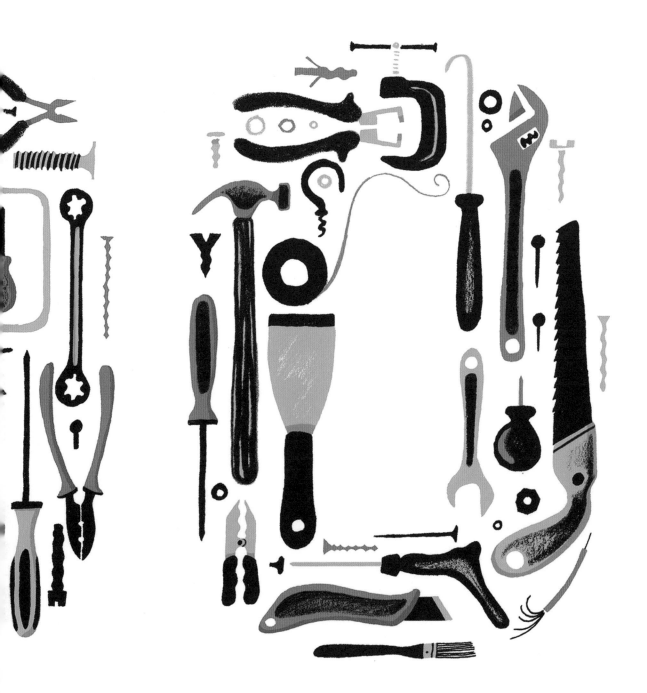

BATHROOMS
AND
KITCHENS

EVERYTHING
YOU NEED
TO GET THE
JOB DONE

RENOVATE GROUT

01

Tiles actually rarely wear out – it's the grout that generally lets the side down. Renovating grout can be a quick and cheap way to freshen up the look of your bathroom or kitchen.

▶ YOU'LL NEED

OLD TOOTHBRUSH AND WASHING-UP LIQUID

MATERIALS FOR GROUTING (SEE PAGE 34)

PLUS, AS NEEDED:

VINEGAR AND BICARBONATE OF SODA

MOULD AND MILDEW REMOVER

⚠ **HOUSEHOLD BLEACH**

◆ **TOOL UP** GROUT RAKE

◆ **TOOL DOWN** CRAFT KNIFE

VACUUM CLEANER WITH NARROW NOZZLE ATTACHMENT

GROUT SEALANT

SANITARY SILICONE SEALANT AND APPLICATOR GUN

GETTING STARTED

Start by cleaning the area with an old toothbrush and washing-up liquid. If the dirt is stubborn, try a paste of vinegar and bicarbonate of soda. If it's mouldy, try a mould and mildew remover or a solution of one part bleach to eight parts water. If dirt or mould persists, you will need to remove and replace the grout.

WHAT TO DO

1 Starting at the top of a vertical joint, gently pull rake or knife down the centre of grout line. Work to a depth of around 3mm. You need enough space for new grout to take hold, but don't go too deep. Repeat for horizontal lines. Be careful not to dislodge tiles and try not to slip and scratch the tile surface.

2 Use an old toothbrush, or the narrow-nozzle attachment on a vacuum cleaner to remove all dust and debris from the joints.

3 If using powdered grout, mix up according to instructions. Apply grout as for *Grout Tiles* (see page 34).

4 Apply grout sealant, and re-apply waterproof silicone sealant, if needed. See *Apply Silicone Sealant* (page 46).

HOW TO NAIL IT!

- You can whiten grout by using a grout pen or reviver that will paint a white or coloured finish on top of old grout.

- If you need to renovate a large section of grout, it's worth investing in a power tool.

- Never wash ANY grout down the drain as it WILL harden in the U-bends and and you will have to cut out the section.

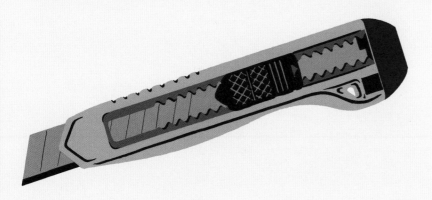

GROUT TILES

02

Grout is the waterproof cement that goes between the tiles. All tiling must be finished off with grouting. This is the really satisfying part! You can create very different looks with coloured grout. For more outlandish combinations, test a small area first. Beware – bold grouts are unforgiving of less-than-perfectly-cut tiles.

▶ YOU'LL NEED

GROUT (PRE-MIXED OR POWDERED)

BUCKET OF WATER,
IF USING POWDERED GROUT

TOOL UP GROUT SPREADER

TOOL DOWN
PLASTIC KITCHEN SPATULA

DAMP SPONGE

TOOL UP GROUT SHAPER

TOOL DOWN YOUR FINGER

CLEAN, DRY CLOTH

GROUT SEALANT, IF NEEDED

GETTING STARTED

If using powdered grout, mix up according to the packet instructions. Always add the powder to the water rather than the other way round. Aim for a thick, creamy texture a bit like toothpaste. Check that you will have enough for the job, but don't make up too much at once.

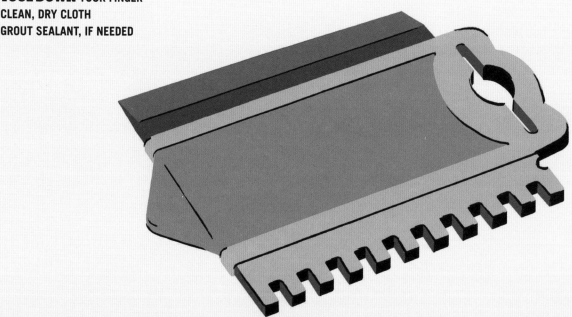

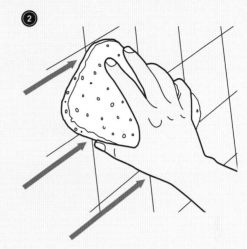

WHAT TO DO

1 Use the grout spreader or spatula to spread golf-ball-sized lumps of grout over the whole tile surface in long, upwards, diagonal strokes. Hold the rubber edge of the spreader at an angle of 45 degrees. Work into all the joints.

2 Use a damp sponge to wipe away any excess grout. Pull sponge lightly across each right angle once. Turn the sponge over to use the clean side, then rinse in bucket of clean water and repeat.

3 When grout has slightly hardened, use a grout shaper or your finger to neaten up the joints. If any gaps appear, apply more grout with your fingertip. Sponge off excess.

4 Allow several hours – preferably overnight – for grout to dry. Polish up the tiles with a clean, dry cloth.

5 Once grout is dry, apply grout sealant, if needed, according to manufacturer's instructions.

HOW TO NAIL IT!

- Work on areas of about one square metre at a time so that the grout doesn't harden before you have finished.

- Sponge off excess without delay as it is horribly difficult to remove hardened grout.

- Never wash ANY grout down the drain as it WILL go hard and block the U-bends and you will have to cut out the section.

CUT TILES

Tiling, especially on a flat, small, regular area, doesn't have to be tricky. It gets more complicated when you need to tile over larger spaces that have plenty of curves and obstacles, but with practice, patience and the right tools, you'll soon be able to master the art of cutting tiles.

▶ YOU'LL NEED

SAFETY GOGGLES
PROTECTIVE GLOVES
RULER
CHINAGRAPH PENCIL
↕ **TOOL UP** FLAT-BED TILE CUTTER FOR STRAIGHT CUTS; JIGSAW, WITH TILE-CUTTING BLADE, PLUS CLAMP, FOR SHAPED CUTS
↕ **TOOL DOWN** TILE SCORER FOR STRAIGHT CUTS; TILE SAW AND CLAMP, OR TILE NIBBLERS, FOR SHAPED CUTS
SANDPAPER OR TILE FILE
WORKBENCH OR OTHER SUITABLE CUTTING SURFACE (SEE PAGE 22)
MASKING TAPE, IF NEEDED

GETTING STARTED

Watch out for your eyes – remember to wear goggles to protect them from flying bits of tile! You could also wear gloves to protect your hands.

A simple tile scorer or flat-bed tile cutter works well for straightforward tiling jobs. However, if you are working on a large area and are not only snapping tiles straight, but cutting tiles for corners or awkward spaces, a jigsaw with tile-cutting blade is a good investment.

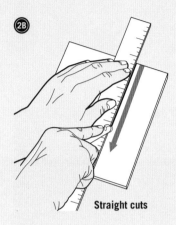

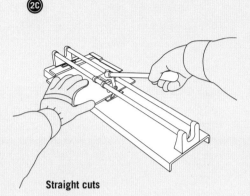

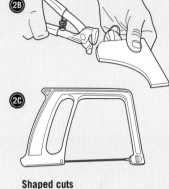

Straight cuts

Straight cuts

Shaped cuts

WHAT TO DO

Straight cuts

1 Measure and mark the line you want to cut along in chinagraph pencil, all the way across the tile.

2 Cut tile using one of the following options:

A Clamp tile to workbench and, wearing protective gloves, cut along line with jigsaw.

B Score tile with tile scorer along marked line. Put on protective gloves and snap tile cleanly in two by hand, using firm and decisive motion.

C Use a flat-bed tile cutter to score and snap the tile, along the line.

3 Smooth cut edges with sandpaper or tile file.

Shaped cuts

1 Mark the line you want to cut along in chinagraph pencil.

2 Cut tile using one of the following options:

A Clamp tile to workbench and, wearing gloves, cut along line with jigsaw.

B Score with tile scorer and use nibblers to shape, nipping off pieces up to line.

C Clamp tile to workbench and cut with a tile saw.

3 Smooth cut edges with sandpaper or tile file.

HOW TO NAIL IT!

- It is very tricky to cut extra bits off a tile once you have made your cut, so cut once, cut right – measure, measure and measure again. The key to shaping tiles is patience, but confidence, with every cut.

- You can place masking tape along the line to be cut before marking with pencil. This should stop the tile snapping in the wrong place.

- To snap a straight cut, hold tile with scored line over edge of table and press firmly on either side. Alternatively, lay pencil under line and push down on either side.

TILE WALL

It's all about the preparation. Start tiling on a bumpy or 'active' wall – with bits falling off it – and don't be surprised if the result is a bit disappointing. The wall should be clean, flat and dry.

► YOU'LL NEED

TILES, TO COVER AREA, PLUS EXTRA

STEEL TAPE MEASURE

PENCIL, PAPER AND RULER

MASKING TAPE

WOODEN BATTEN OR OTHER SUITABLE LENGTH OF WOOD

SPIRIT LEVEL

TILE ADHESIVE (PRE-MIXED OR POWDERED)

BUCKET OF WATER, IF USING PRE-MIXED ADHESIVE

NOTCHED SPREADER

▲ TOOL UP SPACERS

▼ TOOL DOWN MATCHES

MATERIALS FOR CUTTING TILES (SEE PAGE 36)

MATERIALS FOR GROUTING (SEE PAGE 34)

SILICONE SEALANT AND APPLICATOR GUN, IF NEEDED

GETTING STARTED

Measure, measure and measure again. It's worth drawing areas on paper and checking again before starting. Always buy extra tiles as you will almost certainly get some cuts wrong.

Remember to leave spaces for grout and take your time.

To calculate number of tiles needed

Most tiles come in boxes with enough to cover one square metre. Simply measure the length and width of area in metres and multiply to calculate number of tiles to buy. Measure alcoves, bays and L-shapes separately and add in to total. Add ten per cent for wastage and whoopsies.

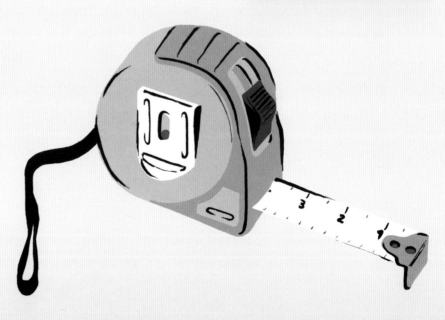

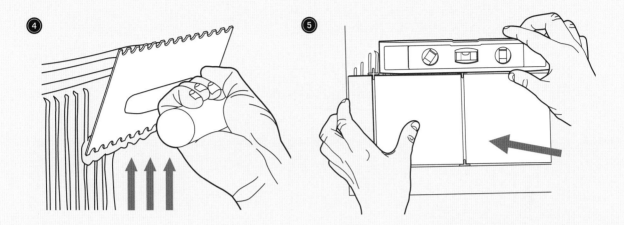

WHAT TO DO

1 Put plugs in the bath and basin and use masking tape to secure.

2 Mark area on wall to be tiled, using pencil and wooden batten. Make sure lines are level using spirit level.

3 If using powdered adhesive, make it up according to manufacturer's instructions.

4 Using notched spreader, spread tile adhesive evenly over one square metre of wall at a time. Use serrated edge to form ridges.

5 Start from the most visible corner and work across, one row at a time, sticking spacers or matches between each tile. Press each tile in place, twisting slightly as you press so that it beds in securely. Check tiles are level as you go. Work in sections. If you need a break, remove tile adhesive from areas not yet covered by scraping off with the other side of the spreader and discarding.

6 Cut tiles as you go along (see page 36).

7 Leave adhesive to harden for 24 hours. Finish with grouting (see page 34) and sealant, if required (see page 46).

HOW TO NAIL IT!

- Always use cut tiles in corners where they will be less obvious.

- Never wash ANY tile adhesive or grout down the drain – it WILL go hard and block the U-bends and you will have to cut out the section.

FIT MOSAIC TILES

Mosaic tiles have been around for many hundreds of years. Once placed one tiny tile at a time, they are now available in easy-to-fit sheets.

YOU'LL NEED

MOSAIC TILES, TO COVER AREA, PLUS EXTRA

PENCIL

SPIRIT LEVEL

TILE ADHESIVE (PRE-MIXED OR POWDERED)

BUCKET OF WATER, IF USING POWDERED ADHESIVE

NOTCHED SPREADER

TOOL UP CLEAN, DRY PAINT ROLLER

TOOL DOWN FLAT PIECE OF SCRAP BOARD AND SHORT LENGTH OF STRAIGHT WOOD

CRAFT KNIFE

STEEL TAPE MEASURE

DAMP SPONGE

MATERIALS FOR GROUTING (SEE PAGE 34)

GETTING STARTED

If you only plan to tile a section of wall, mark out the area using your pencil. Use a spirit level to ensure your lines are level.

If using powdered adhesive, make it up according to manufacturer's instructions.

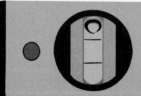

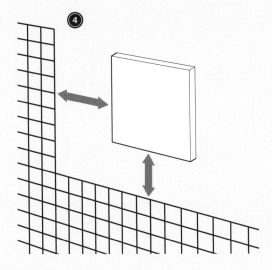

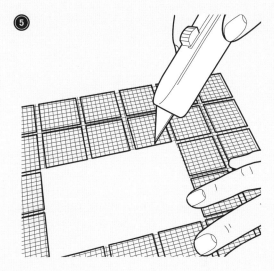

WHAT TO DO

1 Follow instructions for *Tile Wall* (see page 38), remembering to apply small areas of adhesive at a time and making sure the wall to be tiled is clean and flat.

2 Apply the first sheet of mosaic tiles by pressing firmly into the adhesive and ensuring the grout lines are level.

3 To make sure each tile beds into the adhesive, push paint roller firmly over the area, or place scrap board over tiles and tap gently against the wall using a length of wood. Using a craft knife, cut the sheet of tiles to fit, if necessary.

4 To tile around an obstacle, such as a light switch, measure the distance from the last full sheet to the obstacle and measure the dimensions of the obstacle.

5 Use a craft knife to cut out tiles within the obstacle area.

6 Lay the cut sheet in the usual way.

7 Clean away excess adhesive from tile surfaces with damp sponge. Leave tiles for at least 24 hours to set.

8 Finish with grouting (see page 34).

HOW TO NAIL IT!

- Check each sheet of mosaic tiles is the right way up for your pattern before you apply it to the wall.

- Work quickly when applying the tiles to the adhesive; the backing sheet starts to disintegrate in contact with adhesive, so becomes difficult to move.

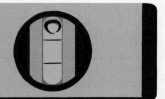

DRILL THROUGH TILES

Ceramic tiles are brittle but they can be drilled through without shattering. You need to use a ceramic tile or masonry bit to break through the glaze without it skidding on, or cracking, the surface.

▶ YOU'LL NEED

PIPE-AND-CABLE DETECTOR

CHINAGRAPH PENCIL AND RULER

MASKING TAPE

⚠ **POWER DRILL, WITH CERAMIC TILE AND MASONRY BIT, IF NEEDED**

WALL PLUG(S)

SCREW(S)

TILE SCORER (OPTIONAL)

GETTING STARTED

These instructions are for drilling into tiles already fixed to the wall, so that an accessory, such as a towel hook, can be hung. Check for pipes and cables using a detector.

WHAT TO DO

1 Mark desired fixing points on tile using chinagraph pencil and ruler.

2 Place masking tape over markings, transferring them to top of tape if they don't show through.

3 Starting on a slow speed, drill hole with ceramic bit. If you have masonry wall behind, change to masonry bit once you have broken through tile.

4 Remove masking tape and fit wall plug into hole. This should be a snug fit.

5 If your accessory requires more than one screw, double-check the position of subsequent holes before repeating steps 2–4.

HOW TO NAIL IT!

• You can create a starter hole in the tile using a tile scorer. This makes the drilling a bit easier.

• Make a cross with two pieces of masking tape over the hole position, for slightly more grip with drill bit.

REPLACE BROKEN TILES

07

If you only have one or two chipped or damaged tiles and a supply of spares to match, it's possible to remove and replace them.

▶ YOU'LL NEED

SAFETY GOGGLES

PROTECTIVE GLOVES

GROUT RAKE

⚠ POWER DRILL, WITH CERAMIC TILE OR MASONRY BIT

HAMMER

⚠ CHISEL

POWDERED TILE ADHESIVE

SMALL BUCKET OF WATER

NOTCHED SPREADER

⬆ **TOOL UP** TILE SPACERS

⬇ **TOOL DOWN** MATCHES

DAMP SPONGE

MATERIALS FOR GROUTING (SEE PAGE 34)

WHAT TO DO

Put goggles and gloves on, as broken tiles are sharp. Loosen grout around the edges of broken tile and rake it out. Also remove 10mm or so of grout in each direction around neighbouring tiles.

1 Drill holes in centre of the broken tile to break it up a little more (see opposite).

2 Remove pieces of tile using hammer and chisel, putting chisel into cracks and applying pressure with hammer. Work from centre out to remove all tile pieces.

3 Scrape away all tile adhesive remaining on wall surface.

4 Make up small amount of tile adhesive according to manufacturer's instructions.

5 Spread tile adhesive on back of replacement tile using notched side of spreader and fit into space on wall. Put tile spacers or matches in four corners to keep tile in position while adhesive dries.

6 Wipe off any adhesive from tile surface with damp sponge.

7 Finish with grouting. See *Grout Tiles* (page 34).

HOW TO NAIL IT!

- Be careful when chiselling the tiles – you don't want to dig into the wall, or yourself!

- Cracks in tiles allow moisture to get where it shouldn't, so replace broken or damaged tiles as soon as you can.

REMOVE SILICONE SEALANT

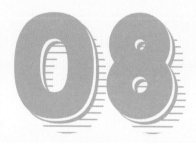

Silicone sealant makes a great waterproof barrier but can be susceptible to mould and mildew. Dirty sealant can make your bathroom look ugly and cleaning it is nearly impossible – so remove it and start again.

▶ YOU'LL NEED

CRAFT KNIFE

DAMP CLOTH AND GENTLE, NON-BLEACH CLEANER

AEROSOL LUBRICANT, SUCH AS WD40; OR SILICONE SEALANT REMOVER

TOOL UP SILICONE-REMOVING TOOL

TOOL DOWN BLUNT CRAFT KNIFE OR SCRAPER

GLASS SCRAPER OR RAZOR BLADE HOLDER

PLASTIC SCOURER

⚠ RUBBING ALCOHOL

GETTING STARTED

First check that what you're removing is actually silicone sealant. Use a craft knife to cut into it: if it's soft and rubbery, it is silicone and easily removable with your tools. If it's hard and crumbly, it is probably grout. See *Renovate Grout* (page 33).

Clean the whole area before you start, to remove soap scum and dirt. Use a damp cloth and gentle, non-bleach cleaner. If you clean after removing the silicone, water will find its way where it shouldn't.

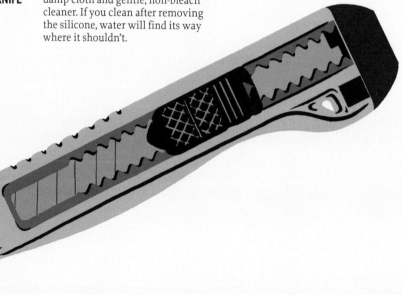

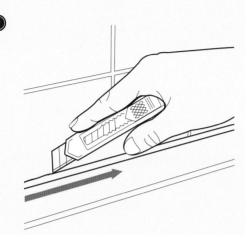

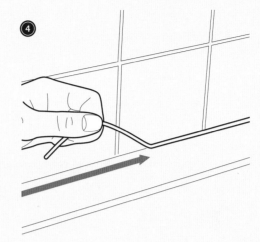

WHAT TO DO

➊ Spray lubricant or sealant remover along the old sealant and leave for 5 minutes. The spray will start to break the sealant down, making it easier to take off. If you're using a specific sealant remover, refer to the instructions for timings.

➋ Run your blunt knife or scraper, or silicone-removing tool, along the top and bottom edges of the seal. Be very careful not to scratch the tiles or bath.

➌ Cut through the silicone at one end with the craft knife.

➍ Prise the end up, grip it firmly and slowly and pull the silicone away in one long thread. Use your knife to loosen any remaining bits as you go. Be patient – you will save yourself time in the long run – but don't expect to do it in one go.

➎ Scrape away remaining silicone with a glass scraper or razor blade holder.

➏ Use a plastic scourer soaked in rubbing alcohol to clean away any last traces of silicone.

HOW TO NAIL IT!

- Go in carefully with your tools to avoid damaging your tiles or bath.

- Be sure to remove all traces of old silicone before applying any more, as new won't stick to old.

- Once you've cleaned away all remaining traces of old sealant, leave the surface completely clean and dry before applying new sealant.

APPLY SILICONE SEALANT

Silicone sealant is ideal as a flexible and waterproof seal around sinks, baths and showers. It's easy to use and, if applied with care, can give an expert finish. Silicone comes in different colours so if you have a coloured suite or tiles, you should be able to find one to match.

YOU'LL NEED

SANITARY SILICONE SEALANT AND APPLICATOR GUN

MASKING TAPE

CRAFT KNIFE

WASHING-UP LIQUID

TOOL UP SILICONE SMOOTHER

TOOL DOWN YOUR FINGER

KITCHEN PAPER

GETTING STARTED

To remove any old silicone sealant, see *Remove Silicone Sealant* (page 44).

Ensure the surfaces are completely clean and dry before you start.

Choose a good-quality brand of sealant that has an anti-mould and anti-mildew ingredient.

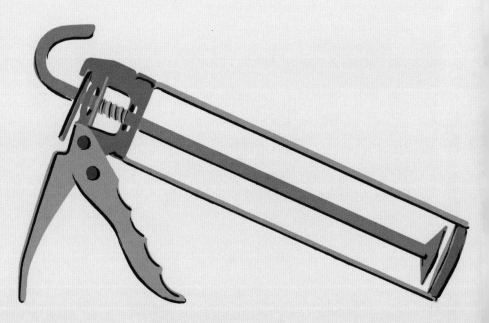

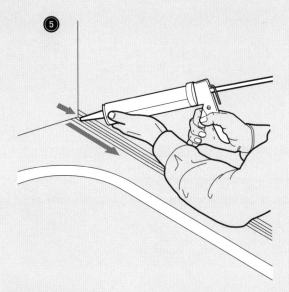

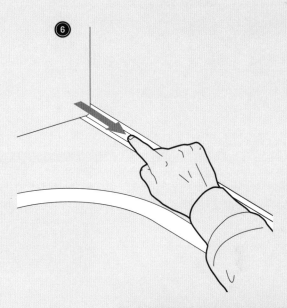

WHAT TO DO

1 Run some masking tape parallel to the edge of the area to be sealed, about 3mm away. Do the same on the other side, ensuring that the gap between the two pieces of tape is even. This will help you keep a neat, straight line.

2 Place the tube of sealant into the applicator gun and then screw the nozzle onto the tube. Using your craft knife, cut the nozzle at a 45-degree angle, to a size that corresponds with the area you are sealing. Cut a little off first; you can always cut more if needed.

3 Fill the bath with cold water. This stops the silicone being stretched and pulling away when you eventually have your well-earned bath.

4 Add a dash of washing-up liquid to a small bowl of water and keep nearby.

5 Starting in the corner, squeeze the silicone steadily and smoothly along the space between the pieces of tape. Be generous and make sure that you don't leave any gaps. Don't worry about blobs – they will be neatened up next.

6 Dip the smoother or your finger into the bowl of water and washing-up liquid. Starting from the same place you began, press the smoother or your finger into the silicone and drag it along between the tape, to a concave line. Wipe away any excess onto kitchen paper. Do 300-400mm at a time, then clean, re-wet and repeat.

7 As soon as you're happy with the finish and have made sure there are no gaps, quickly remove the tape in one steady, even movement. Leave the silicone to set and the water in the bath for three to four hours. (Check specific timings against manufacturer's instructions).

HOW TO NAIL IT!

- Where you cut the end of the applicator controls how much comes out. For a small bead, cut the applicator near the tip; for a larger bead, cut higher up.

- Don't worry too much about mishaps, but if you are nervous, try applying a line on waste paper or cardboard before you begin.

- Start by applying short lengths of silicone until you gain confidence.

REMOVE AND PREVENT MOULD

Mould spores are everywhere in the air, but they will only grow in damp areas, caused mainly by household condensation. This is not only unsightly but can be smelly, not to mention hazardous to your health.

YOU'LL NEED

RUBBER GLOVES
HOUSEHOLD BLEACH
PLUS, IF NEEDED:
RESPIRATOR
PLASTIC SHEETING AND TAPE
SOFT BRUSH
SPRAY BOTTLE
CRAFT KNIFE
PLASTIC WRAP
VACUUM CLEANER
MILDEWCIDE PAINT
AND PAINTBRUSH

GETTING STARTED

Wearing rubber gloves, test suspected mildewy areas by dabbing a little neat household bleach onto the dark area. After one or two minutes, if it has lightened, it is probably mildew; if it remains dark it is probably just dirt. Only do this on walls, not carpet. If you have a very large mould infestation (across more than one square metre, or with a strong, musty smell) take extra precautions to protect yourself and prevent spores spreading. Wear old clothes and a respirator. Open doors and windows to outside and hang plastic sheeting over inner doorways.

WHAT TO DO

❶ Remove mould

Walls: wearing rubber gloves, mix one part bleach to eight parts water. Using a soft brush, scrub with bleach solution until mould disappears. Do not rinse surface. Leave to dry in direct sunlight, if possible.

Wallpaper: spray with water mist to stop spores spreading. Use craft knife to cut away mouldy pieces in sections. Wrap in plastic and tape up for disposal. Vacuum away debris.

Carpets: it is difficult to clean mould from carpet and underlay. It's usually better to remove the carpet entirely.

❷ Prevent mould recurring

Find and fix any leaks or water ingress to area. Check and clear gutters, look at ventilation and deal with causes of condensation. Allow area to dry fully, then repaint walls with paint containing mildewcide. See *Paint Walls* (page 150).

HOW TO NAIL IT!

- Never add another chemical substance to a bleached area. (Ammonia, even if hidden in a detergent, reacts with bleach to create a poisonous gas.)

- Poor insulation can aggravate condensation, which happens when hot damp air meets a colder surface. You can help by limiting steam cooking, and drying clothes outside when possible. Keep doors and windows open when using bathroom, use extractor fans for 20 minutes after cooking, and increase ventilation.

- To tackle mouldy grout, see *Renovate Grout* (page 33).

REMOVE LIMESCALE

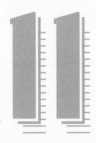

Limescale is the crystalline mineral deposit left behind when water evaporates. The best way to prevent limescale from developing is to keep surfaces dry. Limescale can be removed using natural acids like lemon juice, which are just as effective as man-made products.

▶ YOU'LL NEED

WHITE VINEGAR OR LEMON JUICE
PLUS, IF NEEDED:
COTTON WOOL
RUBBER GLOVES
STRING
PLASTIC SCOURER
LEMON, HALVED
TOOTHPICK
SPONGE SCOURER

GETTING STARTED

Judge how serious your limescale deposits are and act accordingly!

WHAT TO DO

Washing machines and dishwashers

Run an empty wash cycle with a large cup of white vinegar or lemon juice instead of your usual detergent. Place liquid in base of dishwasher rather than in dispenser.

Kettles

❶ Fill kettle up to limescale line (or quarter-full, if no strong line) with white vinegar or lemon juice. Leave to soak for an hour.

❷ Top up kettle to full with water and boil. Pour boiled solution away before it cools. Rinse kettle thoroughly several times.

Taps

Soak cotton wool in vinegar or lemon juice. Wearing rubber gloves, wrap around limescaled parts – secure with string if needed. Leave overnight, then wipe or scrub off.

Shower heads

❶ Remove the shower faceplate from shower head – or just remove the whole shower head. It should unscrew easily.

❷ Soak faceplate or shower head in white vinegar or lemon juice for at least eight hours. Alternatively, place the cut side of half a lemon against the shower head and tie in place with string. Leave overnight and rinse.

❸ Remove any remaining limescale by pushing a toothpick through shower head holes. Scrub clean. Replace showerhead.

Other flat surfaces

Scrub with scourer and vinegar or lemon juice, or rub with the cut side of half a lemon. Leave overnight and rinse.

HOW TO NAIL IT!

- For very thick limescale build-up you can chip it off carefully using a penknife tapped – very gently – with a hammer.

REPAIR CERAMIC OR ENAMEL SURFACE

12

Ceramic and enamel sinks, baths and toilets look great when shiny and new, but when they're chipped or cracked they not only look horrid, but can leak. Often, though, it's a simple job to repair them.

YOU'LL NEED

- SPONGE AND SCOURER
- WASHING-UP LIQUID
- TOWEL
- RUBBER GLOVES
- TOOTHPICK OR RAZOR BLADE
- ⚠ ENAMEL OR EPOXY FILLER
- KITCHEN SPATULA OR PALETTE KNIFE
- COTTON BUD, IF NEEDED
- NAIL VARNISH REMOVER, IF NEEDED

GETTING STARTED

Sponge-wash and scrub the sink, bath or outside of toilet thoroughly with washing-up liquid and hot water to get rid of grease and dirt. Dry it out completely with a towel.

WHAT TO DO

❶ Wearing rubber gloves, use a toothpick or razor blade to spread the epoxy filler smoothly into the chipped or cracked area. Using a spatula or palette knife, scrape it flush to the surface and wipe away any excess.

❷ Allow 24 hours for the filler to dry before touching the surface or exposing it to water.

HOW TO NAIL IT!

- Fix any rough epoxy edges using a cotton bud dipped in nail varnish remover. Do this while the epoxy is drying.
- Don't scrub the sink, bath or toilet for a week after you've filled the cracks.

ADJUST LOOSE TOILET SEAT

Toilet seats can easily loosen through use, but you don't need to live with a seat that shifts to the side every time you sit down on it. Tightening it is easier than fitting a new seat and a quick fix for an annoying problem.

YOU'LL NEED

SCREWDRIVER
ADJUSTABLE SPANNER OR PLIERS

GETTING STARTED

Find the bolts that secure the lid to the toilet pan at the back of the seat. They might be covered by plastic caps, which you can pop open.

WHAT TO DO

1. Use a screwdriver to tighten the bolts. If the bolt just spins in place, use a spanner or a pair of pliers to hold the nut on the underside firmly in place while turning the screwdriver.

2. Turn the nut clockwise to tighten and hold bolt in place.

3. Check the toilet seat and adjust again, if necessary.

HOW TO NAIL IT!

- You can use a flat-head screwdriver to help flip open the plastic caps.
- Don't overtighten the nuts or you risk cracking the seat or – worse – toilet pan.
- It's often easier to take off the toilet seat, clean the toilet thoroughly and refit.

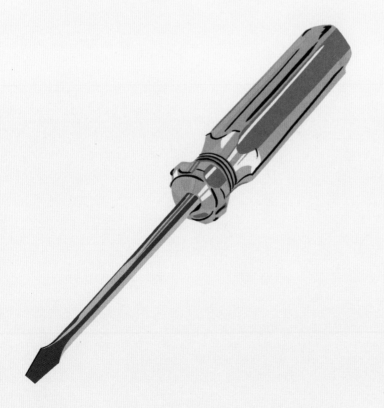

REPLACE TOILET SEAT

14

This is the simplest toilet repair job around and a quick and easy way to give your toilet a feeling of newness when you first move house.

YOU'LL NEED

STEEL TAPE MEASURE

NEW TOILET SEAT AND FIXINGS

SCREWDRIVER
OR ADJUSTABLE SPANNER

⚠ BLEACH AND TOILET CLEANER

PLUS, AS NEEDED:

AEROSOL LUBRICANT,
SUCH AS WD40

MASKING TAPE

⚠ JUNIOR HACKSAW

GETTING STARTED

Check the shape and dimensions of your existing toilet seat before going to the shop. Toilet seats come in a few standard sizes. To be really sure, take your old seat with you.

WHAT TO DO

1 Close the toilet lid and remove the seat from the pan by unscrewing the fastening at the back. The bolts may be covered by caps, which you'll need to open first. Use fingers, screwdriver or spanner as needed.

2 Use the opportunity of the toilet being seat-free to give it a really good clean before putting the new seat on.

3 Align the holes of the new seat with the holes of the pan, insert the new bolts and fasten to secure.

4 Secure the bolts with nuts on the underside and tighten with your screwdriver or spanner. Don't overtighten or you may crack the toilet pan. Fit any caps.

HOW TO NAIL IT!

- If the nuts won't loosen, try spraying on lubricant, leaving a few minutes and trying again.

- If the nuts are totally stuck, protect toilet with masking tape and use a junior hacksaw to cut the bolts off. New toilet seats come with their own bolts so don't worry about destroying the old ones.

- NEVER mix chemical cleaners as dangerous reactions can occur.

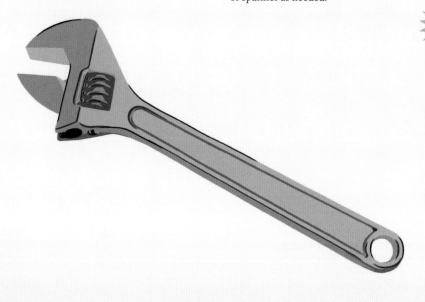

UNBLOCK TOILET

The only things you should flush down the loo are things that would break down in a bucket of water if left for 24 hours. If you do get a blockage, it's worth trying to sort out the problem yourself before calling in a plumber.

YOU'LL NEED

RUBBER GLOVES
OLD NEWSPAPERS
PLASTIC JUG AND BUCKET
PLUNGER
WIRE COAT HANGER OR TOILET AUGER, IF NEEDED

GETTING STARTED

As soon as you notice a problem, use the toilet as little as possible. Don't flush repeatedly or it may overflow and flood the room!

WHAT TO DO

1. Put on rubber gloves.

2. Place old newspapers around the base of the toilet to catch any spills.

3. Bail out excess water from blocked toilet bowl into a bucket, using a plastic jug. You can pour this back down the toilet once it's clear.

4. Cover toilet with cup end of plunger, ensuring plunger is full of water. Push down firmly but carefully and lift slowly, repeating until blockage clears.

5. If blockage persists, try using a wire coat hanger. Unravel it and bend into a curve or snake shape. Push the wire up the toilet canal and wiggle it about to clear the blockage, being very careful not to scratch the toilet.

6. If the blockage persists, use toilet auger. Hold handle and insert wire into drain. Push gently while turning handle.

7. When crank becomes hard to turn, remove auger, clean end with running water and reinsert, repeating until blockage breaks up and clears.

8. When blockage has cleared, flush toilet to check flow.

HOW TO NAIL IT!

- Don't be too rough with your equipment as toilet bowls can easily be damaged.
- You may find that you need to clear from the other end of the blockage – if so, find the manhole cover and use the toilet auger.

MEND TOILET FLUSH

16

If you've got problems with your loo, there are a few easy things to try before calling in the plumber. The most common issues tend to be that the loo won't flush or that water constantly runs into the cistern or pan.

YOU'LL NEED

OLD TOWEL
ADJUSTABLE SPANNER
PLUS, AS NEEDED:
REPLACEMENT PARTS
SCREWDRIVER
SPONGE AND VINEGAR

GETTING STARTED

The first step is identifying the source of the problem. Have an old towel to hand to mop up any spilled water. Take the cistern lid off and flush the loo a couple of times to watch the process. When you push the handle, the chain or rod lifts the flapper, or flap valve, allowing the water from the cistern to fall through into the bowl. As the water in the cistern drains, the float drops.

The float is connected to a valve (ballcock valve or fill valve) that lets water into the cistern when the float is down and should stop when the float is up. There is an overflow pipe that drains water into the bowl if it gets too high.

There are a few standard kinds of replacement part, so it's best to remove the whole part, take to your local DIY shop and buy one to match.

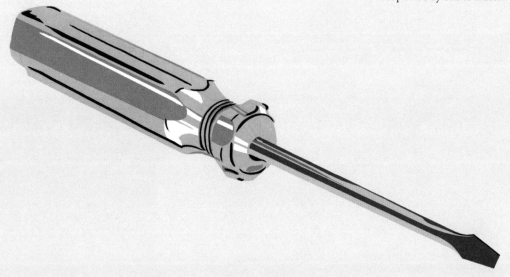

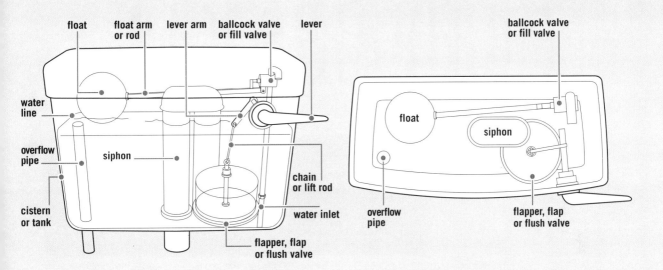

float · float arm or rod · lever arm · ballcock valve or fill valve · lever · water line · overflow pipe · siphon · cistern or tank · chain or lift rod · water inlet · flapper, flap or flush valve · ballcock valve or fill valve · float · siphon · overflow pipe · flapper, flap or flush valve

WHAT TO DO

If the toilet won't flush

Check whether the flushing lever is still attached to the internal workings of the cistern. It should be connected via a chain or lift rod. If it's no longer attached, re-attach or make a replacement from a thick piece of wire.

If the lever is loose

Tighten the nut on the inside of the cistern that holds the lever to the tank.

If the lever or lever arm is broken

1 Remove the support nut attached to the lever. Unclip the chain or rod connecting the float to the rubber stopper and slide the lever and arm out of the hole in the porcelain.

2 Take the lever or lever arm to your local DIY shop and buy a replacement to match.

3 Feed the new arm and lever through the hole into the tank.

4 Tighten the support nut and reattach the chain or rod to the float.

If the cistern keeps filling

If the cistern keeps filling, the overflow will keep running, generally draining into the loo bowl. This can waste a huge amount of water so try to deal with it quickly.

1 Check the water level in the tank. It should be about 25mm below the overflow outlet or in line with a marked water line inside the cistern.

2 If it isn't, try adjusting the float down the arm or bending the float arm. Check to see if water stops rising.

3 If this doesn't work, check whether the float is damaged and holding water. If it is, replace it.

4 If these steps don't solve the issue, there may be a problem with the ballcock valve – the valve that lets water into the cistern. Some have screws to manage the water level so try adjusting these. You could also try cleaning the valve, but if it's worn or split, replace.

If water is continuously flowing or leaking into the bowl

1 Check the water level of the cistern – it may not be full enough. It should be about 25mm below the overflow outlet or in line with a marked water line inside the cistern. Increase the water level by turning the water valve all the way on. To find the water valve, look behind the tank of the toilet. It should be near the floor, usually on the left side of the toilet.

2 If this allows the cistern to fill, the toilet should stop running and the problem is solved.

3 If not, locate and check the flapper, or flap valve. This is the valve which sits at the bottom of the cistern or underneath the siphon that lifts to let the water through to the toilet bowl. Over time, the rubbery part can get old and stiff, or limescale can build up on it or around the valve (also called flush valve).

4 Run a finger carefully around the underside of the flapper and the rim where it sits. If you feel dirt, turn off the water valve and flush to empty the cistern. Try cleaning with a sponge and some vinegar.

5 If the rubber is old and worn, replace.

HOW TO NAIL IT!

- Ensure the float isn't catching on anything or dragging against the side of the cistern.

- If these steps don't help solve the problem, you will need to call in a plumber to check for cracks or a worn gasket.

FIX DRIPPING TAP

On older taps, drips can often be stopped by replacing a washer; on modern taps, by replacing the interior cartridge that houses all the important parts.

YOU'LL NEED

- SCREWDRIVER
- PLIERS
- ADJUSTABLE SPANNER, OR SPANNER TO FIT
- REPLACEMENT CARTRIDGE OR WASHER
- SILICONE GREASE
- HEAVY CLOTH, PIECE OF LEATHER OR DUCT TAPE, IF NEEDED

GETTING STARTED

First turn off the water supply. There is usually a valve under the sink or behind the shower assembly, or you may find a screw slot, which you'll need to turn with a screwdriver until it points across the width of pipe rather than along its length. Otherwise, turn off the water supply to the whole building.

Turn the tap on and wait until you have cleared any residual water from the pipes.

Put the plug in the sink in case any small screws or nuts fall out while you're taking the tap apart. It's a good idea to put these aside somewhere safe so that you can locate them easily when reassembling the tap.

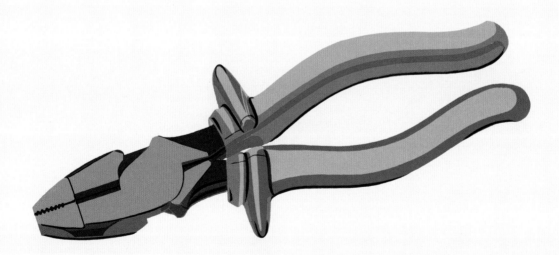

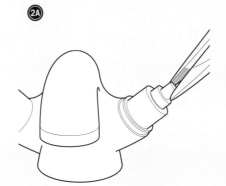

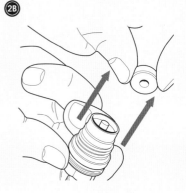

WHAT TO DO

① Remove decorative tap top (often marked 'hot' or 'cold'). Remove screw underneath, then jiggle handle to remove. Screwdriver or pliers may be needed at any stage.

② **A** *Modern taps*: remove interior cartridge using pliers. NB: it may be held in by a lock ring or nut that will need removing first, using a spanner. Replace with new cartridge.

B *Older taps*: use spanner to undo nuts, remove headgear and reveal old washer. Prise out washer and replace with new.

③ Apply silicone grease to screw threads then reassemble tap in reverse sequence.

④ Turn water supply back on. Check for leaks in reassembled taps.

⑤ If the problem continues, you may need to replace the tap.

HOW TO NAIL IT!

- Use a cloth, piece of leather or some duct tape to protect the tap if using pliers on chrome surfaces.

- If the old washer is hard to remove, try levering it off with a screwdriver.

- Check your replacement washer is exactly the same size and style as the old washer.

FIX DRIPPING SHOWER HEAD

A dripping shower head doesn't just waste precious water but can be extremely annoying. If your shower head is cracked, rusty or just falling apart, it's probably time to get a new one. However, if it appears in good condition, it's a simple job to fix.

YOU'LL NEED

- SCREWDRIVER
- WHITE VINEGAR OR LEMON JUICE
- TOOTHPICK
- SPONGE SCOURER
- MASKING TAPE
- REPLACEMENT WASHER OR CONNECTION
- PTFE OR JOINT TAPE, IF NEEDED

GETTING STARTED

First check that shower head is not split or damaged in any way and that the hose is securely screwed on.

Check the shower holes for limescale clogging as this could be causing the dripping. Otherwise, a worn-out washer could be responsible.

The washer may have visible damage such as a split or break. It may also feel brittle and leave behind a dark residue on your fingers.

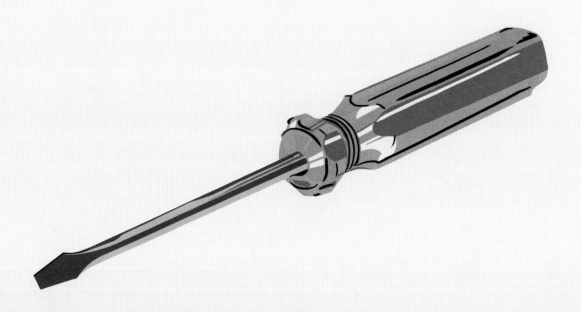

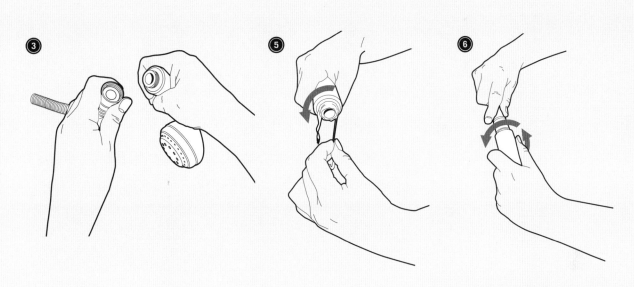

WHAT TO DO

1 Remove the shower faceplate from shower head. It should unscrew by hand.

2 To remove limescale, soak faceplate in white vinegar or lemon juice for at least eight hours. Remove any remaining limescale by pushing a toothpick through shower head holes. Scrub clean with sponge scourer. See also *Remove Limescale* (page 49). Replace faceplate.

3 If this doesn't solve the dripping, you'll need to unscrew shower head from the hose. Before you do this, cover the drain with masking tape or put the plug into the bath.

4 Check connection between hose and shower head. Replace rubber washer or connecting part as necessary.

5 Screw hose back on and check. If shower still drips, try PTFE tape, or joint tape – it helps make threaded fittings watertight. Unscrew head from hose and wrap tape around thread.

6 Screw hose and shower head back together, tightening by hand.

7 Turn water on again and run shower briefly. Turn off, then wait a few minutes to check for drips. If the problem continues, you may need to buy a new shower head or hose, or both.

HOW TO NAIL IT!

- **Check your replacement washer is exactly the same size and style as the old washer.**

UNBLOCK SINK

Bathroom plug holes can easily get blocked with hair; kitchen sinks with waste food or vegetable peelings. You might need to remove the sink's U-bend (waste trap) to clear a blockage, or if you lose something valuable. Use chemical drain cleaner only as a last resort.

▶ YOU'LL NEED

RUBBER GLOVES (OPTIONAL)
DAMP RAG OR KITCHEN CLOTH
PLUNGER
BUCKET
▲ **TOOL UP** PLUMBER'S WRENCH
▼ **TOOL DOWN** PLIERS

GETTING STARTED

Once you notice a blockage, use the sink as little as possible so you don't aggravate the problem. Gather all the tools you will need for the job before starting. If you like, wear rubber gloves to help with grip and to protect your hands against any unpleasant waste.

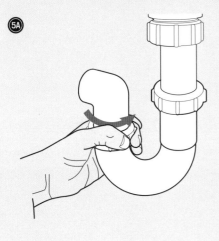

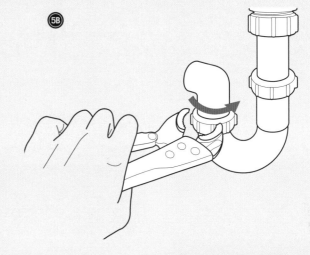

WHAT TO DO

1 Fill the blocked sink halfway with water, if not already full. Block overflow hole with damp rag or kitchen cloth.

2 Cover sink drain opening with the cup end of plunger, ensuring plunger is full of water. Push down firmly but carefully and lift slowly, repeating until blockage clears.

3 When the blockage has cleared, run hot water down the sink drain for several minutes. Unblock overflow hole.

4 If the blockage has not cleared, locate the waste trap – it's the U-shaped pipe that connects the vertical pipe coming from the sink to the horizontal pipe that goes into the wall. Place the bucket under the trap to catch any spills.

5 A Unscrew the trap.

B If too tightly fixed to unscrew by hand, use plumber's wrench or pliers.

6 Pull away the trap; it will be full of dirty water so let it fall into the bucket.

7 Empty the trap into bucket and look for any lost valuables. Clean the trap of any hair or food debris.

8 Reassemble the trap, taking care not to overtighten. Run hot water for several minutes to ensure blockage is clear. If blockage persists, check outside drains .

HOW TO NAIL IT!

- If you lose something valuable down the sink, turn off the water as soon as possible so the item doesn't get washed out of reach.

- Use plug strainers to help minimise future blockages.

- If the U-bend hasn't been undone for a while and you need to use a plumber's wrench or pliers, protect the pipe with a cloth so you don't damage it.

CONNECT WASHING MACHINE OR DISHWASHER

This job should not take long and with some plumbing know-how you can avoid calling out the professionals. These instructions assume you are replacing existing appliances so the plumbing will be ready to connect.

▶ YOU'LL NEED

NEW WASHING MACHINE
OR DISHWASHER, PLUS HOSES
PLUS, AS NEEDED:
WASHING MACHINE
OR DISHWASHER SINK TRAP,
WITH NON-RETURN VALVE
WASTE JUNCTION
ADJUSTABLE SPANNER,
OR SPANNER TO FIT

GETTING STARTED

Remove all the packaging from outside and inside the appliance. Make sure you keep hold of the instructions. Don't forget to recycle packaging wherever possible.

⚠ STAY SAFE!

Make sure your washing machine or dishwasher is not plugged into the mains, before you start work.

For washing machines, remove bolts that secure drum whilst in transit, with adjustable spanner.

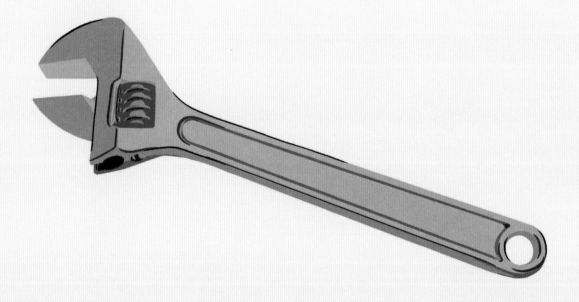

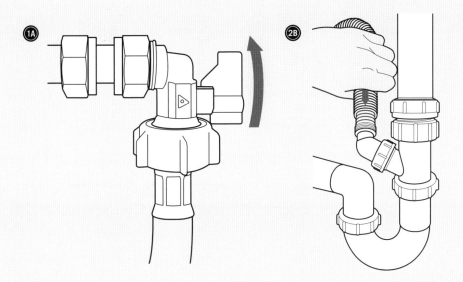

WHAT TO DO

1 Fit water pipes to the appliance, following the manufacturer's instructions and using supplied hoses. There may be a red for hot and a blue for cold, or just a cold pipe.

A Check the valve(s) on the existing household plumbing are turned off.

B Screw the hose onto the valve(s). Check connection is tight before turning on the valve.

2 If you are replacing like for like, you need only push waste pipe into the existing machine drain. If not, either fit waste pipe to sink drain, if machine is close to sink, or fit to vertical waste pipe.

A To connect waste pipe to sink drain: swap the sink trap for a washing machine or dishwasher trap and join the machine waste pipe to the trap.

B To connect waste pipe to existing waste supply, add junction, if needed, to existing pipe and attach waste pipe from appliance to this.

HOW TO NAIL IT!

- Don't try to tackle any electrical jobs while connecting your machine. Call in a professional electrician instead.

- If you are getting rid of an old washing machine or dishwasher, contact your local council or the manufacturer for advice on how to recycle it.

RENOVATE KITCHEN UNITS

You can make a huge difference to the look of your kitchen with just some simple renovations to the units. By repainting cupboard doors and updating the handles, you'll refresh the heart of your home without the need for a full redesign.

► YOU'LL NEED

SCREWDRIVER

STEEL TAPE MEASURE

DUSTSHEET, NEWSPAPER OR OLD CLOTH

NEW DOOR HANDLES, HINGES AND FITTINGS, AS DESIRED

FINE- AND MEDIUM-GRADE SANDPAPER

TOOL UP POWER SANDER

TOOL DOWN SANDING BLOCK

SOFT CLOTH

PAINTBRUSH

PRIMER

PAINT

GETTING STARTED

If you find it easier, use a screwdriver to remove your cabinet doors, drawer fronts and their hinges and handles, and move them to your workspace.

If you are replacing handles, take your old ones with you to the shop to ensure you choose something that has the same-size fittings. Remember to note how many you will need.

Also, if any of the handles were held on by more than one screw, note the distance between the two screws, as you will need to find replacements with the same distance between – or, be prepared to fill and drill new holes.

It's a good idea to buy one sample first, to check the fit, before investing in a full set.

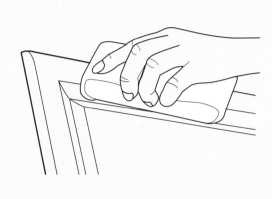

WHAT TO DO

1 Lay down dustsheet, newspaper or old cloth to protect your floor.

2 Using medium-grade sandpaper, sand down front and edges of wooden, painted or varnished doors or drawer fronts, with power sander **(A)** or sanding block **(B)**. No sanding or priming is needed for melamine doors, but you do need to use the right paint. Wipe off dust and give the doors a good clean.

3 Paint on a coat of primer, leave to dry and apply another coat.

4 When dry, rub down surfaces with fine-grade sandpaper. Wipe off dust.

5 Apply the first coat of paint and leave to dry overnight. Repeat with another coat of paint, for a more durable finish. See also *Paint Interior Woodwork* (page 168). Replace handles with new, if desired.

6 Replace doors and drawer fronts using a screwdriver to tighten hinges.

HOW TO NAIL IT!

- If you have a number of cabinet doors to remove, label them on the back so you can easily find the right place for the right door when you have finished.

- If your cabinet doors and drawer fronts do not completely cover the front of the units, you can prepare and paint those surfaces in the same way. A good time to do this is while the cabinet doors are drying.

- If you want to save time, you can buy undercoat and primer in one, eliminating one of the stages.

REPAIR GRANITE WORKTOP

22

Granite is a great choice for a kitchen worktop as it can withstand the heat of a saucepan and is easy to keep clean. It's a very durable material, but prone to chipping if you drop something hard on it. Fortunately, these chips can be fixed quite easily.

▶ YOU'LL NEED

SPONGE

WASHING-UP LIQUID

CLEAN, DRY TEA TOWEL

MASKING TAPE

RUBBER GLOVES

⚠ GRANITE EPOXY RESIN AND HARDENER

KITCHEN SPATULA OR PALETTE KNIFE

RAZOR BLADE

GRANITE SEALER

PAINTBRUSH

GETTING STARTED

Clean grease and dirt from the damaged area with a sponge and warm, soapy water. Dry with tea towel and leave to air-dry for one hour.

Mask off area to be repaired using masking tape.

WHAT TO DO

1 Wearing rubber gloves, mix epoxy resin and hardener, according to instructions.

2 Use a spatula or palette knife to apply resin to the damaged area.

3 Scrape off excess with a razor blade.

4 Leave to dry for one hour, or as per instructions.

5 After 24 hours, apply granite sealer with a paintbrush. Leave to dry before using worktop.

HOW TO NAIL IT!

- If the chipped area is in any way wet or greasy it will not hold the glue.

- When you're scraping off the excess, hold the razor blade perpendicular to the countertop or you could risk pulling the resin out.

REPAIR LAMINATE WORKTOP

Laminate is one of the most affordable and popular materials for a kitchen worktop. It comes in hundreds of different colours and styles. Small scratches, gouges and chips can be disguised with the help of adhesive sealant.

► YOU'LL NEED

- RUBBER GLOVES
- CLEAN RAG
- ⚠ SOLVENT
- KITCHEN SPATULA OR PALETTE KNIFE
- ADHESIVE SEALANT
- SPONGE
- WASHING-UP LIQUID

GETTING STARTED

Wearing rubber gloves, clean grease and dirt from damaged worktop area using a rag soaked in appropriate solvent. Check with your local DIY store that it won't damage your surface.

Smooth down the surface as far as possible using a spatula to remove any fragments that are sticking out.

WHAT TO DO

1. Put a generous blob of adhesive sealant on the spatula or palette knife, gently press it down into the scratch and smooth it out.

2. Repeat application until scratch has been filled and built up to level of worktop.

3. Smooth off the top with the spatula.

4. Use the solvent-moistened rag to wipe around sealed area.

5. Leave 24 hours for sealant to harden before cleaning with sponge and warm soapy water.

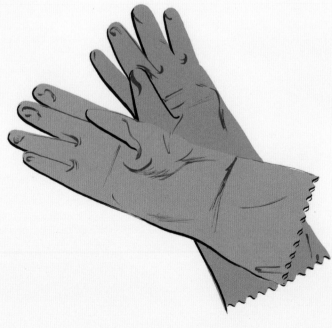

HOW TO NAIL IT!

- You may be lucky enough to find a sealant that matches the colour of your laminate worktop. If not, opt for a clear one.

- If a strip of laminate has come loose from one of the front or side edges of the worktop, place a clean, folded tea towel over it and carefully press with a medium-hot iron. This should reactivate the glue so that it sticks back in place.

REPAIR WOODEN WORKTOP

24

The beauty of a solid wood worktop is that if you mistreat it – causing surface damage or scratches – you can simply sand it down and apply a few coats of oil to reveal a lovely new surface.

▶ YOU'LL NEED

MASKING TAPE

MEDIUM- AND FINE-GRADE SANDPAPER

⚡ TOOL UP POWER SANDER

⚡ TOOL DOWN SANDING BLOCK

DAMP CLOTH

RUBBER GLOVES

COTTON BUDS

⚠ HOUSEHOLD BLEACH

WORKTOP OIL

LINT-FREE CLOTH

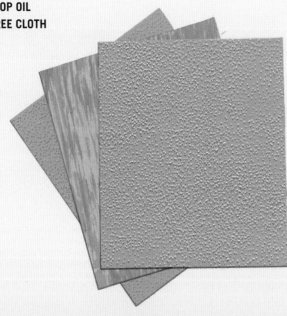

GETTING STARTED

Allow any dark stains on wood to dry before starting work.

Look carefully over the worktop to locate all the marks you'll need to repair – knife marks are typical.

Use masking tape to protect taps and other areas that could get damaged by sandpaper.

WHAT TO DO

1. Using power sander or sanding block, sand carefully over the areas to be repaired. Start with medium-grade sandpaper, then smooth off with fine-grade sandpaper.

2. Remove dust from sanded surfaces with a damp cloth. Leave to dry.

3. Wearing rubber gloves, use cotton buds dipped in bleach to remove any remaining black stains. Apply and leave for one hour to work.

4. Apply worktop oil using a lint-free cloth. Leave overnight or at least eight hours to dry.

5. Sand down gently using fine-grade sandpaper.

6. Repeat steps 4 and 5 until two coats have been applied. Apply third coat and leave to dry.

HOW TO NAIL IT!

- For a thorough job, remove the silicone from the joint between the worktop and wall before sanding, then re-apply when you have finished (see pages 44 and 46).

DOORS
AND
WINDOWS

EVERYTHING YOU NEED TO GET THE JOB DONE

CUT DOWN INTERIOR DOOR

Over time, moisture in the air can cause doors to swell and become hard to open. Sometimes, they stick because they've been painted too often. Sanding or planing off some of the door can bring it back to its full use. This job is best done with a helper.

▶ YOU'LL NEED

DOOR WEDGES

SCREWDRIVERS

PLIERS

COARSE- AND MEDIUM-GRADE SANDPAPER

⚠ **TOOL UP** POWER SANDER

▽ **TOOL DOWN** SANDING BLOCK

⚠ **TOOL UP** POWER PLANER

▽ **TOOL DOWN** PLANER

WORKBENCH, OR OTHER SUITABLE SURFACE (SEE PAGE 22)

PAINTBRUSH

WOOD PRIMER

PAINT

GETTING STARTED

Look over all the door edges to find the area that's sticking. Check for scrape marks on the paint or wood.

If the sticking point is on the top or upper edge you should be able to fix the door in position. If it is sticking near the floor, remove the door from its hinges and fix it on a workbench.

To remove door, open it and put wedges or screwdrivers underneath to hold it off floor. With a helper, unscrew hinges from the frame. Lift door away.

If your door has hinge pins, wedge door, then use pliers to remove the bottom hinge pin, then the top one. Lift door up and away. Sometimes a door will separate itself from the frame as soon as pins are removed, so be careful.

1B

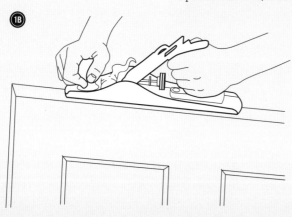

WHAT TO DO

1 **Tackle the sticking point**

A *For small areas:* sand away high spot with coarse-grade sandpaper and block.
B *For larger, high areas:* use planer to shave off excess wood. Sand with medium-grade sandpaper or power sander.

2 Prime the wood and repaint it. See *Paint Interior Woodwork* (page 168).

3 To re-hang the door, if needed, screw hinges back on door. With helper, lift door into position and screw in frame hinges. For hinge pins, position door in frame and hold in place with wedge or screwdrivers. Have helper hold the door while you replace top hinge pin, then lower one.

HOW TO NAIL IT!

- If you need to use the planer close to the lock, remove the lock first, to avoid damaging it. Simply unscrew and pull away.

- Never remove more than 10mm from each side of a door, and not more than 5mm from a panel door, or you will weaken the structure.

REPLACE DOOR HINGES

26

Door hinges can get squeaky or floppy with age. See *Fix Squeaky Door* (page 72), as a first step to resolving squeaks. Replacing them is a relatively straightforward way to relieve stress on your door. This job is best done with a helper.

YOU'LL NEED

DOOR WEDGES

SCREWDRIVERS

PLIERS, IF NEEDED

NEW HINGES

⚠ POWER DRILL, WITH WOOD BIT, IF NEEDED

⚠ CHISEL AND MALLET, IF NEEDED

GETTING STARTED

Remove the old hinges (see step 1) and take them to the hardware shop before buying replacements. This way, you'll know you're buying exactly the right size and quantity.

WHAT TO DO

1 Put door wedges or screwdrivers under door to hold it open. For fixed hinges, unscrew hinges from doorframe. With helper, pull door away and unscrew hinges from door. For hinge pins, remove pins following instructions, opposite.

2 Buy replacements.

3 To rehang, screw new hinges on door first, then lift into position with helper and screw into original holes on frame. For hinge pins, hold door in position and put pin in.

4 If your new hinges are a different size, or if you need to re-position the hinge, you may need to drill new small pilot holes first in door and frame before screwing into place. Use chisel to create recess on door and frame as necessary, to fit.

3

HOW TO NAIL IT!

- The number of hinges needed will depend on the weight of the door, so don't scrimp by replacing three hinges with two.

FIX SQUEAKY DOOR

27

Squeaky doors always seem to be at their worst at night when you're trying to be quiet. At any time of day, the noise is very annoying. Whether the squeak comes from the hinge or the handle, it is usually a very easy job to fix.

▶ YOU'LL NEED

WARM, SOAPY WATER

SOFT CLOTH

▲ **TOOL UP** AEROSOL LUBRICANT, SUCH AS WD40

▼ **TOOL DOWN** OLIVE OIL AND PAINTBRUSH OR CLOTH

PLUS, AS NEEDED:

PLIERS

STEEL WOOL AND SOAP

HAMMER

GETTING STARTED

Work out which part of the door the squeak is coming from.

Make sure the hinges are free of dust and grime by wiping with warm, soapy water.

WHAT TO DO

1 Spray lubricant or dab a small amount of olive oil onto hinge mechanism.

2 Open and close door a few times to allow lubricant or oil to work its way through.

3 Wipe away excess.

4 If your door has hinge pins and is still squeaking, remove one pin at a time with pliers. See *Cut Down Interior Door* (page 70). Wipe with steel wool and rub with soap. If bent, tap into shape with hammer. Replace and repeat with second pin. Alternatively, replace with new.

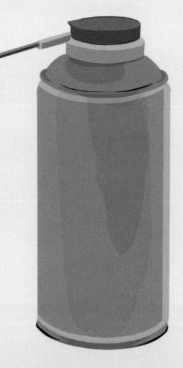

HOW TO NAIL IT!

- Using olive oil rather than an aerosol lubricant is not only better for the environment, but smells much nicer. Avoid using vegetable oils as they can oxidise and go rancid and tacky.

FIT CATFLAP

28

Catflaps that work with magnets are a popular option but can allow other cats with magnetic collars to get in. They can also attract metallic debris. Microchipped catflaps are more expensive, but allow access to your cat only, as long as it, too, has been microchipped.

YOU'LL NEED

STEEL TAPE MEASURE

CATFLAP, WITH TEMPLATE AND FIXINGS

MASKING TAPE

SPIRIT LEVEL

⚠ POWER DRILL, WITH 13MM AND 6MM WOOD BITS

PENCIL AND LONG RULER

⬆ **TOOL UP** POWER JIGSAW

⬇ **TOOL DOWN** PADSAW

MEDIUM-GRADE SANDPAPER

SCREWDRIVER

⚠ JUNIOR HACKSAW, IF NEEDED

GETTING STARTED

Refer to manufacturer's instructions before you start.

WHAT TO DO

1 Choose a position the cat will be able to reach, in a thinner part of the door, if possible. This should be about 100-150mm off the ground, as a rough guide. Tape the fixing template in position on the door and, using a spirit level, check it is level.

2 Drill holes at each inner corner of the catflap template, using the 13mm bit. This is to mark where you will cut out the inner slot.

3 Remove template and draw lines connecting holes using a pencil and ruler.

4 Insert saw into a corner hole and cut along the lines to remove panel and reveal the hole. See *Fit Letterbox* (page 74). Smooth out rough edges with medium-grade sandpaper.

5 Hold flap in position over hole and check it is level. Mark and drill screw-fixing holes through door with 6mm bit.

6 Screw catflap in place and fasten nuts supplied.

HOW TO NAIL IT!

- If the supplied bolts are too long for your door, fit the nuts, then cut bolts to size with a hacksaw.

- Make sure you install the catflap the right way round, or the cat may be able to get in, but not out.

- You can also fit a catflap tunnel into a solid wall. If you want to fit into glass, you should contact your local glazier to make the hole.

FIT LETTERBOX

29

This is a straightforward job, but you should always double-check all your measurements before drilling a hole in your front door.

▶ YOU'LL NEED

LETTERBOX AND FIXINGS

PENCIL

LONG RULER

SPIRIT LEVEL

⚠ **POWER DRILL, WITH 13MM AND 6MM WOOD DRILL BITS**

⬆ **TOOL UP** POWER JIGSAW

⬇ **TOOL DOWN** PADSAW

MEDIUM-GRADE SANDPAPER

SCREWDRIVER

⚠ **JUNIOR HACKSAW, IF NEEDED**

GETTING STARTED

Choose whether you want your letterbox to come with a knocker and/or an interior draught-excluding plate. If your door is panelled, you must fit your letterbox to a strong, non-panelled section of the door. If you have a solid wood door, the letterbox can go anywhere. It's common to fit it in the centre of the door, just below the door handle.

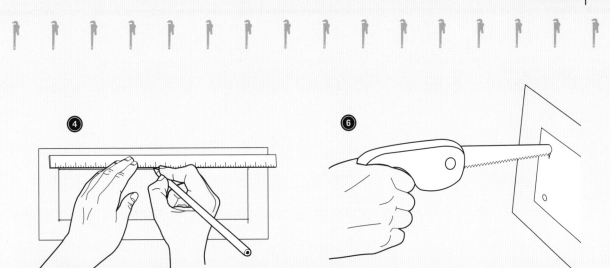

WHAT TO DO

1 Find centre point of door at the height you have chosen and mark with pencil.

2 Place letterplate centred across the mark and draw around the outside of it with your pencil.

3 Measure the distance between the outside edge of the letterbox and the top, bottom and sides of the inner flap. Make a note of these and mark up on the door.

4 Join your pencil marks, using a pencil and ruler, so that the inner flap and its position are now clearly outlined on the door. Double-check outline is straight using a spirit level.

5 Drill holes at each inside corner of the inner flap, using the 13mm bit.

6 Insert saw into a corner hole and cut along the pencil lines to remove the panel and reveal the hole.

7 Smooth out rough edges with medium-grade sandpaper.

8 Mark and drill holes for fixing bolts, using the 6mm bit. Start on one side of the door and when the drill protrudes, finish off from the other side.

9 Screw letterbox in place and fasten nuts supplied.

10 Screw letterbox cover to the inside of the door, if supplied.

HOW TO NAIL IT!

- If the supplied bolts are too long for your door, fit the nuts, then cut bolts to size with a hacksaw. Be careful to leave enough length to attach the nuts.

- If the supplied bolts are too short, use a larger drill bit and countersink the nuts. See *Back to Basics* (page 18).

FIT ARCHITRAVE

Architrave is the timber moulding that hides the joint between the door frame and the wall. Adding one to your door frame is a simple matter of cutting and fixing three lengths of moulding.

YOU'LL NEED

- PENCIL AND RULER
- ARCHITRAVE MOULDINGS, TO FIT THREE SIDES OF DOOR FRAME
- **TOOL UP** COMPOUND MITRE SAW
- **TOOL DOWN** MITRE BOX AND TENON SAW
- GRAB ADHESIVE
- PANEL PINS
- HAMMER
- WOOD ADHESIVE
- NAIL PUNCH
- DAMP CLOTH
- DECORATOR'S CAULK AND APPLICATOR GUN
- FINE-GRADE SANDPAPER
- PAINTBRUSH
- PRIMER
- PAINT

GETTING STARTED

If you are also fitting skirting boards to your room, fit the architrave first.

Using a pencil and ruler, mark points 6mm away from door frame at intervals all around frame **(A)**. Draw a continuous line through these points. This is where your architrave will be positioned.

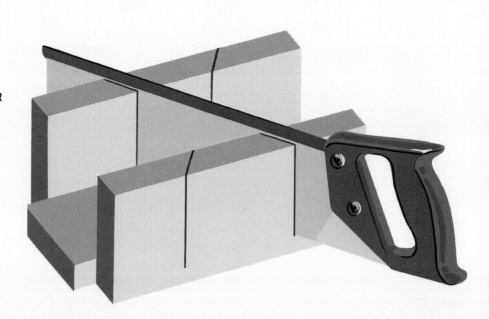

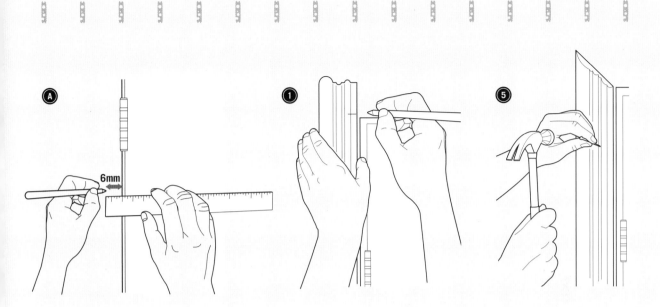

WHAT TO DO

1 Hold length of moulding up alongside door frame. Mark in pencil on moulding the level of the top corner of door.

2 Cut 45-degree angle at the marked point using mitre saw, or mitre block and saw. See *Fit Skirting Boards* (page 132). Before you cut, make sure the angle is facing the right way. For the upright mouldings, it should go upwards and outwards, with the lowest part starting from the side of the architrave closest to the door.

3 Repeat with other lengths of architrave, remembering to cut two mitres from each end of the overhead length and checking the angle before you cut.

4 Apply a line of grab adhesive to back of one vertical length of architrave. Place architrave with the moulded edge facing the doorway, on your 6mm line.

5 Loosely fix architrave with one panel pin, but don't nail pin in all the way.

6 Repeat steps 4 and 5 with the second vertical architrave.

7 Apply line of grab adhesive to back of overhead architrave and apply wood adhesive where mitres meet. Place overhead architrave in position, adjusting side sections to get a good fit.

8 Pin all three sections in place, banging the panel pins in every 300-400mm, all the way, with a nail punch.

9 Wipe away any adhesive. Use caulk to fill any discrepancies in the mitres, behind the architrave or over the nail holes (see *How to Nail It!*, page 133). Sand down when dry.

10 Prime and paint to finish. See *Paint Interior Woodwork* (page 168).

HOW TO NAIL IT!

- Don't hammer the panel pins in all the way or you risk damaging the architrave with the hammer. Finish off the job with a nail punch.

- If you want to save time on painting, buy ready-primed MDF architrave moulding.

- If your doorway is not quite 'true', ie: not straight vertically and horizontally, it's often best to follow the line of your door.

INSTALL DOORBELL

31

Some doorbells are battery-powered and wireless and really easy to install. Others take a small amount of wiring, but if you're replacing an old one, this can be done without an electrician. If in any doubt, however, consult a professional.

▶ YOU'LL NEED

- DOORBELL KIT, WITH FIXINGS
- BATTERIES, IF NEEDED
- ⚠ POWER DRILL, WITH MASONRY AND WOOD BITS, AS NECESSARY
- SCREWDRIVER
- MULTI-PURPOSE DETECTOR
- WALL PLUGS, IF NEEDED
- HAMMER
- PINS AND PLASTIC CLIPS

GETTING STARTED

Doorbells are generally supplied as two units: the button and the bell or chime. Both units require power, which can come from batteries or the mains. They can be wired together to receive the same power source or powered separately by a combination of batteries and mains electricity.

Determine whether your bell will be powered by batteries or the mains and whether the button and bell will be wired together or communicate wirelessly. If you don't already have mains wiring for a doorbell, a battery-powered or plug-in device is best.

Battery-powered: these units are easy to fix as you don't need to worry about tapping into your mains supply, but you will need to replace the batteries periodically.

Mains-powered: these run on very low voltage and you won't need to worry about the power running out. If you are replacing an existing mains-powered bell, you just need to do some simple wiring. If you are installing a mains-powered doorbell for the first time, you will need to employ an electrician to run a wire out of the mains for you.

Combination: some modern doorbell units communicate wirelessly, so each unit needs its own power supply. The button is powered by batteries, and the bell unit is also battery-powered or plugged in to a normal household socket. This combination style is the easiest to install as you don't need to connect any wires, and you can carry the bell unit about with you if you have far-away parts of your home.

Choose the best place for the bell unit. This should be somewhere that will be heard through the house, like a hallway.

⚠ STAY SAFE!

Before attempting to connect wiring to the mains power supply, ensure mains electricity is turned off. If in doubt, consult a professional.

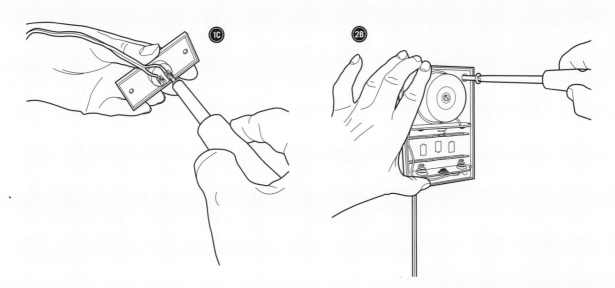

WHAT TO DO

① Fit button

A Choose a position on the doorframe at chest height and drill a small hole all the way through frame for the wire, if not a wireless device. Drill small pilot holes for screws.

B For wired mechanism, pass wires through hole from inside to outside.

C Strip back insulation and connect wires to button unit, following manufacturer's instructions.

D Screw back plate of button unit onto doorframe and secure front cover.

E Fit batteries (if needed) to button unit, according to manufacturer's instructions.

② Fit bell unit

A Check chosen position for pipes and cables using detector and locate studs, if not fixing to masonry. Hold bell unit in place. Mark positions for fixing screws.

B Drill holes to depth of wall plugs, if using, and insert. Secure back plate to wall.

C If your unit is mains-powered, turn off mains electricity first. For wired mechanism, strip back insulation on wire ends and join wire from button to bell unit.

D Replace bell unit cover. Connect existing wiring following manufacturer's instructions.

E Fix wire discreetly alongside doorframe or skirting board as appropriate, using hammer, pins and small plastic clips.

HOW TO NAIL IT!

- If the wiring has any kinks in it, you can try warming it by rubbing your hands over it a few times. This should allow it to be smoothed out.

- Change batteries as soon as they have run down; if they stay in place, they may corrode and damage the main unit.

- Try to keep the wire between battery-powered units as short as possible as the further the electricity has to travel, the faster your batteries will run down.

FIT FRONT DOOR KNOCKER

32

Fitting a front door knocker is a straightforward job and a quick way to give the front of your house a makeover. There are many different styles out there, so find one that blends well with the other fittings on your door.

► YOU'LL NEED

- KNOCKER, WITH FIXINGS
- STEEL TAPE MEASURE
- PENCIL
- BRADAWL OR NAIL
- ⚠ POWER DRILL, WITH WOOD BITS TO MATCH BOLT SIZE
- SCREWDRIVER
- ⚠ JUNIOR HACKSAW

GETTING STARTED

Choose the position for your knocker. It will probably look best centred, so measure the width of the door to find the mid-point. Choose a good height. Mark chosen point with pencil.

WHAT TO DO

1. Measure the door knocker and note the distance between fixings.

2. Use measurements to mark fixing positions on the door with bradawl or nail, either side of the central point. Repeat measurements to double-check for accuracy.

3. Starting from one side, drill most of the way through fixing marks, then finish the holes from the other side. This will help keep the wood from splitting as the drill comes through. Blow sawdust out of holes.

4. Screw knocker into door and fix nuts on. Trim any excess bolt length with hacksaw.

HOW TO NAIL IT!

- Make sure you drill through the door in a straight line, not at an angle.
- Before you fully tighten the screws, check the knocker is hanging straight.
- Take care to keep your fingers well out of the way when using a hacksaw.

FIT WEATHERBOARD

A weatherboard is a slanted piece of wood at the bottom of your external door. It keeps water away from your doorframe and stops it running back into your house. It's worth fitting one, as it's easier to replace a weatherboard than a whole door!

YOU'LL NEED

STEEL TAPE MEASURE

WEATHERBOARD MOULDING, TO FIT MEASUREMENTS

⚠ HANDSAW OR TENON SAW, IF NEEDED

WORKBENCH OR OTHER SUITABLE CUTTING SURFACE (SEE PAGE 22)

FINE-GRADE SANDPAPER

PAINTBRUSH

WOOD PRIMER

PAINT

PENCIL

⚠ POWER DRILL, WITH WOOD BIT AND COUNTERSINK OR LARGE BIT

BRADAWL OR NAIL

WOOD ADHESIVE

WOOD SCREWS

SCREWDRIVER

WOOD FILLER

GETTING STARTED

Measure the width of the door from the outside, with door in closed position. Subtract 10mm from measurement to ensure the board won't catch on the frame as the front door closes. Make a note of the measurement.

WHAT TO DO

1 Ideally, buy weatherboard moulding to fit, or cut to size with handsaw or tenon saw. Sand down for a smooth finish.

2 Prime and paint the back and bottom of the weatherboard. Wait until dry.

3 Hold board in position against door, making sure bottom of board is level with the bottom of the door, but not touching the sill. Mark the top of weatherboard onto door in pencil.

4 On workbench or other suitable surface, drill three or four evenly-spaced pilot holes through narrowest part of weatherboard (at the front, near top).

5 Countersink the pilot holes. See *Back to Basics* (page 18).

6 Hold weatherboard in place and mark through holes with bradawl or nail. Remove and drill pilot holes at marks to depth of screw – don't go through door.

7 Apply adhesive to back of weatherboard. Line up against pencil line and screw to door, sinking screws all the way into wood. If weatherboard catches, sand board down until door opens smoothly.

8 Prime and paint board to match door. See *Paint Exterior Woodwork* (page 170).

HOW TO NAIL IT!

• A hardwood weatherboard will last longer than one made from soft wood, but check what the door is made from first: there's little point in fitting a hardwood weatherboard to a softwood door, as the weatherboard will outlast the door!

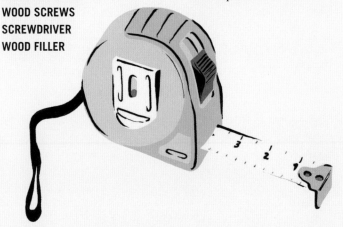

REPAIR ROTTEN WINDOW FRAME

34

Weather will eventually take its toll on wooden window frames. If paint wears away and moisture is allowed to get in, the wood underneath can get damp and will crack and rot. Repair damaged areas as soon as possible to stop the spread.

▶ YOU'LL NEED

- PENKNIFE
- ⚠ CHISEL OR NARROW SCRAPER
- ⚠ WOOD PRESERVATIVE
- PAINTBRUSH
- RUBBER GLOVES
- EXTERIOR WOOD REPAIR COMPOUND
- PUTTY KNIFE
- WATERPROOF FRAME SEALANT, IF NEEDED
- COARSE- AND MEDIUM-GRADE SANDPAPER
- ⚡ **TOOL UP** POWER SANDER
- ⚡ **TOOL DOWN** SANDING BLOCK
- WOOD PRIMER AND EXTERIOR-GRADE PAINT

GETTING STARTED

Test for rot by poking a penknife into the wood. It will sink easily into rotten wood. Identify the areas for replacing this way.

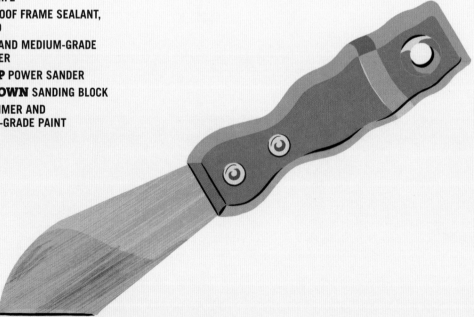

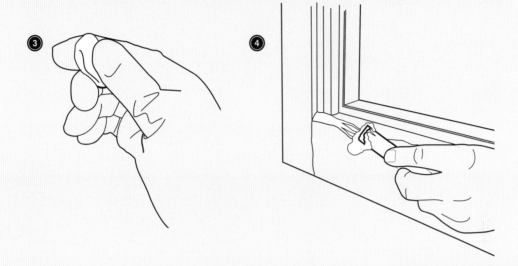

WHAT TO DO

❶ Remove all rotten wood using chisel or scraper. Dig down until the wood is sound, but don't damage healthy wood. Clean away all the debris.

❷ Ensure area is fully dried out. Paint wood preservative over the whole window surface.

❸ Wearing rubber gloves, knead repair compound.

❹ Use putty knife to apply repair compound in layers to damaged area. Press in well to avoid air bubbles. Keep going until the putty is worked up to the level and form of the rest of frame.

❺ Seal any gaps between the frame and wall with waterproof frame sealant.

❻ Leave sealant to dry for 48 hours.

❼ Using power sander or sandpaper and block, sand entire window frame with coarse-grade, then medium-grade sandpaper so that the only difference between repaired area and original frame should be colour.

❽ Prime and paint window frame in chosen colour. For best finish, use two coats in chosen colour. See *Paint Exterior Woodwork* (page 170).

HOW TO NAIL IT!

- Work on a dry day when the weather won't be competing against your hard work.

- If more than ten per cent of your window frame is rotten, the structure isn't sound and the whole frame will need to be replaced.

REPLACE BROKEN PANE OF GLASS

Broken glass doesn't just let the weather in, or heat out – it can also be dangerous and a security risk. You should be able to replace small panes of glass yourself, but you'll need to get a whole new unit made if your window is double-glazed.

▶ YOU'LL NEED

- NEWSPAPER OR OLD SHEET
- PROTECTIVE WORK GLOVES
- SAFETY GOGGLES
- HAMMER, IF NEEDED
- STEEL TAPE MEASURE
- HARDWOOD OR PLYWOOD, IF NEEDED
- ⚠ JUNIOR HACKSAW, IF NEEDED
- WORKBENCH OR OTHER SUITABLE CUTTING SURFACE (SEE PAGE 22)
- PANEL PINS OR WEATHERPROOF SILICONE SEALANT, IF NEEDED
- REPLACEMENT PANE OF GLASS
- ⚠ CHISEL, IF NEEDED
- PUTTY KNIFE
- PLIERS, IF NEEDED
- MEDIUM-GRADE SANDPAPER AND SANDING BLOCK
- WOOD SEALANT
- PAINTBRUSH
- WOOD PRIMER
- LINSEED OIL PUTTY (500G WILL FILL 4M)
- PANEL PINS OR METAL GLAZING CLIPS
- LINSEED OIL
- EXTERIOR-GRADE PAINT

GETTING STARTED

Wear sturdy boots to protect your feet from broken glass.

If pane is smashed, lay down newspaper or old sheet on both sides of window. Put on protective gloves and goggles. Work each piece of glass loose, from top down. Tap any remaining glass out with hammer. Wrap in newspaper and dispose of at tip.

Measure space for replacement pane in a few locations in case wood is warped or uneven. Measure to rebate – the recess that holds the pane – and subtract 2–3mm from height and width to ensure pane will fit easily.

For temporary repair, cut piece of hardwood or plywood to fit. Secure with panel pins or weatherproof silicone sealant.

If glass is cracked only, seal cracks with silicone sealant.

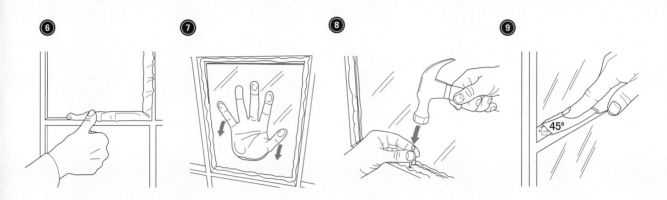

WHAT TO DO

1 Lay new pane on a pad of newspaper – not a hard surface – well away from working area.

2 If cracked pane is still in place, remove putty so that you can take out whole pane of glass. Chip out old putty using chisel or putty knife, taking out panel pins or metal clips with pliers as you go. Save any that can be reused.

3 Sand down exposed wood, fill in any holes or cracks with wood sealant and brush with wood primer.

4 Clean out any debris from the rebate and wet your hands to prevent putty sticking.

5 Knead the putty until it is pliable and take a palm-sized ball to work with.

6 Roll out putty into long strip. Place this along rebate and press down with your thumb to a thickness of around 3mm.

7 Sit the new pane into the bottom edge of frame and gently push it into place in the putty. Allow putty to squish out of the rebate to form a weatherproof seal.

8 Secure glass by carefully tapping panel pins or clips into the putty, flat against surface of glass. Space pins at 20mm intervals.

9 Roll another worm of putty and press firmly into edges. Wet putty knife and smooth putty neatly with the knife at a 45-degree angle, so panel pins are covered. If knife sticks, dip into linseed oil, wipe off excess and use again.

10 Remove surplus putty from both sides of glass with the putty knife.

11 Leave putty for two weeks to harden, then prime and paint window frame. See *Paint Exterior Woodwork* (page 170).

HOW TO NAIL IT!

• Save a piece of the broken glass to take to the glazier to ensure you order the right width. If in doubt, it's always best to buy thicker glass rather than thinner.

• If the old putty is hard to remove, use a heat gun, soldering tool or hairdryer to soften it.

• If you need to remove excess oil from the new putty, roll it over some newspaper before using.

CURTAINS AND BLINDS

EVERYTHING YOU NEED TO GET THE JOB DONE

PUT UP CURTAIN POLE

Curtain poles can be decorative features in themselves, so choose carefully and think about how they blend with other features in the room.

YOU'LL NEED

STEEL TAPE MEASURE

CURTAIN, WITH RINGS OR LOOPS

CURTAIN POLE AND FITTINGS

⚠ JUNIOR HACKSAW, IF NEEDED

WORKBENCH OR OTHER SUITABLE CUTTING SURFACE (SEE PAGE 22)

MULTI-PURPOSE DETECTOR

PENCIL

LONG SPIRIT LEVEL

⚠ POWER DRILL, WITH MASONRY OR OTHER SUITABLE BITS

SCREWS AND WALL PLUGS, AS NEEDED

SCREWDRIVER

GETTING STARTED

Choose position and length of curtain pole. Make sure curtains can be pulled back at least 50mm from the edge of the window, to allow for maximum light. Heavy fabric will take up more space.

Choose height of curtain pole above window recess (usually 50-120mm). See also *Put Up Curtain Track* (page 88).

If necessary, cut the curtain pole to the right length with a junior hacksaw.

Make sure you are fixing to solid brick. If not, locate studs using a detector and fix to these, if possible. Choose wall plugs, screws and drill bits to suit your wall. See *Back to Basics* (pages 18-20).

If you're concerned about where your hidden pipes and cables are, use a detector to make sure you don't drill into anything important!

WHAT TO DO

❶ Mark the positions for the end bracket screws (and central, if needed) on the wall in pencil. Check the marks are level using a long spirit level.

❷ Drill at pencil marks to depth of wall plug, if using, and insert. Screw brackets into place.

❸ Thread curtain rings or loops onto pole, secure pole to bracket and leave one ring or loop outside each end bracket. Secure finials or curtain stops to ends.

HOW TO NAIL IT!

- If you are hanging heavy curtains, ensure the screws holding up the pole are long enough to support the weight properly.

- For curtain poles longer than 1.8m or for heavy curtains, you will need to add a support bracket in the centre as well as at the two ends.

- Remember to check length of curtain when deciding on height of pole.

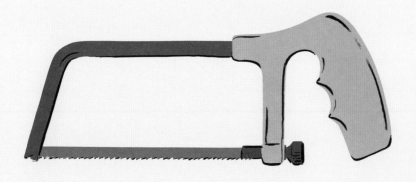

PUT UP CURTAIN TRACK

37

Although curtain tracks can look plain, they are a good solution for tight areas or if you want to use pencil-pleat curtains. Remember to allow for overlap when measuring for your curtains.

▶ YOU'LL NEED

STEEL TAPE MEASURE

CURTAIN TRACK AND FITTINGS (GLIDERS AND HOOKS)

CURTAIN, WITH HEADER TAPE ATTACHED

⚠ JUNIOR HACKSAW

MULTI-PURPOSE DETECTOR

WORKBENCH OR OTHER SUITABLE CUTTING SURFACE (SEE PAGE 22)

PENCIL

LONG SPIRIT LEVEL

⚠ POWER DRILL, WITH MASONRY OR OTHER SUITABLE BITS

SCREWS AND WALL PLUGS, AS NEEDED

SCREWDRIVER

GETTING STARTED

Choose position and length of curtain track. Make sure curtains can be pulled back at least 50mm from the edge of window to allow for maximum light. Heavy fabric will take up more space.

Choose height of curtain track above window recess (usually 50-120mm).

Cut the track to the right length with a junior hacksaw.

Make sure you are fixing to solid brick. If not, locate studs using a detector and fix to these, if possible. Choose wall plugs, screws and drill bits to suit your wall. See *Back to Basics* (pages 18-20).

If you're concerned about where your hidden pipes and cables are, use a detector to make sure you don't drill into anything important!

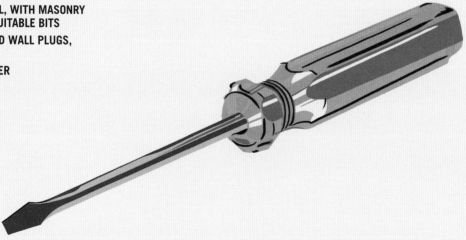

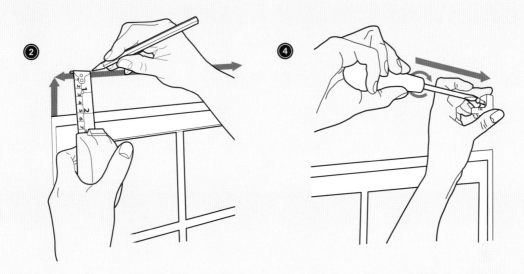

WHAT TO DO

1 Use pencil and tape measure to mark positions of the brackets, at least 50mm above the window or window recess. Mark the two side positions first, at 50mm in from the track ends.

2 Now measure the interim brackets at regular intervals, depending on width of window recess and weight of curtain, and always at the same height above the window. Check marks are level using a long spirit level.

3 Drill into wall at each bracket mark to depth of wall plug, if using, and insert. If fixing to studs, drill pilot holes.

4 Screw brackets into position.

5 Fit the stops to the track ends and click the track into each bracket.

6 Fit curtain to track using gliders and hooks.

HOW TO NAIL IT!

- Use flexible curtain track to fit around bay and curved windows.
- If the screws that come with your curtain track aren't long enough to fit the track securely to the wall, swap for longer screws.

HANG BLINDS

Blinds often give a sleeker look than curtains and can let in far more light when pulled up. Blackout blinds are great for helping young children stay asleep on very light summer mornings.

YOU'LL NEED

STEEL TAPE MEASURE

BLIND AND FITTINGS

MULTI-PURPOSE DETECTOR

PENCIL

LONG SPIRIT LEVEL

⚠ POWER DRILL, WITH MASONRY OR OTHER SUITABLE BITS

SCREWS AND WALL PLUGS, AS NEEDED

SCREWDRIVER

PLUS, FOR ROLLER BLINDS:

⚠ JUNIOR HACKSAW

WORKBENCH OR OTHER SUITABLE CUTTING SURFACE (SEE PAGE 22)

SANDPAPER

RULER

CRAFT KNIFE OR SHARP FABRIC SCISSORS

GETTING STARTED

Choose the position for your blind and measure the width and drop length before you go shopping.

For a window recess, you'll need to be exact about the measurements. Allow for some clearance on either side of the blind and take into account projecting window handles.

You have more flexibility on size if the blind's going on the outside of a recess. Add at least 25mm on each side to ensure window is well covered.

Make sure you are fixing to solid brick. If not, locate studs using a detector and fix to these, if possible. Choose wall plugs, screws and drill bits to suit your wall. See *Back to Basics* (pages 18-20).

If you're concerned about where your hidden pipes and cables are, use a detector before drilling.

TYPES OF BLINDS

- **Roller blinds** come in different designs and colours, so can add an accent to an otherwise plain room. These blinds can also be cut down to size more easily than other types and can be rolled away completely.

- **Roman blinds** are great for bringing cosiness to a bedroom. They can be good for blocking out light. Bear in mind that even when open, the fabric will 'stack' at the top of the window, reducing visibility but adding colour and character.

- **Venetian blinds** can help vary the amount of light in a room during the day. They also allow light in, whilst maintaining some privacy.

- **Vertical blinds** have a functional look that might remind some of a doctor's surgery but can work well on patio doors and large windows.

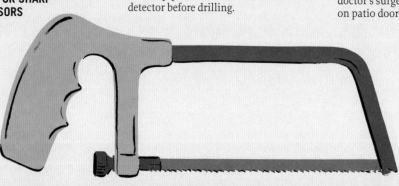

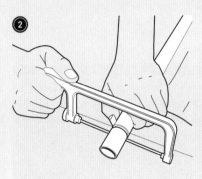

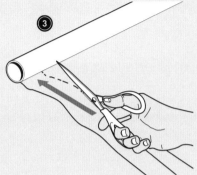

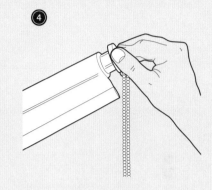

WHAT TO DO

Hang roller blinds

1 Check your measurements once you're back home with the blind and mark the bracket positions in pencil. Use a spirit level to check marks are level. Allow at least 5mm between drill holes and wall edges and corners.

2 Cut blind down to size: unroll the blind, take out the roller tube (if you can), mark required width on roller tube and cut through with hacksaw. Sand off rough edges.

3 Mark required width on reverse of roller blind with pencil and ruler – this should be 15mm shorter than the cut roller tube. Cut out along the line with a craft knife or scissors.

4 Reinsert the roller tube. Fit the control end of blind into the end of roller tube you wish to operate blind from and fit the dummy end into other. Push in firmly.

5 Drill holes at marks to depth of wall plug, if using, and push in. If fixing to studs, drill pilot holes. If you find you have a concrete lintel, you will need to use the hammer-action setting on your drill. Screw in brackets.

6 Slot blind into brackets and test.

Hang Roman and Venetian blinds

Always fit in a recess. Follow the instructions for roller blinds, omitting steps 2–4. Your blind will either be made-to-measure or you should get the best fit possible.

Hang vertical blinds

Always fit in a recess. Follow the instructions for roller blinds, omitting steps 2–4.

HOW TO NAIL IT!

- Looped cords on blinds can be a serious hazard for small children so make sure the cords are kept well out of reach. You can find safety devices to keep them out of the way of little fingers.

- Open the window to test the location of projecting window handles at their fullest length before you decide where to fix the blind. You may need to move blind further away from window to accommodate it.

FIT SHUTTERS

Wooden shutters can be a stylish way to shut out light and maximise privacy. Like curtains and blinds, they are fitted either inside or outside the window recess. You will need to recruit a helper to lift the frame into position.

▶ YOU'LL NEED

- SHUTTERS AND FITTINGS
- STEEL TAPE MEASURE
- MULTI-PURPOSE DETECTOR
- HAMMER
- OLD CARDBOARD
- PENCIL
- LONG SPIRIT LEVEL
- PAPER AND PEN
- BRADAWL OR NAIL
- SCREWDRIVER
- ⚠ POWER DRILL, WITH MASONRY OR OTHER SUITABLE BITS
- SCREWS AND WALL PLUGS, AS NEEDED
- DECORATOR'S CAULK AND APPLICATOR GUN

GETTING STARTED

Choose whether your shutters will go inside or outside the window recess and measure accordingly.

For inside mounting, measure at three different heights across window. Note down the smallest width and drop and remove 2mm to allow space for fitting.

For outside mounting, remember to add on the extra space needed for the frame. Refer to the shutter manufacturer for their specifications.

Shutters will need to be made-to-measure for the best possible results. When they arrive, the shutter frames will be marked with the window or position they were ordered for, so ensure the right frames are in the right rooms before you start. They will also come with predrilled holes.

Make sure you are fixing to solid brick. If not, locate studs using a detector and fix to these, if possible. Choose wall plugs, screws and drill bits to suit your wall. See *Back to Basics* (pages 18–20).

If you're concerned about where your hidden pipes and cables are, use a detector before drilling.

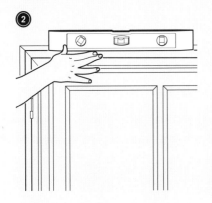

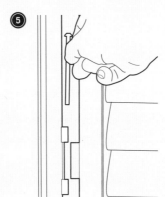

WHAT TO DO

1 Using a hammer, tap fixings into the frame corners to assemble shutter frame. Work on top of cardboard to protect frames.

2 With a helper, lift frame into position at window. Mark fixing points with bradawl or nail, through predrilled holes in frame. Check they are level by placing spirit level on top of frame.

3 Drill all frame fixing holes to depth of wall plugs, if using, and push in. If fixing to studs, drill pilot holes.

4 Fix frame with just one screw on each side. Do not tighten.

5 Put the panels in the frames by lifting into position and adding the hinge pin to fix. The panels will be labelled with their position from left to right.

6 Once panels are in, screw in remaining frame screws and tighten.

7 Screw in the remaining screws to fix the frames to the wall. Add in any screw caps.

8 Add a line of caulk between window and shutter frame to finish (see *How To Nail It!*, page 133).

HOW TO NAIL IT!

- For sash windows and inward-opening windows, it's best to fix shutters outside the recess. It sounds obvious, but shutters can only be inside-mounted if the window recess is deep enough.

- It's really important to get accurate window measurements for your shutters, so use a steel tape measure. Measure once, take a break then come back and measure again.

- If you have old windows that aren't exactly square, use the smallest measurement in each dimension.

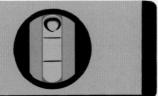

HANG NET OR VOILE CURTAINS

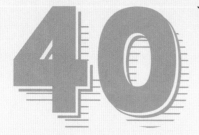

Net curtains have a terrible reputation for being twitched by nosy old neighbours but, used right, they do a good job of keeping out the busybodies while letting in a good amount of light, and are super affordable.

YOU'LL NEED

- NET OR VOILE CURTAINS
- STEEL TAPE MEASURE
- FABRIC SCISSORS
- NET CURTAIN HEADING TAPE AND SEWING MACHINE, IF NEEDED
- LONG SPIRIT LEVEL
- MULTI-PURPOSE DETECTOR, IF NEEDED

TO HANG CURTAINS:

- NET POLE, NET ROD, NET WIRE OR STICKY-BACKED VELCRO TAPE
- L-SHAPED SCREW-IN HOOKS, FOR NET POLE
- ⚠ POWER DRILL, WITH MASONRY OR OTHER SUITABLE BITS, IF NEEDED
- WALL PLUGS, AS NEEDED
- HOOKS AND EYES, FOR NET WIRE
- HAMMER AND PLIERS, IF NEEDED
- IRON, FOR VELCRO

GETTING STARTED

Choose whether to hang your curtains on a pole, rod or wire, or with Velcro.

Ⓐ Net pole: tension rod stretches across the window recess to hang curtain close to window, allowing room for larger curtains to hang in front, outside the window recess. Very easy to fit.

Ⓑ Net rod: extending plastic-coated metal rod, useful for hanging curtains above the window recess. Hangs on L-shaped, metal, screw-in hooks.

Ⓒ Net wire: fixed with hooks wherever you want. Cheap and easy to fit, but prone to sagging across wider windows.

Ⓓ Velcro: easy to fix and keeps the curtains in position.

Net and voile curtains sometimes come complete with heading tape that allows you to use regular curtain hooks, or holes to thread a pole through. If not, you may have to add your own (see step 3, opposite).

If fitting screw-in hooks for a rod or wire, try and fix to solid brick. Otherwise, use a detector to locate studs and fix to these. Choose wall plugs, screws and drill bits to suit your wall. See *Back to Basics* (pages 18-21).

If you're concerned about where your hidden pipes and cables are, use a detector before any drilling.

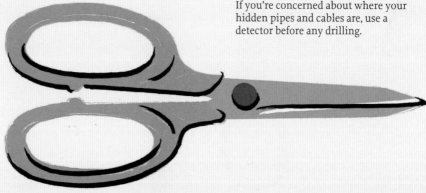

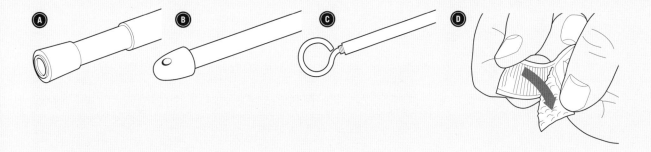

WHAT TO DO

① Measure window space width and drop, depending on whether you want your curtains inside or outside the recess. For a ruffled look, multiply width by 1.5 (or more) before cutting fabric. If you are mounting the curtains outside the recess, add 50mm to either side for clearance of the wall edges.

② If not supplied as made-to-measure, cut curtains to chosen dimensions.

③ If your curtains do not already have holes or hooks fitted for hanging, measure net heading tape to fit curtain width and cut. Sew heading tape to top of curtain.

④ Hang the curtain:

Net pole: thread curtain onto pole, extend pole to fit window width and twist to fix in place.

Net rod: drill holes to depth of wall plugs, if using, and push in. For studs, drill pilot holes. Screw in L-shaped hooks.

Net wire: mark the height you want the curtains to hang from. Drill holes to depth of wall plugs, if using, and tap curtain wire hooks in position in the wall. Cut curtain wire to desired length with pliers and thread through heading tape or top hem. Add ring to both ends of wire and attach wire to hooks.

Velcro: cut length to match width of curtain. Iron soft side of Velcro to curtain and stick rough edge at desired height on wall or window frame. Stick Velcro together.

HOW TO NAIL IT!

- To get a really neat, bistro look, you can hem the bottom edge of your net curtains and add a second pole or wire to keep them taut.

- Be careful your curtain wire isn't too long so it sags, or too short that it pulls on the wire hooks.

- If using Velcro, it's best to choose a colour that won't be seen through the curtains.

HANG BLACKOUT CURTAINS

Blackout curtains are great when you want a very dark room for sleeping – but they also muffle sounds from outside and help insulate the room to keep heating bills down.

YOU'LL NEED

READY-MADE BLACKOUT LINING, TO FIT EXISTING CURTAIN SIZE

STANDARD CURTAIN HOOKS

OR, FOR SEPARATE BLACKOUT CURTAINS:

STEEL TAPE MEASURE

BLACKOUT CURTAIN AND FIXINGS, TO FIT MEASUREMENTS

CURTAIN POLE AND FITTINGS OR CURTAIN TRACK AND FITTINGS

MATERIALS FOR FIXING CURTAIN POLE OR TRACK (SEE PAGES 87 AND 88)

GETTING STARTED

You can hang a curtain made of blackout fabric – ready-made ones are available – or add blackout fabric lining to your existing curtains. Where possible, hang outside the recess, as wide and long as you can for best results.

If you are replacing an existing curtain with a blackout curtain you can reuse your curtain track or pole, but check first that it is strong enough to hold the heavier blackout fabric, and wide enough to allow a minimum of 50mm each side of the window area to be covered.

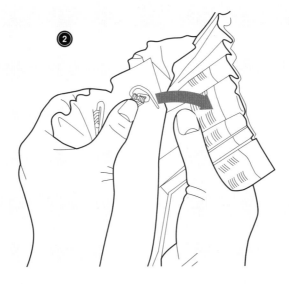

WHAT TO DO

Add blackout lining to existing curtains

1 Remove existing curtain and place face-down on floor or table. Lie blackout lining face-up on top of curtain, lining up the two heading tapes.

2 Insert curtain hook first into blackout lining tape then into curtain tape and twist hook around. Repeat across width of fabrics, so the two are fastened wrong-sides together.

3 Use curtain hooks to fix the lined curtain back onto curtain pole or track as before.

Hang separate blackout curtain

1 First measure for curtain dimensions by measuring window recess and adding at least 50mm on each side and as much as possible above and below.

2 If you need to put up a new curtain pole or track, see *Put Up Curtain Pole* (page 87) or *Put Up Curtain Track* (page 88).

3 Hang curtain onto pole, or fit to track, as necessary.

HOW TO NAIL IT!

- Blackout curtains come in all sorts of fabrics, so look around for something that suits your room.

- Remember, the blackout curtain or lining will be visible from the other side of the window, so choose colour mindfully if the view from the street is important to you.

- Some blackout curtains come in pairs with magnetic strips down the middle to help keep them drawn together.

HANG DOOR CURTAIN

42

A heavy curtain hung over an exterior door can be a cosy way of keeping out draughts, but you'll need to consider how you use your door. Think about how often you will be pulling the curtain across to go in and out and whether there is enough clearance for post to come through the letterbox.

YOU'LL NEED

CURTAIN POLE, PORTIÈRE ROD OR DOOR ROD WITH SWING ARM, PLUS FITTINGS

CURTAIN, TO FIT MEASUREMENTS

STEEL TAPE MEASURE

⚠ JUNIOR HACKSAW, IF NEEDED

WORKBENCH OR OTHER SUITABLE CUTTING SURFACE (SEE PAGE 22), IF NEEDED

PENCIL

LONG SPIRIT LEVEL

⚠ POWER DRILL, WITH MASONRY BITS

SCREWS AND WALL PLUGS, AS NEEDED

GETTING STARTED

Choose whether you want the curtain fixed by a static curtain pole, portière rod or door rod with swing arm.

Ⓐ **Static curtain pole:** hanging the curtain above the door recess covers more of the door area so keeps out most draughts, but the pole and curtain will need to be sturdy and securely fixed to withstand all the pulling and moving each time you go through the door.

Ⓑ **Portière rod:** designed to fit onto the door so that the curtain moves with the door when it opens. Convenient for an often-used door, but as the curtain only extends a little way past the door edges, it's less effective at keeping out all the draughts.

Ⓒ **Door rod with swing arm:** fixed to the wall at just one end, the rod and curtain can swing with the door as it opens, and stay 'parked' in an open or closed position. Suitable for light-weight or medium-weight fabrics only.

Make sure you are fixing to solid brick. If not, locate studs using a detector and choose wall plugs, screws and drill bits to suit your wall. See *Back to Basics* (page 18–21).

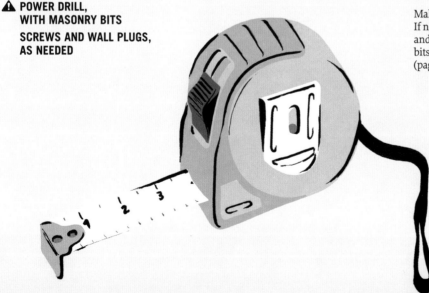

WHAT TO DO

1 Measure the space to determine curtain dimensions and length of pole or rod, bearing in mind the type of fitting you have chosen. Ensure the pole or rod is at least 50mm above the door and long enough to allow curtain to be pulled right back to one side, without obstructing door. If necessary, cut pole or rod to right length with junior hacksaw.

2 Mark chosen positions for fixings using pencil and spirit level.

3 Drill holes as necessary. Refer to manufacturer's instructions, fitting wall plugs, if needed, and screws where fixing brackets to wall.

4 Thread curtain onto pole, or attach to rings or hooks and hang up. Fit any filials or curtain stops.

HOW TO NAIL IT!

- Door curtains need to be fairly heavy so make sure the supporting pole is sturdy and well secured with screws that are long enough and wall plugs that are suitable for your wall type.

HANG CURTAIN AS ROOM DIVIDER

Curtains are a flexible way of dividing up rooms, perhaps to make one area seem cosier, or to zone off open-plan living spaces. You can hang a light-weight curtain across a wide area using a high tension wire. To hang a heavier dividing curtain over a shorter distance, see *Hang Door Curtain* (page 98).

▶ YOU'LL NEED

STEEL TAPE MEASURE

MULTI-PURPOSE DETECTOR

PENCIL

⚠ POWER DRILL, WITH MASONRY OR OTHER SUITABLE BITS

SCREW-IN HOOKS WITH ANCHORS (THESE LOOK LIKE THEY HAVE A WALL PLUG ATTACHED)

STEEL HANGING WIRE, TO FIT MEASUREMENTS, PLUS 500MM EXTRA

2 TURNBUCKLES

APPROX 6 WIRE ROPE CLIPS, TO FIT WIRE

CURTAIN, TO FIT MEASUREMENTS

WIRE CUTTERS

GETTING STARTED

To ensure you buy the correct size of curtains, measure the distance across the room where you want the curtain to hang, and the drop height. Multiply width distance by 1.5 or more to allow the curtain to gather nicely across the space.

Make sure you are fixing to solid brick. If not, choose wall plugs, screws and drill bits to suit your wall. See *Back to Basics* (pages 18-21).

If you are worried about drilling into hidden pipes or cables, use a detector before drilling, or a multi-purpose one if you also want to locate studs (see page 21). It can be useful to fix the hooks into studs, especially if you are using heavy fabric.

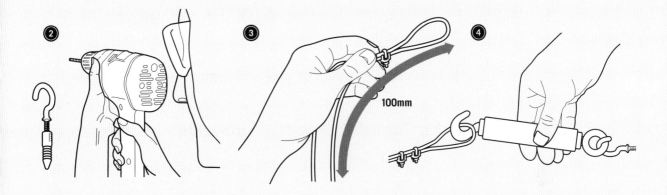

WHAT TO DO

1 Using a pencil, mark positions for hooks on each opposing wall. Measure carefully to ensure they are at the same height.

2 Drill holes at markings and tap in screw-in hooks with anchors.

3 Make a loop at one end of wire, with at least 100mm of spare wire held alongside length. Place wire rope clips along loop at intervals to secure.

4 Unscrew turnbuckle to expand, insert eye end into hook and the wire loop into other end of turnbuckle.

5 Stretch wire to other side of room and thread curtain onto wire.

6 Pull wire taut and repeat turnbuckle fixing at other end of cable. Use wire cutters to cut off excess.

7 Turn turnbuckles at either end to fine-tune the tautness.

HOW TO NAIL IT!

- A quick and easy way of adding a light-weight curtain to an empty doorway, between rooms, is to drill two holes 50mm above the doorframe, 50mm out from each corner. Insert wall plugs, if needed, and screw in two hooks. Thread the curtain onto a light-weight pole – a length of dowelling would also work well – and place it on the hooks.

- If you want to hang very heavy-weight curtains, use a pole with fixings all the way along to distribute the weight.

FIT WINDOW FILM

If you have glass doors or windows with an ugly view, or facing a busy street, window film is an affordable alternative to frosted glass panels and a modern alternative to nets. Go for a simple frosted look or opt for a pattern.

YOU'LL NEED

- SPRAY BOTTLE WITH SOAP SOLUTION (50ML WASHING-UP LIQUID TO 1L WARM WATER)
- SQUEEGEE
- WINDOW SCRAPER
- LINT-FREE CLOTH
- STEEL TAPE MEASURE
- PENCIL AND RULER
- WINDOW FILM
- SCISSORS
- STRAIGHTEDGE
- CRAFT KNIFE

GETTING STARTED

Clean the window with soapy spray and squeegee, scraping off until all grease and dust is removed. Dry with a lint-free cloth.

Measure dimensions to be covered by film and add 30mm in each direction. Mark lightly on backing paper with pencil and ruler. Cut out film with scissors.

WHAT TO DO

1 Wet window with soapy solution using fine spray. Ensure all of glass is covered.

2 Place film onto the glass with adhesive side facing you.

3 Peel off liner and spray adhesive side liberally with soapy solution.

4 Taking care not to let film curl up, reverse film so adhesive side is against window, with a little film overlapping window edges on all sides. Slide film until position is accurate.

5 If any dirt is caught under film, peel back, remove with scraper, re-wet and reapply.

6 Once in position, smooth out film using palm of your hand, in a swooping motion, from centre out. Repeat using a squeegee, carefully moving all the liquid out from underneath. This is easier to do if the surface is wet.

7 Slide straightedge against each window edge and use as a guide to cut off excess film with craft knife.

8 Repeat step 6 to strengthen bond, re-wetting film surface to help squeegee to move.

9 Leave to dry for two days before touching.

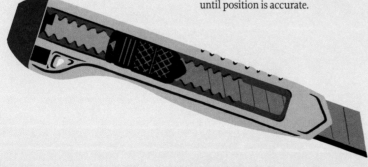

HOW TO NAIL IT!

- If any of the window isn't wet when you apply the film, it will stick to the dry areas and air bubbles will get in.
- If you're covering large windows, call in another pair of hands to help you keep the film straight, while turning it around.

FLOORS
AND
WALLS

EVERYTHING
YOU NEED
TO GET THE
JOB DONE

PATCH CARPET

If your carpet has a scorch mark, burn, stain or worn area, which can't be hidden by furniture – and if you can find a piece of matching carpet, you can patch it. The job is easier on plain carpet but you can still do a good job with care on patterned carpets.

► YOU'LL NEED

SPARE CARPET
CRAFT KNIFE
⚠ **CARPET ADHESIVE**
VACUUM CLEANER

GETTING STARTED

Find spare carpet to provide the replacement patch. Ideally, you will have leftover scraps from fitting the carpet, but if not, you can ask the shop for a matching remnant. In the worst-case scenario, you could take a piece from under or behind a piece of never-moved furniture.

WHAT TO DO

1. Cut out damaged area using a craft knife with sharp blade, taking care to leave underlay intact.

2. Use cut-out piece as a template to cut out a new patch from spare carpet. Be careful to align pile direction and any patterning before cutting.

3. Spread carpet adhesive on back of replacement patch and on edges surrounding hole.

4. Press replacement patch into hole and use fingers to roughen up the pile.

5. Leave six hours to dry then vacuum the patched area.

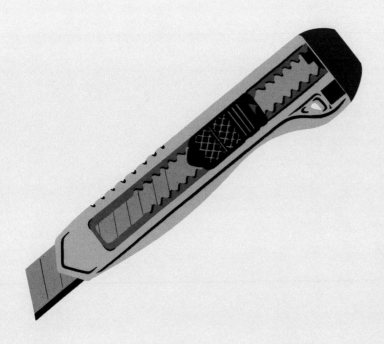

HOW TO NAIL IT!

- If you accidentally cut through the underlay, tape it up with heavy-duty carpet tape.

LAY CARPET AND UNDERLAY

46

A cheap carpet, well laid, can look fab – an expensive carpet laid badly will always look terrible. If you're laying a carpet for the first time, start with a small room, if possible. You can rent the necessary equipment from a large DIY store or hire company.

YOU'LL NEED

- MATERIALS FOR PREPARING FLOOR (SEE *GETTING STARTED*)
- STEEL TAPE MEASURE
- CARPET, TO FIT SPACE, PLUS EXTRA
- UNDERLAY, TO FIT SPACE, PLUS EXTRA
- PIPE-AND-CABLE DETECTOR
- PENCIL
- HEAVY-DUTY GLOVES
- KNEE PADS (OPTIONAL)
- GRIPPER ROD, FOR PERIMETER OF ROOM, EXCLUDING DOORWAYS
- ⚠ JUNIOR HACKSAW
- WORKBENCH OR OTHER SUITABLE CUTTING SURFACE (SEE PAGE 22)
- ⚠ GRAB ADHESIVE, IF NEEDED
- HAMMER
- DOOR THRESHOLD, WITH FIXINGS
- ⚠ POWER DRILL, WITH BIT SUITABLE FOR FLOOR
- SCREWDRIVER
- PAPER LINING, TO FIT SPACE
- CARPET TACKS, STAPLE GUN OR
- ⚠ SPRAY ADHESIVE
- HEAVY-DUTY CRAFT KNIFE OR CARPET KNIFE
- CARPET TAPE
- CARPET TUCKER AND STRETCHER

GETTING STARTED

Remove old carpet, vinyl or other floor coverings and ensure surface is dry, firm and level. If laying over concrete, test for moisture. See *Lay Laminate Flooring* (page 110).

Carpets should always be fitted with an underlay to help them last longer and feel comfortable. Fit the best quality you can afford: hessian- or woven-backed carpets are generally better quality than foam-backed carpets.

Measure the room. When ordering carpet and underlay, add about 100mm in each direction to allow for cutting to exact size. Include alcoves and halfway into any doorways.

Use a pipe-and-cable detector to locate any hidden pipes and cables under the floor and mark positions in pencil. In these places you'll need to attach the gripper with adhesive rather than nails.

WHAT TO DO

① Fit gripper around the edge of the room

A Wearing heavy-duty gloves and kneepads, if liked, cut gripper rod with hacksaw to lengths needed.

B Position with angled edge facing skirting board (teeth pointing to wall) and lengths butted together. Leave 7mm gap between gripper and skirting board. If you have a curved area, cut the gripper into small pieces to follow curve. If the gripper can't be nailed, apply grab adhesive and press in place.

C Use hammer to secure rest of gripper in place, taking care not to damage skirting boards.

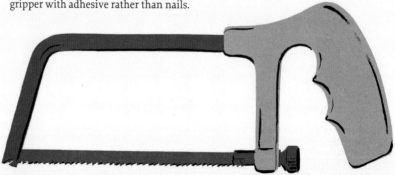

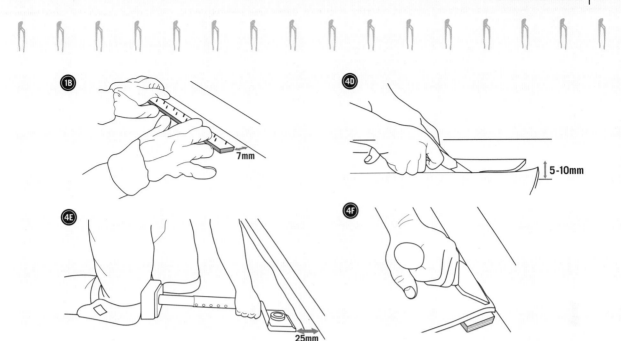

2 Fit door threshold

At doorway, check for hidden pipes and cables, then drill holes to secure threshold bar to floor with screws.

3 Fit underlay

A Roll out paper lining to cover space, butting up to grippers and overlapping strips by around 25mm. Secure with tacks, staples or adhesive.

B Loosely lay underlay on floor, rubber-side down. Use craft knife to cut underlay flush with gripper rods. Butt up different sections of underlay and secure with carpet tape. The underlay should be as smooth and level as possible so don't overlap the strips.

4 Lay carpet

A Roll carpet out loosely into position, leaving 50-100mm excess at each edge.

B At internal corners, cut triangular notches out of spare carpet to help it lie flat. At external corners, cut slit down from edge. In both cases, leave around 100mm excess. See *Lay Vinyl Tiles*, steps 3 and 4 (page 113).

C Work one wall at a time. Starting at end of longest wall and working backwards towards the doorway, crease carpet firmly against skirting using a carpet tucker. This will make a fold line for cutting.

D Cut along carpet edge with heavy-duty craft knife or carpet knife leaving 5-10mm excess. Be careful not to damage the skirting board.

E Use carpet stretcher to hook carpet onto gripper: place the stretcher, teeth-down, about 25mm from skirting and push against the padded end with your knee.

F In this position, use carpet tucker to push excess down between skirting board and gripper.

G Repeat steps C-F, moving across the room to fit carpet up to wall opposite the one you've just done. Finish with adjacent walls. At door threshold push carpet edge underneath bar with screwdriver.

HOW TO NAIL IT!

- Carpet looks best with the pile facing away from the window. Rub your hand over the carpet: one way will feel smooth and the other will feel rough. The carpet should feel smooth when running your hand away from the window.

- If your carpet has a pattern, stand in the doorway to check it looks square on before you fix it in place.

- Some carpets come with an integral underlay. In this case, skip the underlay stage, but don't forget to lay lining paper first.

LAY NATURAL FLOORING

47

There's now a large range of floor covering made from natural fibres, which are more ecologically friendly than synthetic carpet and often woven by hand into interesting patterns and textures. Be warned, though, these are not the easiest carpets to clean.

▶ YOU'LL NEED

- MATERIALS FOR PREPARING FLOOR (SEE *GETTING STARTED*)
- STEEL TAPE MEASURE
- FLOORING, TO FIT SPACE, PLUS EXTRA
- KNEE PADS (OPTIONAL)
- 'BLIND' GRIPPER (NO PINS, OR VERY SHORT ONES)
- PIPE-AND-CABLE DETECTOR
- ⚠ POWER DRILL, WITH BIT SUITABLE FOR FLOOR
- DOOR THRESHOLD, WITH FIXINGS
- ⚠ CARPET ADHESIVE
- NOTCHED SPREADER
- HEAVY-DUTY CRAFT KNIFE OR CARPET KNIFE
- CARPET TUCKER
- SCREWDRIVER

GETTING STARTED

Remove old carpet, vinyl or other floor coverings and ensure surface is dry, firm and level. If you have a concrete floor, test for moisture. See *Lay Laminate Flooring* (page 110).

Measure the room to be covered by multiplying its length by its width. Allow around 100mm excess at each edge. Include alcoves and halfway into any doorways.

Unroll the natural floor covering in the room it will fill and leave to acclimatise for 24-48 hours before laying. If you can't lay it out completely, loosely unroll the carpet.

Make sure the room you are working in is well ventilated. This job can be hard on the knees so knee pads are helpful.

TYPES OF NATURAL FLOORING

Coir fibres come from coconut husks. They are extracted by hand, softened in seawater and woven into flooring that is durable and good value. Stains easily, so spray with protective coating.

Jute fibres are extracted from the stalks of giant corchorus plants that grow in the tropics. The fibres are fine and soft underfoot, so jute flooring is well suited to bedrooms, but not hard-wearing enough for elsewhere. Jute has a 'tweedy' look.

Seagrass grows in tropical meadows and riverbanks. The fibres are extracted by hand, dried and spun, before being woven. Seagrass is very durable, but as it retains moisture, it is not suitable for bathrooms and kitchens.

Sisal fibres come from an agave plant. The fibres make hardwearing flooring suitable for hallways and stairs. They are easily dyed so can come in a range of colours.

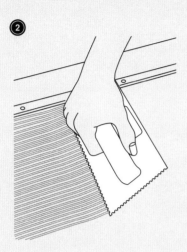

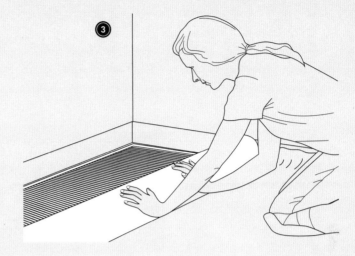

WHAT TO DO

1 Fit blind gripper to perimeter of room. At doorway, check for hidden pipes and cables, then drill holes to secure threshold bar to floor with screws.

2 Spread carpet adhesive over first third of floor using notched spreader, starting at wall edge furthest from door.

3 Unroll carpet onto adhesive, leaving about 100mm excess at floor edges and pressing as you go, to ensure complete coverage.

4 Repeat for next third of floor and again until floor is covered.

5 Remove excess by running craft knife or carpet knife around edge of wall, leaving around 5mm extra. Be very careful not to mark the skirting boards. At doorway, cut to line up with door threshold bar.

6 Tuck carpet edge behind gripper using carpet tucker. See *Lay Carpet and Underlay*, step 4F (page 107). At doorway, tuck flooring underneath door threshold with screwdriver.

7 Leave flooring for at least 24 hours before moving furniture into room. Check manufacturer's instructions for timings.

HOW TO NAIL IT!

- Ensure the carpet adhesive you use has a low water content. Natural fibres absorb moisture so should be kept away from it as much as possible.

- Be generous with adhesive as the textured backing of the carpet takes a lot to be completely covered. Without enough adhesive the carpet won't bond properly to the floor and may shrink.

- When cutting the carpet at room edges, try to follow straight lines along the weave, rather than cutting across weave patterns.

LAY LAMINATE FLOORING

Laminate flooring is hard-wearing, easy to clean and easy to install. You don't have to spend much to get a really professional look. This job can be very hard on the knees, so knee pads are helpful.

YOU'LL NEED

MATERIALS FOR PREPARING FLOOR (SEE *GETTING STARTED*)

STEEL TAPE MEASURE

LAMINATE FLOORING, TO COVER FLOOR SPACE, PLUS EXTRA

MATCHING FLOORING TRIM, TO COVER PERIMETER, PLUS EXTRA

UNDERLAY, FOR LAMINATE FLOORS

SCISSORS OR CRAFT KNIFE

STICKY TAPE

TOOL UP JIGSAW

TOOL DOWN JUNIOR HACKSAW

WORKBENCH OR OTHER SUITABLE CUTTING SURFACE (SEE PAGE 22)

EXPANSION SPACERS, PENCIL

GRAB ADHESIVE

HAMMER AND PANEL PINS OR HEAVY BOOKS

GETTING STARTED

Remove old carpet, vinyl or other floor coverings and ensure surface is dry, firm and level. You can lay laminate on top of ceramic or vinyl tiles if you don't want to remove those first.

If you're laying on top of concrete, check surface for damp by taping one square metre of plastic sheeting onto the concrete floor – ensure all edges are taped down – and leave overnight. If any condensation has appeared, consult a damp-proofing specialist.

Work out how many packs of laminate flooring you'll need. Measure room width and length at widest points, then multiply to calculate surface area. Add extra for wastage. Divide this total by the surface area provided by each pack. Round up to the nearest whole number.

Next, measure the perimeter of the room to calculate the amount of flooring trim needed and buy ten per cent extra.

Allow the floorboards to acclimatise by leaving them for 48 hours in the room they will cover, before laying.

Decide which direction to lay the floorboards:

• Running floorboards lengthways, towards a light source, is the most forgiving for visible joints. It will also make a room feel longer.

• Running floorboards across the width of the room will make it feel wider.

• If laying laminate over a timbered floor, lay the boards at 90 degrees to the floorboards below for the strongest result.

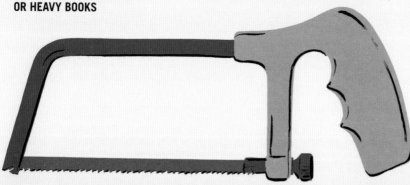

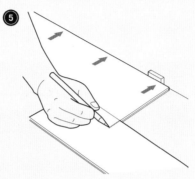

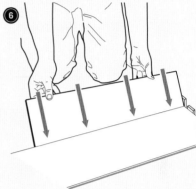

WHAT TO DO

1 Lay out underlay over the entire floor. Trim to fit with scissors or a craft knife. Tape joins securely, with no overlap.

2 Loosely lay out the first row of boards, end to end, to ensure there won't be a very short strip at one end. If the last board will need to be cut to less than one-third of its length, cut the first board to less than a full length so that neither board is too short. Repeat this process for the width of the room to ensure neither first or last board is too narrow.

3 Lay the first board in the corner, with an expansion spacer between it and the wall on both edges. Expansion spacers allow for natural movement of the boards, and should be placed wherever the boards meet the wall.

4 Fit the next board end-on, slotting the tongue into groove at a 30-degree angle. Lower the board to lock into place.

5 Continue along the row until you'll need to cut. Turn the end board around so tongue-end is against wall and positioned alongside penultimate board. Mark a line on the end board at level of penultimate board.

6 If the offcut is more than 300mm long, use it to start the next row. If not, cut another board in half and start laying the second row next to where you started first. With cut end against the wall, angle the new board against first board with tongue in groove. Click down to lock in place. Repeat along the row.

7 To finish, remove expansion spacers and add matching trim, cutting mitres at corners. Measure and cut lengths of trim and glue back to skirting board. Press in place and hold firm by hammering in panel pins or placing heavy books on top, until dry.

HOW TO NAIL IT!

- Choose a combined underlay and damp-proof membrane if you are at all worried about damp.

- If you have an uneven floor, choose a thick underlay such as wood fibre. This will also insulate for sound and heat. You can add a damp-proof membrane underneath, if necessary.

- Cut boards outside or in another room, if possible, to avoid dust getting into underlay.

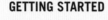

LAY VINYL FLOORING

49

Vinyl flooring is hard-wearing and comes in all sorts of colours and designs. It is much easier to clean than carpet and suits areas that are exposed to a lot of moisture, such as bathrooms.

YOU'LL NEED

MATERIALS FOR PREPARING FLOOR (SEE *GETTING STARTED*)

STEEL TAPE MEASURE

ROLL OF VINYL FLOORING, TO FIT SPACE, PLUS EXTRA

SCISSORS

SOFT BROOM

STEEL STRAIGHTEDGE OR RULER

CRAFT KNIFE

SMALL BLOCK OF WOOD

⚠ VINYL SPRAY ADHESIVE AND MASK

⬆ **TOOL UP** FLOOR ROLLER

⬇ **TOOL DOWN** ROLLING PIN OR CLEAN PAINT ROLLER

PIPE-AND-CABLE DETECTOR

⚠ POWER DRILL, WITH BIT SUITABLE FOR FLOOR

DOOR THRESHOLD, WITH FIXINGS

SCREWDRIVER

GETTING STARTED

Remove old carpet, vinyl or other floor coverings and ensure surface is dry, firm and level.

Timber floor: put down 9mm exterior-grade plywood, to take out the ridges. Screw into boards below at 300mm intervals. Fill and sand any joins to ensure surface is perfectly smooth.

Concrete floor: if you have a concrete floor, test for moisture. See *Lay Laminate Flooring* (page 110). If laying over bumpy concrete or tiles, you can use a self-levelling compound to achieve a smooth base. Basically, over time, bumps show through vinyl so

it's best to get your floor as smooth as possible. Once the floor is flat, paint primer on any porous surface such as cement, plywood, hardboard or chipboard, before you begin.

Measure the room to be covered by multiplying its length by its width. Add about 100mm to measurements at each edge. Include alcoves and halfway into any doorways.

Vinyl sheets come in different widths, so choose one that will cover the whole floor, or in a sensible number of strips. Work out how many you will need by measuring the length of longest wall and dividing by width of roll. Measure adjacent wall and multiply by number of strips to work out length needed.

Leave vinyl in room for 48 hours to acclimatise. In cold weather, put heating on to stop it becoming brittle.

The method you use for fixing the vinyl will vary. Some vinyls come with peel-off adhesive, some only require sticking at doorways, seams and edges and some require no glueing. If using adhesive, consult manufacturer's recommendations.

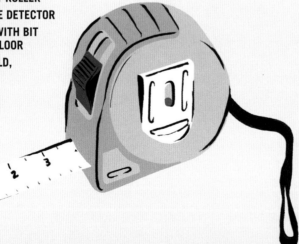

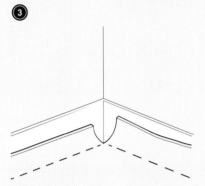

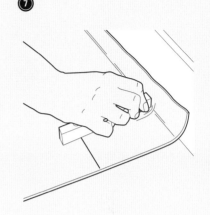

WHAT TO DO

1 Take off shoes to avoid treading grit into underside of vinyl.

2 Unroll vinyl face-up against longest continuous wall. Using scissors, roughly cut edge down to leave an excess of about 100mm against skirting. You can trim more precisely once it is all in place.

3 At internal corners, cut triangular notches out of 'spare' vinyl to help sheet lie flat.

4 At external corners, make straight cut down from vinyl edge to floor level.

5 Use soft broom to brush surface, removing air pockets.

6 Where more than one piece of vinyl is required, fit largest piece first, then lay next rough-cut piece so that it overlaps the first by 35-50mm. To cut seam, place straightedge or ruler with guiding edge alongside edge of lower piece of vinyl. Hold firmly and cut through both layers with craft knife. Go slowly and do not attempt in one stroke! Remove cut strip.

7 Press vinyl sheet against base of skirting boards or wall using small block of wood to help crease.

8 Hold sheet hard to skirting board with metal straightedge and cut along crease with sharp craft knife. Move knife carefully, removing waste frequently to check cut is accurate.

9 To fix with adhesive, roll back 50 per cent of vinyl. Wear mask and apply glue to floor. Press vinyl firmly and slowly onto adhesive to ensure a good bond. Use a rolling motion to reduce air bubbles and follow with a floor roller, rolling pin or clean paint roller. Roll from the centre of the floor out with firm pressure. Repeat with other half of vinyl. Roll again between one and four hours later.

10 At doorway, cut vinyl to line up with flooring in next room. Check for hidden pipes and cables, then drill holes to secure threshold bar to floor with screws. Push vinyl edge underneath with screwdriver.

11 Avoid walking on floor for at least 24 hours after installation. Check manufacturer's instructions for timings.

HOW TO NAIL IT!

- If you're using vinyl flooring on kitchen or bathroom floors, seal the edges with silicone sealant to make a waterproof barrier. See *Apply Silicone Sealant* (page 46).

- Try to avoid joining strips of vinyl in doorways or areas of heavy wear.

- To lay around a curve, make a paper template. Take a piece of paper (wider than the curved object) and cut slits 10-20mm wide along one edge. Place paper with slits up against curve, crease slits against curve and draw pencil line around crease. Remove paper and cut along curved line. Place template on vinyl and draw around line. Using sharp craft knife or scissors cut, check and trim for a perfect fit.

LAY VINYL TILES

Laying soft vinyl tiles is easier than laying vinyl sheeting. If you make a mistake you have only wasted one tile, rather than a whole sheet. The first tile to be laid is called the key tile; find a helper and take time to get its position right. You can buy self-adhesive tiles if you prefer.

▶ YOU'LL NEED

MATERIALS FOR PREPARING FLOOR (SEE *GETTING STARTED*)

STEEL TAPE MEASURE

SOFT VINYL TILES, TO FIT SPACE, PLUS EXTRA

PENCIL OR CHALK

CHALK LINE

STRING

CHINAGRAPH PENCIL OR ORDINARY PENCIL

CUTTING BOARD OR SCRAP HARDBOARD

CRAFT KNIFE

STRAIGHTEDGE

FOR NON-ADHESIVE TILES:

⚠ **TILE ADHESIVE**

NOTCHED SPREADER

SMALL ROLLER

DAMP CLOTH OR SPONGE

GETTING STARTED

Remove old carpet, vinyl or other floor coverings and ensure surface is dry, firm and level.

Timber floor: you will need to put down 9mm exterior-grade plywood first, to take out the ridges. Screw into boards below at 300mm intervals. Fill and sand any joins to ensure surface is perfectly smooth.

Concrete and tiles: if you have a concrete floor, test for moisture. See *Lay Laminate Flooring* (page 48). If laying over bumpy concrete or tiles, you can use a self-levelling compound to achieve a smooth base. Basically, over time, bumps show through vinyl so it's best to get your floor as smooth as possible.

Once the floor is flat, you need to paint primer on any porous surface such as cement, plywood, hardboard or chipboard, before you begin.

Measure area to be tiled. Measure tiles and calculate number of tiles needed for the area. See *Tile Wall* (page 38).

Check all the packets of tiles have the same batch or item numbers or you may find they have colour differences.

Leave the tiles in the room they will cover for 24 hours to acclimatise.

To get the best symmetrical results, tile from the centre out.

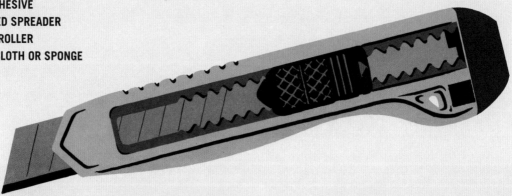

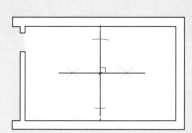

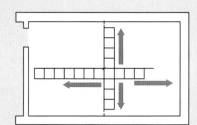

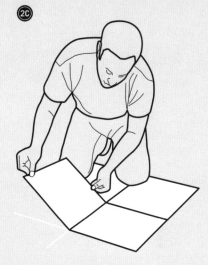

WHAT TO DO

① Find centre of room

A Measure one wall, find its midpoint and mark with pencil on the floor. Repeat on opposite wall and stretch a chalk line between the two points.

B Mark mid-point of this line. Attach pencil or chalk to one metre of string. With one person holding the string end at the mid-point, draw semicircles at two intersections with chalk line.

C Move end of string to intersection of points and draw two semicircles towards centre of room, at either side of chalk line. Repeat at other mark so you have two crosses where the semicircles intersect.

D Make chalk line between two intersection points. The cross point will be a perfect right angle in centre of room.

② Lay tiles

A Without sticking, loosely lay out a test row of tiles starting at the centre line and working towards the wall. If the last tile would be cut too narrow, move start tile back half a tile-width and repeat test row. Adding onto initial row, lay test rows towards other walls, adjusting start positions so each row ends with at least half a tile. Mark final start position for key tile on floor with pencil or chalk.

B *For self-adhesive tiles:* peel backing paper off first tile and press down in start position, as above.

For non-adhesive tiles: spread tile adhesive over floor with notched spreader, covering an area of one square metre at a time. Make sure you can still see chalk lines for starting position. Press first tile into adhesive so each part of it is in contact.

C Lay second tile on other side of chalk line butting up to first tile. Lay first four tiles in a square of tiles then continue until half the room is tiled. Don't fill edge gaps until the end.

D *For non-adhesive tiles:* use a small roller to ensure all tiles are well stuck-down, paying attention to edges. Wipe away any adhesive that comes through joins with damp cloth or sponge.

③ Cut and lay tiles for gaps at skirting

A Place tile to be cut exactly on top of last full tile. Place a second tile on top with its edge butting up to wall. Mark along edge of top tile onto face of tile below using chinagraph or ordinary pencil. See *Lay Ceramic Floor Tiles, step 3A* (page 117).

B On cutting board or scrap board, cut part-way through marked line using craft knife and straightedge. Break tile along score mark by bending until it snaps. See also *Cut Tiles* (page 36).

C Check fit of cut tile before sticking in place.

HOW TO NAIL IT!

- When calculating number of tile packs to buy, always round up and err on the side of caution as some tiles will be wasted.

- Once tiles are laid, leave floor for at least 24 hours before walking on. Check manufacturer's instructions for timing.

LAY CERAMIC FLOOR TILES

51

Ceramic tiles are hard-wearing, easy to clean and resistant to spills and stains. They are expensive, though, so take extra care when laying them. Ask your local DIY store for guidance on finding the right grout for your tiles.

YOU'LL NEED

MATERIALS FOR PREPARING FLOOR (SEE *GETTING STARTED*)

STEEL TAPE MEASURE

TILES TO FILL SPACE, PLUS EXTRA

PENCIL, CHALK LINE AND STRING

⚠ TILE ADHESIVE

NOTCHED SPREADER

⬆ **TOOL UP** TILE SPACERS
⬇ **TOOL DOWN** MATCHES

SPIRIT LEVEL, TROWEL

CHINAGRAPH PENCIL

⬆ **TOOL UP** FLAT-BED TILE CUTTER FOR STRAIGHT CUTS; JIGSAW, WITH TILE-CUTTING BLADE, PLUS CLAMP, FOR SHAPED CUTS

⬇ **TOOL DOWN** TILE SCORER FOR STRAIGHT CUTS; TILE SAW AND CLAMP, OR TILE NIBBLERS, FOR SHAPED CUTS

SANDPAPER OR TILE FILE

CERAMIC TILE SEALANT (IF LAYING NATURAL OR POROUS TILES)

FLOOR TILE GROUT (PRE-MIXED OR POWDERED)

RUBBER GLOVES (OPTIONAL)

STRIKING TOOL OR DOWEL

SPONGE AND CLOTHS

FLEXIBLE SEALANT, IN SAME COLOUR AS GROUT, AND APPLICATOR

GETTING STARTED

Prepare the existing floor.

Concrete floor: clean with detergent and water. Ensure it is thoroughly dry.

Timber floor: strengthen by laying 9mm exterior-grade plywood. Screw into boards below at 300mm intervals.

Ceramic/quarry tiles: check all tiles are securely stuck down and clean.

Vinyl flooring: check all tiles are securely stuck down and clean.

Measure the area to be tiled. Measure tiles and calculate the number of tiles needed for the area. See *Tile Wall* (page 38).

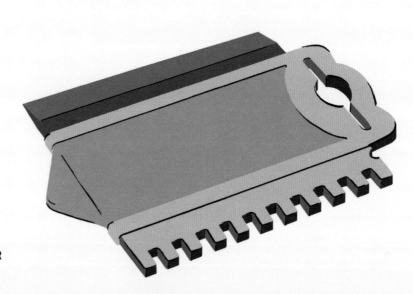

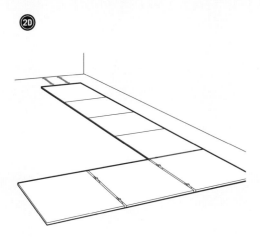

WHAT TO DO

❶ Find centre of room, then locate best position for key tile. See *Lay Vinyl Tiles*, step 1 (page 115).

❷ Lay tiles

A Cover about one square metre of floor at a time with adhesive, using notched spreader. Make sure you can still see chalk lines for starting position.

B Lay first key tile, giving slight twist to bed into adhesive properly.

C Work a single row out towards one wall, fitting spacers or matches to keep tiles evenly spaced. Use spirit level to check tiles are level.

D Lay next row at a right angle out from key tile towards wall, then work one row at a time to fill this quarter of room.

E Repeat process, filling a quarter of a room at a time, until all but cut tiles at edges are laid.

F Use trowel to clean out adhesive in gaps around the walls before it sets. Leave tiles for 24 hours before cutting and laying edge tiles.

❸ Cut and lay tiles for gaps at skirting

A Place tile to be cut exactly on top of last full tile. Place a third tile on top with its edge butting up to wall. Mark along edge of top tile onto face of tile below using chinagraph pencil.

B Cut just short of marked line to allow space for grout. See *Cut Tiles* (page 36).

C Apply adhesive to back of each cut tile and lay in place. Leave for 24 hours.

❹ Grout tiles

A If your tiles are natural stone or very porous, apply chemical sealant before and after grouting.

B When adhesive has set, if using powdered grout, mix it to fairly dry consistency. Take advice from tile retailer for consistency needed. See also *Grout Tiles* (page 34). Leave for a few minutes to stand. A dry grout mix needs to be applied carefully with fingers to prevent staining of tile surface. Wear rubber gloves, if you prefer. If tiles are glazed, pour grout mix over tiles and spread with rubber edge of spreader.

C As grout starts to set, press and smooth it into joints with striking tool, dowel or finger, to create neat concave line. Compacting it like this makes it water-resistant. Wipe off excess grout with a damp sponge.

D Leave grout to harden for one hour. Wipe with damp cloth then polish with dry cloth.

E Seal edge of floor with flexible sealant.

F Leave floor for at least 24 hours before walking on, and at least 48 hours before using it heavily.

HOW TO NAIL IT!

- Because freshly laid tiles have to be left untouched for 48 hours, don't find yourself unable to use the kitchen. Tile half a room at a time before taking a long break and make sure you leave an exit path so you don't have to tread on any tiles.

- Push tile spacers well below the surface of the tile so they won't protrude through the grout at the end.

- A short length of hose pipe works well to smooth and shape grout.

REPAIR SCRATCHES IN FLOORBOARDS

The best way to get an even wooden floor is by sanding, but if you just have a few scratches, small holes or gaps, they can be repaired without embarking on such a big job.

YOU'LL NEED

FLOOR OR MULTI-SURFACE CLEANER AND SOFT CLOTHS

STEEL WOOL

FINE-GRADE SANDPAPER

⚠ WHITE SPIRIT

PUTTY KNIFE

WOOD FILLER, TO MATCH FLOOR COLOUR

MATERIALS FOR VARNISHING FLOOR (SEE PAGE 127)

GETTING STARTED

See how deep your scratch is. Light scratches can be dealt with using steel wool but deeper scratches will need fine-grade sandpaper.

WHAT TO DO

❶ Clean area with floor or multi-surface cleaner.

❷ Rub over scratch with steel wool or fine-grade sandpaper, taking care to go in direction of wood grain and only over scratch.

❸ Clean and smooth the area with white spirit on a soft cloth.

❹ Use putty knife to press wood filler into scratched area. Leave to dry.

❺ Sand excess dried filler to the level of the wood, using fine-grade sandpaper. Clean away dust.

❻ Re-varnish repaired area to match the rest of the floor. See *Varnish Floorboards* (page 127).

HOW TO NAIL IT!

- If you have recently sanded your floor, salvage the sawdust from the sander, mix with wood adhesive and use to fill small holes in the wood.

- Always sand along the grain of the wood or you risk damaging it further.

FIX CREAKING FLOORBOARDS

Floorboards can creak either because their fastening screws have come loose, or they've swollen and now rub against each other. Once you've found the problem, it's easy to fix. If a floorboard covers an area of pipes or cables, fixing it with a screw instead of a nail will allow easy access.

YOU'LL NEED

- TALCUM POWDER
- OLD KNIFE
- PLIERS OR CLAW HAMMER
- WIDE-BLADED CHISEL, IF NEEDED
- 60MM SCREWS
- ⚠ POWER DRILL, WITH COUNTERSINK BIT
- SCREWDRIVER
- FLOORBOARD NAILS

GETTING STARTED

Remove any floor coverings and press on the boards with your feet to pinpoint the problem place. Sprinkle talcum powder along the cracks and work in with a knife. This may be enough to solve the problem.

If the floorboard still creaks, you will need to screw it down or re-nail to secure and stop the movement. You can screw directly into existing nail holes if they're in good condition.

WHAT TO DO

❶ Use existing nail holes

A Prise out old nails with pliers or claw hammer – if you need to lift board slightly to pull nails higher, drive a wide-bladed chisel between the boards and prise up a little. Push board back down, leaving nails proud, and remove.

B Screw in 60mm screws and secure tightly. If screw heads sit proud of surface, remove, countersink (see *Back to Basics*, page 18) and screw back in.

❷ Use new nail holes

Drive nails in away from old holes but near enough so you go into joist underneath. If in doubt, prise board up, as above, and take a look, marking the position of the joist on floorboard.

If you are driving nails in near the very end of board, drill small pilot holes (smaller than width of your nail) first, to help stop board from splitting.

HOW TO NAIL IT!

- If board end doesn't fix to joist, screw a 25mm x 50mm batten onto nearest joist end, to provide anchor for board.

FILL FLOORBOARD GAPS

54

As good as stripped floorboards look, the gaps between them can let cold air circulate. Stop the draughts by sealing up the gaps. The amount you'll save on heating bills will pay for the job within a year.

YOU'LL NEED

HAMMER

NAIL PUNCH

RAG

WARM, SOAPY WATER

FOR WOOD SLIVER METHOD:

SLIVERS OF RECLAIMED WOOD

WOOD ADHESIVE

⚠ CHISEL AND MALLET

FOR PAPIER MÂCHÉ METHOD:

WALLPAPER ADHESIVE
(PRE-MIXED OR POWDERED)

PILE OF OLD NEWSPAPERS,
SHREDDED

OLD KNIFE

COLOURED ACRYLIC SEALANT,
TO MATCH FLOOR OR DARKER

APPLICATOR GUN, IF NEEDED

FOR RUBBER SEAL METHOD:

SCISSORS

RUBBER SEAL, APPLICATOR

OLD CREDIT CARD
OR BLUNT KNIFE

GETTING STARTED

First, choose your method by looking at the size of the gaps, deciding whether the boards will be covered afterwards and how beautiful you want the finish to be. The key is to allow for flexibility because floorboards move and fillers can crack.

For best results: hammer and glue in wedge-shaped slivers of reclaimed wood, then sand and treat to match the floor. Although this can be time-consuming, it is worth it, particularly if you are going to sand and treat the floorboards anyway.

Cheapest way: fill gaps with a papier mâché of shredded newspaper and wallpaper paste, then top with a bead of acrylic sealant in a colour to match the floor. This is messy, but cost-effective and can be done without needing to sand the floor afterwards.

Easiest methods:

A *Branded, v-shaped plastic tape.* Simply press down between boards and tape expands to fill gaps of any size. Also prevents smells wafting up, and there's no need to treat floor afterwards. However, gaps remain and dirt can collect in the tape, which becomes hard to clean.

B *Rubber seal.* Easy to install and comes in different sizes to fit range of gaps and in dark grey colour to mimic natural shadows.

For small gaps up to 6mm: see *Repair Scratches in Floorboards* (page 118).

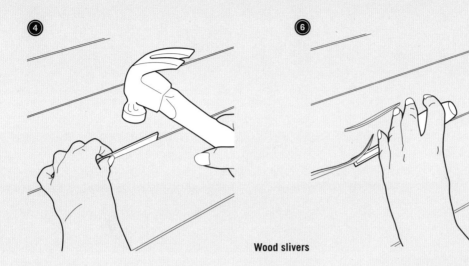

Wood slivers

WHAT TO DO

Wood slivers

❶ Use a hammer and nail punch to push any protruding nails to 3-4mm below the surface of the floorboard.

❷ Clean out all floorboard gaps as thoroughly as possible and leave to dry.

❸ Test out the wood slivers in the gaps for general fit. If OK, remove and apply glue down each side of sliver.

❹ Place sliver into gap and hammer all over its surface to wedge it in as tightly as possible.

❺ Repeat to fill all gaps in room then leave at least four hours to dry.

❻ Using a chisel and mallet, carefully cut off tops of slivers to level of floor.

❼ Clean away dust and dirt. Sand and varnish entire floor, as required (see pages 122-127).

Papier mâché

❶ Follow steps 1 and 2 for wood slivers.

❷ If using powdered adhesive, make up small amount. Mix newspaper with adhesive. Don't make it too sloppy; it needs to be able to hold up within gaps.

❸ Push mixture into holes, lower than the floorboard surface. Use old knife to fill small gaps. Leave to dry thoroughly.

❹ Apply acrylic sealant on top of papier mâché and leave to dry. Make sure your sealant is acrylic, not silicone – you can clean up, sand and paint over acrylic sealant.

Rubber seal

❶ Follow steps 1 and 2 for wood slivers.

❷ Using scissors, push end of rubber seal into gap near skirting board. Switch to old credit card or blunt knife, and push seal in for next 50mm.

❸ Use applicator to insert remainder across floor, inserting final 50mm with card or knife. Cut to fit at other end.

❹ Push in cut end with scissors.

HOW TO NAIL IT!

- Don't use wood filler to plug gaps – manufacturers exclude floorboard filling as a use. The main reason is that it isn't flexible enough to cope with the board movements and will fall between the gaps, leaving you back where you started.

- If using wood slivers for filling gaps, try to use old or reclaimed wood. New wood can shrink over time and your gap will open up again.

- Don't use sealant on its own in floorboard gaps; it needs to rest on the papier mâché in order to be held in place.

SAND FLOORBOARDS

Whether you are revealing your floorboards for the first time, or just re-finishing them, this is a rewarding, but very, very dusty job. Make sure you wear goggles and a dust mask.

▶ YOU'LL NEED

MATERIALS FOR PREPARING FLOOR SURFACE (SEE *GETTING STARTED*)

MASKING TAPE

DUSTSHEETS, IF NEEDED

SANDER AND EDGER

COARSE-, MEDIUM- AND FINE-GRADE SANDPAPER DISCS, AS NEEDED

SAFETY GOGGLES AND MASK

SANDPAPER SHEETS AND SANDING BLOCK, OR CHISEL

VACUUM CLEANER

SOFT CLOTH

⚠ WHITE SPIRIT

MATERIALS FOR FINISHING FLOOR, AS NEEDED

GETTING STARTED

Replace and countersink any old or loose nails. See *Back to Basics* (page 18). Fill any gaps in the floorboards and repair or replace broken floorboards (see pages 119-121). The floor surface must be flat and without obstructions.

Empty the room of all furniture, pictures and curtains. Close and seal internal doors and cupboards with masking tape. It's best if room is completely empty, but cover anything left with dustsheets. Open windows and external doors for ventilation.

Hire the right sander for your room size and get an edger to complete the job. Read safety instructions before starting.

WHAT TO DO

1 Fit sander with coarse-grade sandpaper discs (or if floorboards are in good condition and not stained, you can go straight to medium-grade sandpaper). Put on goggles and dust mask.

2 Work diagonally across the room, moving constantly and slowly, in overlapping strips.

3 If floor is deeply stained, work a second time across the room in opposing diagonal direction.

4 Switch to medium-grade sandpaper and work up and down room in same direction as boards.

5 Repeat step 4 with fine-grade sandpaper.

6 Use edger to sand around edges of room, working through grades of sandpaper, as before.

7 Sand awkward corners with sandpaper wrapped around block, or use a chisel to scrape away dirt.

8 Wearing clean socks to avoid marking bare, untreated floor, remove all tools from room and vacuum floor. Remove fine dust using soft cloth dampened with white spirit.

9 Your freshly sanded floor will need some sort of protection or it will stain and absorb anything spilled on it. See pages 124-127 for guidance on oiling, staining and varnishing floorboards. For advice on painting floors, see page 156.

HOW TO NAIL IT!

- Buy more sanding discs than you think you will need. Most hire companies will buy back unused discs – check with yours first.

- Check sander dust collection bags regularly and empty when full, to prevent them from bursting. Small amounts of dust from the bags can be used to fill small holes in floorboards (see page 118).

- See *Back to Basics* (page 23) for more tips on sandpaper and sanding.

OIL FLOORBOARDS

Oils and waxes penetrate into the wood fibres and protect from within. Most oils and waxes are non-toxic, hypo-allergenic and easy to do minor repairs with. You'll need to re-apply every one to two years. They are not as shiny or durable as other finishes. Apply oil only to freshly sanded floor. See *Sand Floorboards* (page 122).

▶ YOU'LL NEED

STEEL TAPE MEASURE

FLOOR OIL, TO COVER AREA, PLUS EXTRA

BROOM, MOP AND FLOOR CLEANER

RUBBER GLOVES

WIDE FLOOR BRUSH

SMALL PAINTBRUSH, FOR EDGES

LINT-FREE CLOTHS

RAGS OR OLD CLOTHS

⬆ **TOOL UP** POWER SANDER

⬇ **TOOL DOWN** FINE-GRADE WIRE WOOL OR SANDPAPER AND BLOCK

⚠ STAY SAFE!

Oil-saturated cloths can spontaneously combust as the oil cures. Place in water after use, then dispose of carefully in sealed metal container filled with water.

GETTING STARTED

Measure the room to calculate the area to be oiled. Check tin for guidance on coverage and remember to buy extra if you are applying more than one coat.

Make sure room is well ventilated. Remove all furniture.

Always read and follow manufacturer's guidelines. Wear old clothes. Floorboards should be clean and dust-free.

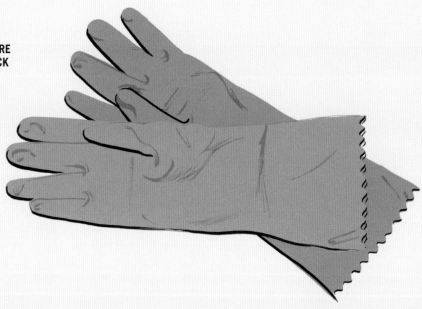

WHAT TO DO

1 Wearing rubber gloves, apply oil, starting from the corner of the room farthest from the door. Apply an even layer of oil all over the floor, using wide floor brush or paintbrush. Use a small paintbrush for edges.

2 Let the wood absorb the oil for 20 minutes.

3 Add more oil if the floor is very absorbent and wait another 20 minutes.

4 Buff oil into the wood using lint-free cloths.

5 Use rags or old cloths to wipe all remaining oil from the wood.

6 You may need two or three further applications, depending on manufacturer's guidelines. Before applying further coats, remove any nibs or dust. You can do this very lightly with a power sander, or with very fine-grade wire wool or sandpaper. Wipe over with damp cloth and allow to dry thoroughly.

7 Do not walk on floor for 12 hours after final application.

HOW TO NAIL IT!

- UV oil is a good choice if you are looking for more durability. It gives a warm, natural look and the durability of a lacquer.

- To keep your floor looking lovely, make your own floor polish by mixing equal parts olive oil and white vinegar. Add drops of lavender, orange or lemon essential oil and use spray bottle to apply.

STAIN FLOORBOARDS

57

Stains and dyes colour your wood, but offer no protection. They can be applied under either oil or varnish/lacquer. This job is best done by two people in one continuous process without a break. Apply stain only to a freshly sanded floor. See *Sand Floorboards* (page 122).

YOU'LL NEED

- STEEL TAPE MEASURE
- STAIN, TO COVER AREA, PLUS EXTRA
- BROOM, MOP AND FLOOR CLEANER
- FINE-GRADE SANDPAPER
- LARGE BIN BAG
- ROLLER TRAY
- RUBBER GLOVES
- PAINT PAD
- SMALL PAINTBRUSH, FOR EDGES
- LINT-FREE CLOTHS

GETTING STARTED

Measure the room to calculate the area to be stained. Check tin for guidance on coverage and remember to buy extra if you are applying more than one coat. Make sure room is well-ventilated. Remove all furniture.

Always read and follow manufacturer's guidelines. Wear old clothes. Floorboards should be clean and dust-free.

All stain colours are affected by the individual colour of your sanded boards, so patch-test on as many inconspicuous areas as possible, then sand back again once you have made your choice.

WHAT TO DO

❶ Spread out bin bag, put tray on it and pour in stain.

❷ Wearing gloves, start at corner farthest from door and apply stain with paint pad, working across two or three boards at a time. Use small paintbrush for edges. Apply quite liberally and work at brisk pace following line of boards. Try to cover entire boards, and do not overlap onto neighbouring ones. One person should apply the stain, while the other follows behind one minute later, wiping off excess with cloth and working along the grain.

❸ Allow at least six hours to dry before varnishing or oiling – overnight, if possible.

HOW TO NAIL IT!

- If you have to work on your own, apply stain with pad across small area then go back to the beginning and wipe off before moving on to the next boards.

- Painting your floorboards is a cost-effective way of adding colour and getting a great look when your floorboards aren't so great! See *Paint Floors* (page 156).

- You can buy stains that are combined with oil, if you want colour as well as the natural look of oil.

VARNISH FLOORBOARDS

Varnishes or lacquers are usually either solvent-based (highly toxic) or water-soluble (less toxic and easier to use at home). They form a durable, protective layer on top of the wood and are water-resistant. Varnishes come in various gloss levels. Apply varnish only to a freshly stained or sanded floor. See opposite and *Sand Floorboards* (page 122).

▶ YOU'LL NEED

STEEL TAPE MEASURE

VARNISH OR LACQUER TO COVER AREA, PLUS EXTRA

BROOM, MOP AND FLOOR CLEANER

RUBBER GLOVES AND MASK

LARGE PAINTBRUSH, PAINT PAD OR ROLLER, PLUS ROLLER TRAY

SMALL PAINTBRUSH, FOR EDGES

TOOL UP POWER SANDER

TOOL DOWN FINE-GRADE WIRE WOOL OR SANDPAPER AND BLOCK

DAMP CLOTH

GETTING STARTED

Measure the room to calculate the area to be varnished. Check tin for guidance on coverage and remember to buy extra if you are applying more than one coat. Make sure room is warm and well-ventilated. Remove all furniture.

Always read and follow manufacturer's guidelines. Wear old clothes. Floorboards should be clean and dust-free.

⚠ STAY SAFE!

Check manufacturer's instructions before disposing of used rags as they can be combustible.

WHAT TO DO

❶ Put on rubber gloves and mask. If using paint pad or roller, decant varnish into roller tray.

❷ Dip pad or brush in varnish.

❸ Starting in corner farthest from door, drag pad or brush towards you along floorboard in long, smooth strokes. Use roller, if covering large area. Use small paintbrush for edges. For brush, apply along grain of wood.

❹ Apply two to three coats, allowing two hours between each for varnish to dry.

❺ Before applying final coat, remove any nibs or dust. You can do this very lightly with a power sander, or with very fine-grade wire wool or sandpaper.

❻ Wipe over with damp cloth and allow to dry thoroughly, according to manufacturer's instructions.

❼ Apply final coat and leave overnight.

HOW TO NAIL IT!

- If you are varnishing on top of a stained floor, apply at least three coats of varnish to protect stain and give depth to the colour.

- Choose combination stains-and-varnish to give colour as well as protection.

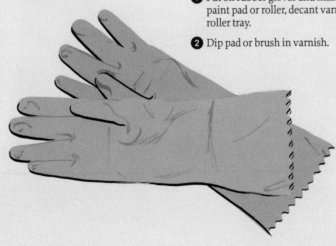

FIT COVING AND CORNICING

Coving is the pre-made decorative moulding which covers the space where the wall meets the ceiling. Cornicing is the name for more ornate coving, as found in period homes. Coving can be made from plaster or lighter materials such as polystyrene, plastic or wood. Most will look similar once painted – the most important thing is the shape.

▶ YOU'LL NEED

STEEL TAPE MEASURE

COVING OR CORNICING, TO COVER PERIMETER OF ROOM, PLUS EXTRA

FINE-GRADE SANDPAPER AND SANDING BLOCK

SCRAPER

DAMP SPONGE

▲ **TOOL UP** COMPOUND MITRE SAW
▼ **TOOL DOWN** MITRE BOX AND TENON SAW

WORKBENCH OR OTHER SUITABLE CUTTING SURFACE (SEE PAGE 22)

PENCIL

CRAFT KNIFE

COVING ADHESIVE, WITH APPLICATOR GUN

HAMMER

PANEL PINS

PLIERS

FILLER

PAINT AND PAINTBRUSH

GETTING STARTED

Fit coving and cornicing before you decorate a room.

Measure the room to find the length of coving or cornicing needed and add 20 per cent for wastage.

Clean the area of loose plaster or flaking paint by sanding gently, or using a scraper. Wipe with damp sponge.

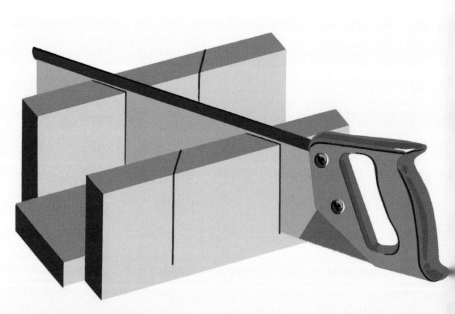

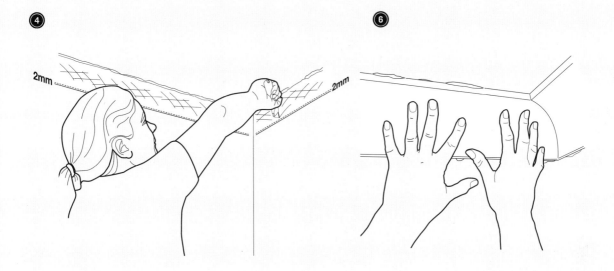

WHAT TO DO

1 Cut all lengths of coving using mitred cuts, following instructions for *Fit Skirting Boards* (page 132).

2 Hold a piece of coving up in position and mark its dimensions on wall and ceiling in pencil, all around the room.

3 Remove any wallpaper from area to be covered, by cutting it away with a sharp craft knife, staying 2mm within borders of the pencil marks at each side. Pull off waste paper with a scraper.

4 'Key' the area within guidelines by scoring the plaster with a craft knife in a criss-cross pattern. This will give the adhesive more grip.

5 Apply coving adhesive along both back edges of the first length of coving, either with applicator gun or by spreading with scraper.

6 Press coving into place within pencil guidelines, ensuring firm contact all along length. Excess adhesive will squeeze out.

7 Remove excess adhesive with finger or scraper. Use it to fill any gaps at mitred corners or where two lengths join.

8 Using hammer, tap panel pins into wall just below bottom edge of coving to support as adhesive dries.

9 Repeat steps 2-8 until whole area has been covered.

10 Fill any gaps with adhesive and wipe with damp sponge. Leave adhesive to dry.

11 Lightly sand joints and corners with fine-grade sandpaper.

12 Once moulding is securely in place, remove panel pins carefully with pliers, fill holes and paint over.

HOW TO NAIL IT!

- If a wall is longer than a single length of coving, join two mitred lengths by butting them together with adhesive.

- Wipe away any splashes of adhesive with a damp sponge.

FIT DADO RAILS AND PICTURE RAILS

Dado rails divide the lower portion of the wall (the dado) from the top. Traditionally, this lower part would have been panelled. The rails can act as protection, but are mainly decorative. Picture rails are usually placed 300-500mm below ceiling height and dado rails at 900mm from the floor.

YOU'LL NEED

STEEL TAPE MEASURE

RAILING, TO FIT PERIMETER OF ROOM, PLUS EXTRA

MULTI-PURPOSE DETECTOR

SCREWS AND WALL PLUGS, AS NEEDED

PENCIL

SPIRIT LEVEL

LONG STRAIGHTEDGE

TOOL UP COMPOUND MITRE SAW

TOOL DOWN MITRE BOX AND TENON SAW

WORKBENCH OR OTHER SUITABLE CUTTING SURFACE (SEE PAGE 22)

FINE-GRADE SANDPAPER

POWER DRILL, WITH COUNTERSINK BIT, WOOD BIT AND BIT SUITABLE FOR WALL TYPE

SCREWDRIVER

BRADAWL OR NAIL

WOOD FILLER

PALETTE KNIFE (OR USE FINGER)

PAINTBRUSH

PRIMER

PAINT OR VARNISH

GETTING STARTED

Measure the room to find the length of rail needed and add 20 per cent for wastage.

Use a detector to note positions of hidden pipes and cables and avoid fixing there. If not fixing to masonry, locate studs using a detector and fix to these, if possible.

See *Back to Basics* (pages 18-23) for advice on choosing screws, wall plugs and drill bits to suit your wall, and for tips on sawing and drilling.

WHAT TO DO

1. Choose the height of your rail. Bear in mind how the rail interacts with other features of the walls such as fireplaces and doorways. Mark chosen position in pencil at each corner of room, measuring carefully up from floor or down from ceiling.

2. Use a spirit level to get straightedge horizontal at your mark height and draw along it with pencil. Repeat across all walls.

3. Cut rail for longest wall first. Use mitre box or mitre saw to cut mitre end, paying attention to which way angle needs to go. See *Fit Skirting Boards* (page 132). Sand any rough edges.

4. If a wall is longer than a single length of rail, join two lengths with opposite mitre cuts. Ensure both lengths are at least 300mm long.

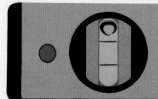

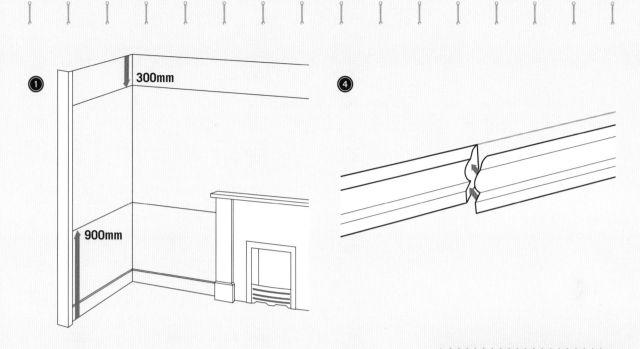

① 300mm

④

900mm

⑤ Drill small pilot holes through rail, one 300mm from each end and no more than 1m apart.

⑥ Countersink holes to ensure screw head will be flush with surface (see page 18).

⑦ Hold rail in position against wall and mark through holes with bradawl or nail.

⑧ Use appropriate bit to drill holes at fixing points to depth of wall plug, if using. If fixing to studs, drill pilot holes. Push in wall plug, if using. Screw rail into place.

⑨ Repeat steps 3-7 for all the walls, making sure you cut the angle the correct way each time.

⑩ Cover each screw hole in the rail with wood filler. Level with palette knife or finger.

⑪ When dry, sand off excess filler. Prime and paint or varnish as required. See *Paint Interior Woodwork* (page 168).

HOW TO NAIL IT!

• If you are confused about which way a mitre cut should go, remember that the back of the rail is always the same length as the wall.

• Don't rush the job. Measure twice and cut once.

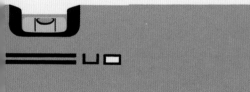

FIT SKIRTING BOARDS

Gaps are needed between the floor and walls to allow for expansion and contraction with the weather. Skirting board is the decoration that hides these gaps. It's easier to prime skirting before it goes on. Better still, buy pre-primed boards.

YOU'LL NEED

SCRAPER

PRYING BAR OR CROW BAR

STEEL TAPE MEASURE

SKIRTING BOARD, TO FIT PERIMETER OF SPACE, PLUS EXTRA

MULTI-PURPOSE DETECTOR

SUITABLE FIXINGS FOR WALL TYPE

PENCIL

TOOL UP COMPOUND MITRE SAW

TOOL DOWN MITRE BOX AND TENON SAW

WORKBENCH OR OTHER SUITABLE CUTTING SURFACE (SEE PAGE 22)

FINE-GRADE SANDPAPER

PLUS, AS NEEDED:

PANEL PINS AND COPING SAW

⚠ **POWER DRILL, WITH COUNTERSINK BIT, WOOD BIT AND BIT SUITABLE FOR WALL TYPE**

BRADAWL OR NAIL

SCREWDRIVER

⚠ **GRAB ADHESIVE**

HAMMER

WOOD OFFCUTS OR HEAVY BOOKS

WOOD FILLER

DECORATOR'S CAULK AND APPLICATOR GUN

PAINTBRUSH AND PAINT/VARNISH

GETTING STARTED

To remove old skirting board, gently tap a scraper down the back of the top of the boards to break the bond with the paint or any filler. Insert prying bar or crow bar and prise carefully along length of skirting.

Measure the room to find the length of skirting board needed and add extra for wastage.

Use a detector to note positions of hidden pipes and cables in walls and avoid fixing there.

Skirting board can be fixed to the wall using nails, screws or adhesive. Adhesive is quick, but it can be difficult to press the board close to the wall, so you may end up with gaps to fill.

Nails work well if there is something wooden to attach them to, such as a stud. Don't use nails on plasterwork.

Masonry walls: use screws and wallplugs.

Stud walls: use standard oval wire nails to fix into the studs. Use a detector to find and mark studs low down on wall.

Timber blocks: if your skirting board was originally fixed to timber blocks (a traditional way of fixing skirting), reuse these fixing points with lost-head nails, which are stronger than oval wire nails.

Damp-proof course: to avoid penetrating the damp-proofing with nails, you'll need to glue the skirting board with wood adhesive.

See *Back to Basics* (pages 18–23) for more advice on choosing screws, wall plugs and drill bits to suit your wall, and for tips on sawing and drilling.

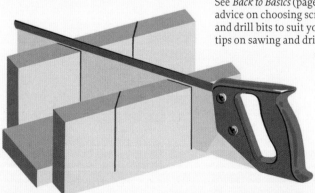

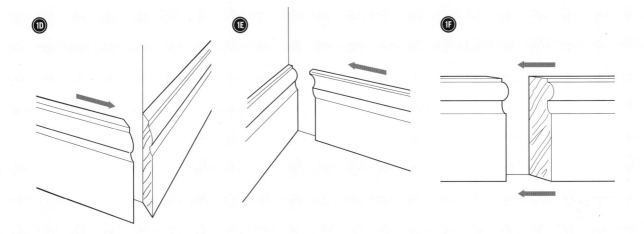

WHAT TO DO

① Cut skirting board

A Measure length of longest wall and mark position for cut in pencil on face of board. Leave shortest walls until last.

B If wall needs more than one length of skirting, place skirting board into mitre saw or box and cut at a 45-degree angle. Cut other board with opposite mitre to fit. Sand any rough edges.

C Before cutting for corners, sketch out a plan for how mitres will fit together.

D *External corners:* cut joining ends as a mitre, at a 45-degree angle, so that longest side of board is away from wall. Check pieces fit together before fixing.

E *Internal corners:* fit one board with flat edge into corner and secure with panel pin, tapping it in lightly. Hold second board butted at right angles to first and mark its outline on end of first board. Remove first board and cut along pencil mark with a coping saw. Refit the boards with second uncut board pushed into corner and the first board overlapping it. If you don't have a coping saw, cut boards with 45-degree mitres, so that the longest part of board is against the wall.

F *At door or architrave:* cut as a flat edge.

② Fix skirting board

Secure skirting board with appropriate fixings at existing positions or space 600mm apart, halfway up flat part of board.

A If using screws, drill small pilot holes through board where you want them positioned, adding more if skirting needs pulling in due to uneven wall. Countersink to ensure screw head will be flush with surface (see page 18).

Hold skirting to wall and mark through the holes with a bradawl or nail.

Use appropriate bit to drill holes at fixing points to depth of wall plug. If fixing to studs, drill pilot holes. Push in wall plugs, if using, and screw board into place.

B If using nails, mark positions of studs on skirting boards. Secure with adhesive, then nail in place. Ensure nails are long enough to penetrate at least 20mm into studs or blocks behind. If using adhesive only, apply to back of board. Press and hold in position with wood offcuts or heavy books as props, until set.

③ To finish

A Sand corners pointing into the room and fill any gaps at joins and nail holes with wood filler.

B Line the gap between skirting and wall with decorator's caulk (see *How to Nail It!*, below). Leave to dry.

C Paint or varnish, as required.

HOW TO NAIL IT!

- Fit skirting board before fitting new carpet (see page 106). If you're laying tiles or wooden flooring, fit skirting board last.

- Decorator's caulk is a flexible filler for imperfect joints or gaps between walls and skirting boards, architraves and window frames. Unlike silicone, it can be smoothed with a wet finger or damp sponge and easily wiped away if you go wrong.

- For mitre cuts, remember that the back of the skirting board is always the same length as the wall.

FIT TONGUE-AND-GROOVE PANELLING

You can add character and texture to a room with tongue-and-groove panelling. It's easy to install and can be painted to great effect. This type of interior timber cladding is generally used to cover the bottom third of walls but can just as easily cover the whole height or even the ceiling.

YOU'LL NEED

STEEL TAPE MEASURE

MULTI-PURPOSE DETECTOR

PENCIL

SPIRIT LEVEL

⚠ POWER DRILL WITH COUNTERSINK BIT, WOOD BIT AND BIT SUITABLE FOR WALL TYPE

50MM X 13MM (2IN X ½IN) BATTEN

BRADAWL OR NAIL

WALL PLUGS, IF NEEDED

50MM SCREWS AND LONGER SCREWS FOR SOCKETS

SCREWDRIVER

TONGUE-AND-GROOVE PANELS, TO COVER SPACE, PLUS EXTRA FOR WASTAGE

⬆ **TOOL UP** JIGSAW OR CIRCULAR SAW

⬇ **TOOL DOWN** TENON OR SMALL HANDSAW

WORKBENCH OR SUITABLE CUTTING SURFACE (SEE PAGE 22)

FINE-GRADE SANDPAPER

HAMMER

PANEL PINS AND NAIL PUNCH

BEADING OR WOOD TRIM, TO COVER TOP EDGE

WOOD ADHESIVE

GETTING STARTED

Measure the full width of every wall you want your panelling to cover. It's better to space your panelling slightly so that it fits without you having to cut individual panels into thin slithers.

Double the width measurement to work out how much batten you will need. The batten is the horizontal support that sits behind the panelling at the top and bottom.

Use a detector to note positions of pipes and cables and avoid fixing there. If not fixing to masonry, locate studs using a detector and fix to these.

See *Back to Basics* (pages 18-23) for advice on choosing screws, wall plugs and drill bits to suit your wall, and for tips on sawing and drilling.

⚠ STAY SAFE!

If you are unsure about working with electricity consult a qualified electrician before attempting step 11.

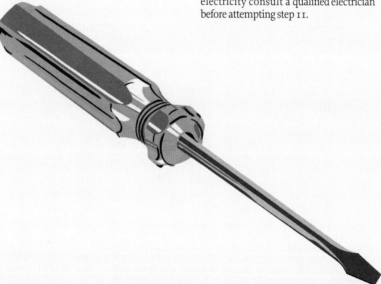

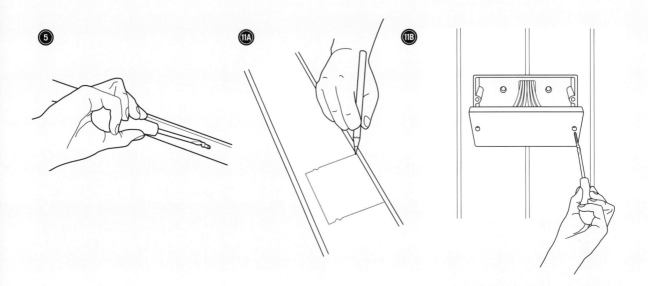

WHAT TO DO

1 Measure and draw chosen top line on wall with pencil, using spirit level to keep line straight. For lower batten, mark position as far down as possible, or just above skirting.

2 Drill small pilot holes all the way through battens, at intervals along its length. Countersink to ensure screws lie flush with surface. See *Back to Basics* (page 18).

3 Hold batten to align top edge with top pencil line and mark fixing points through pilot holes onto wall with bradawl or nail.

4 Use appropriate bit to drill holes at fixing points to depth of wall plug. If fixing to studs, drill pilot holes.

5 Push in wall plugs, if using. Screw in battens so screws are flush with surface. Repeat for lower batten.

6 Saw tongue-and-groove panels to appropriate length. Sand off any rough edges.

7 Starting at one end of room, hammer in first panel with two panel pins at top and bottom, securely fixing it to the batten behind. Use a spirit level to check panels are straight. Recess nails just beyond wood using nail punch.

8 Slide next panel into position and nail as before. Don't push panel in too tight – you should leave a millimetre or so to prevent buckling.

9 Continue along length of wall. If you have to cut a panel at the end, use a jigsaw or circular saw and workbench. If you have not attempted this before, get it cut professionally.

10 Start next wall by beginning at furthest point and working back, butting corners together.

11 A Cut around sockets. Before fitting panel, turn off mains power and unscrew plug socket. Mark position of plug socket on relevant panel(s) and cut smaller hole with tenon saw or jigsaw.

B Fit panel(s), then fix plug socket back on with longer screws so it sits on top of panelling.

12 For a neat finish, attach beading to top of panels using panel pins and wood adhesive. Fit skirting board around the bottom. See *Fit Skirting Board* (page 132).

HOW TO NAIL IT!

- If your wall is smooth, flat and dry and if you don't think you'll be pulling off the panelling any time soon – then panels can be glued directly on to the wall with panel adhesive and without the use of battens. Use panel pins to hold panelling in place whilst glue sets.

- Fill nail punch holes with wood filler before painting.

- As long as you attach a batten measuring the same depth at the top, you can use existing skirting board as a lower batten.

HANG PICTURES AND MIRRORS

63

One way of hanging pictures is from a picture rail (see page 130). If you would rather fix the pictures and mirrors individually, there are certain steps you should take to avoid pock-marking your plaster with evidence of failed attempts.

▶ YOU'LL NEED

MULTI-PURPOSE DETECTOR

PENCIL

SCRAP PAPER

MASKING TAPE

BRADAWL OR NAIL

⚠ POWER DRILL, WITH BITS SUITABLE FOR WALL TYPE, OR HAMMER

HANGING DEVICE (NAIL, SCREWS AND WALL PLUGS, PICTURE HOOKS OR VELCRO STRIPS)

SCREWDRIVER

STEEL TAPE MEASURE

GETTING STARTED

It's useful to create a dummy out of paper if your picture or mirror is heavy, or if you find it hard to visualise the best position for it. Otherwise, measure carefully before drilling any holes.

See *Back to Basics* (pages 18-21) for advice on choosing screws, nails, wall plugs and drill bits to suit your wall, and for tips on drilling.

The most secure practice is to drill into studs or fix with wall plugs to masonry. Locate studs using a detector. In most houses, studs are positioned 400mm apart and are 40mm wide. Mark positions at top or bottom of wall in pencil – leave for future reference. For light loads use hollow-wall fixings away from studs on plasterboard.

Use a detector to note positions of hidden pipes and cables and avoid fixing there.

WHAT TO DO

❶ Picture or mirror with static fixing

A Lie the picture or mirror on floor and place scrap paper (thicker than newspaper, preferably) over the top, taping sheets together, if necessary, to create a dummy of the same dimensions. Transfer fixing point to the paper, too. Use this as an easier-to-handle guide for marking up fixing point on the wall.

B Hold dummy against the wall to try out positions, taking note of studs, if needed, and marking them on paper. Tape dummy in place.

C Use bradawl or nail to punch through dummy and mark wall. Remove paper, then either tap in nail with hammer, or drill hole using appropriate bit to depth of wall plug, or to depth of screw, if fixing to studs. Insert wall plug, if using, and screw in hanging device.

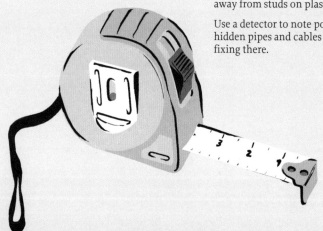

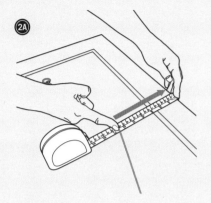

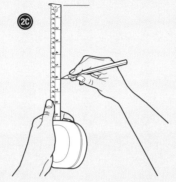

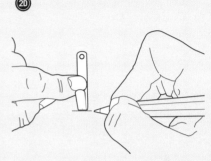

② Picture or mirror with wire fixing

A Pull wire taut towards top of picture or mirror. Measure from the highest point of wire to the top of picture or mirror.

B Position on wall. Mark top of picture or mirror with pencil.

C On wall, measure down from here the distance you just noted and mark again with pencil.

D Position bottom of hanging device against the lower mark and mark fixing point. Drill hole at marked fixing point to depth of wall plug. If fixing to stud, drill pilot holes.

E Insert wall plug, if using, and screw in hanging device.

③ Light picture or unframed canvas

Simply tap a picture hook or small nail into your chosen position, so 10mm sticks out, angled upwards.

④ Using velcro picture strips

These strips allow you to hang pictures and frames without the use of nails, drills or screws. They lock together, holding the picture firmly to the wall and are easy to remove, leaving no marks, damage or nail holes.

Placing pictures and mirrors

Take time to consider where to hang your picture or mirror – it's great to be creative, but there are a few things to bear in mind when choosing position.

- If you place a picture so that you have to look up at it, or down to it, you'll distort its perspective.

- Generally, pictures look better when they are proportionate to the size of wall, i.e. a large picture looks better on a large wall, a small picture on a small wall. If a picture is too small for your wall, add two pictures either side of it, or more, to create a group.

- If pictures are too high, they will have little connection to the furniture beneath them. As a general rule, hang 150-300mm above the back of the sofa.

- When hanging in an empty space, hang pictures so their mid-point is somewhere around 1.5m above the floor.

- Treat groups of pictures as one picture. On the floor, arrange how you want them to fit together. Decide on your focal point, hang this at the optimum position, then fit the others around it.

- Mirrors are a great addition to any wall and not just for vanity. If hung cleverly, they can add a window to a room. They increase light and help a room look bigger.

- Ensure mirrors are hung high enough so that your head is not cut off when you check your reflection.

HOW TO NAIL IT!

- **Never drill without checking for pipes and cables.**

- **Ensure you use the right screws for your walls and the weight of your picture or mirror, or it may come crashing down when you least expect it.**

WALL-MOUNT TV

Flat-screen televisions are well suited to being mounted on the wall: they are lightweight enough and can sit more or less flush. You can opt for a fixed position, a mount that will give you a small tilt, or a full-motion bracket. Stud or solid, masonry walls are the sturdiest choice to hang heavy items from.

▶ YOU'LL NEED

TELEVISION MOUNT, WITH SUITABLE FIXINGS (SEE *GETTING STARTED*)

MULTI-PURPOSE DETECTOR

PENCIL OR BRADAWL

STEEL TAPE MEASURE

SPIRIT LEVEL

⚠ **POWER DRILL, WITH BITS SUITABLE FOR WALL TYPE**

SCREWDRIVER

CABLE TIES AND TACKS, IF NEEDED

GETTING STARTED

Check fixings supplied are appropriate for wall type. For masonry walls, you'll need wall plugs and screws. For cavity walls, you will need cavity wall bolts. For stud walls, simply screw into stud. Check the wall mount to ensure it will carry the weight of your television.

Check for hidden pipes and cables. Choose a position where the television can be seen well. If you hang it in a place you might hang a picture, you could end up with neck strain.

Flat-screen televisions are best watched head-on, so should be at seated eye-level. Make sure direct sunlight doesn't affect the screen or it will be hard to see.

See *Back to Basics* (pages 18-21) for advice on choosing screws, wall plugs and drill bits and for tips on drilling.

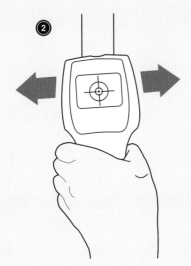

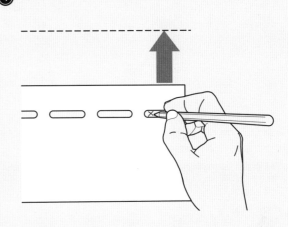

WHAT TO DO

❶ Attach brackets to the back of the TV, according to manufacturer's instructions. Remove plugs on the back of TV set to reveal screw holes, if necessary. Ensure both pieces of bracket are fixed in same place so they line up evenly. Do not rest your plasma TV face-down on the floor – it's not good for the set.

❷ If not fixing to a masonry wall, find and mark studs using a detector. In most houses, studs are positioned 400mm apart and are 40mm wide. Mark central point of each stud. See *Back to Basics* (page 21) for more tips on finding studs.

❸ To mark correct position for wall mount, measure the height of television. Loosely attach the wall part of the bracket to the television and measure from top of wall bracket to the top of television. Use measurements to find the best height for the television and mark line on wall.

❹ Hold bracket against wall, line up the fixing points with the studs, if using, and mark locations of fixing holes on wall with pencil or bradawl.

❺ Use spirit level to check marks are level. Use appropriate bit to drill holes at fixing points to depth of wall plug, if using. If fixing to studs, drill pilot holes. Push in wall plugs, if using.

❻ Secure wall mount to wall with supplied fixings. Check bracket is still level before tightening screws.

❼ To hang the television on the wall: plug cables into TV, unless bracket allows enough space to reach sockets, in which case do this afterwards. With a helper, lift television up onto wall bracket.

❽ Check set is level once more.

HOW TO NAIL IT!

- A tilting wall bracket is helpful, as it allows you some access to the back of the set while installing.

- If you want a really neat finish, use a qualified electrician to provide a power source to be hidden behind the television. You can also neaten cables with ties and tack them with cable tacks around skirting.

- You may need to purchase extra-long AV cables to account for the new, longer distance from the TV to the power source.

PAINTING
AND
DECORATING

EVERYTHING YOU NEED TO GET THE JOB DONE

SAND WALLS

Careful preparation is essential if you want a professional paint finish on your interior walls. The first step is to sand walls down. If they have been professionally skim-plastered, you won't need to do this, but if not, sanding will give you the best starting point.

▶ YOU'LL NEED

MATERIALS FOR PREPARING WALLS (SEE *GETTING STARTED*)

DUSTSHEETS

MASK AND SAFETY GOGGLES

COARSE-, MEDIUM- AND FINE-GRADE SANDPAPER

⚡ **TOOL UP** POWER SANDER

🔧 **TOOL DOWN** SANDING BLOCK

DAMP CLOTH

VACUUM CLEANER

GETTING STARTED

To remove any wallpaper, see *Strip Wallpaper* (page 160).

WHAT TO DO

❶ Locate any dents, nail holes or small cracks and fill them (anything larger may require a professional plasterer to apply skim layer). See *Fill Cracks in Plaster* (page 145) and *Fill Holes in Plaster* (page 146).

❷ Lay down dustsheets to protect floors and furniture. Make sure area is well ventilated. Wearing mask and goggles, sand wall with coarse-grade sandpaper, using power sander or sanding block. Wipe with damp cloth to remove dust.

❸ Repeat with medium-grade sandpaper, then fine-grade sandpaper, wiping away dust with damp cloth after each sanding.

❹ Repeat filling and sanding steps until wall is as smooth as you require. Vacuum away dust.

HOW TO NAIL IT!

- Choose the most expensive sandpaper you can afford as the quality does make a difference.

- You can do this job by hand or with a small power sander. For larger areas, a power sander will save you a lot of time and effort.

- See *Back to Basics* (page 23) for more tips on sandpaper and sanding.

COVER DAMP STAIN

Covering an unsightly damp patch on the wall or ceiling is easy to do, as long as the original cause of the damp has been dealt with.

YOU'LL NEED

MATERIALS FOR PREPARING SURFACE (SEE *GETTING STARTED*)

DAMP CLOTH

DUSTSHEETS

STEPLADDER, IF NEEDED

TIN OR SPRAY CAN OF STAIN-BLOCKING DAMP SEALANT

PAINTBRUSH, IF NEEDED

SAFETY GOGGLES, IF NEEDED

GETTING STARTED

Before you begin, repair any holes, cracks or surface imperfections. See *Fill Cracks in Plaster* (opposite) and *Fill Holes in Plaster* (page 146). Sand down any rough areas. Make sure the surface of your stain is clean and dust-free by wiping down with damp cloth.

WHAT TO DO

1 Cover nearby furniture and carpets with dustsheets.

2 Open all windows and doors to help ventilate the room.

3 If damp stain is on ceiling or high up on wall, put stepladder carefully in position, on level surface. Spray or brush damp sealant over stain. Work sealant in well, covering affected area and beyond.

4 Leave for 24 hours before painting or wallpapering.

HOW TO NAIL IT!

- There are a number of good products on the market for covering stains. Ask your local decorators' merchant for recommendations.

- Keep the area as well ventilated as possible for as long as you can. Wear safety goggles if you are spraying stain block above your head.

- If the damp patch is on top of wallpaper, you will need to cut back the affected area and treat the cause of damp before covering the stain and re-papering. See *Hang Wallpaper* (page 162).

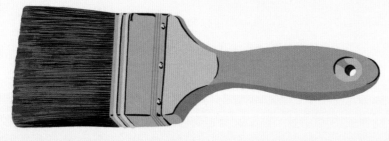

FILL CRACKS IN PLASTER

67

Plaster can crack over time purely through exposure to central heating and age. Rather than paint over the cracks, fill them properly and you shouldn't be bothered by them again. It's easier to fix big cracks than small ones, so you may need to increase the crack before you start.

▶ YOU'LL NEED

FILLING KNIFE OR SCRAPER

SMALL PAINTBRUSH

DAMP CLOTH

CRAFT KNIFE

VACUUM CLEANER

WATER-BASED ADHESIVE, SUCH AS PVA, DILUTED 1 PART TO 3 PARTS WATER

FINE-GRADE FILLER

PUTTY KNIFE, IF NEEDED

FINE-GRADE SANDPAPER

PRIMER

GETTING STARTED

Carefully scrape away any loose or crumbling material with a filling knife or scraper. Use dry paintbrush to remove any dirt or debris from around the crack. Wipe with damp cloth.

WHAT TO DO

1. Gently turn craft knife inside crack to enlarge it slightly. Remove debris and vacuum up any dust.

2. Wet crack area, including edges, with diluted PVA, or brush dipped in water.

3. Load fine-grade filler on to filling knife or putty knife and draw firmly across crack, pressing in. Scrape excess off.

4. Leave to dry for 24 hours. Sandpaper over dried filler.

5. If filler has shrunk at all, re-wet and fill again, repeating steps 3 and 4.

6. Paint primer over filled crack, ready for redecoration.

HOW TO NAIL IT!

- It's important to use primer before you redecorate the repaired area, or you'll always be able to see where the patch in the plaster was.

- Repaint the area using the same method (brush or roller) with which the wall was originally painted.

FILL HOLES IN PLASTER

If your existing plaster has some areas that are loose or need fixing, you can fill the problem areas without touching the 'good' plaster. For dealing with cracks in plaster, see *Fill Cracks in Plaster* (page 145).

▶ YOU'LL NEED

⚠ **CHISEL**
SMALL PAINTBRUSH
DAMP CLOTH
WATER-BASED ADHESIVE, SUCH AS PVA, DILUTED 1 PART TO 3 PARTS WATER
POWDERED OR PRE-MIXED PLASTER
CLEAN BUCKET AND STICK (IF USING POWDERED PLASTER)
PLASTERING TROWEL
PIECE OF WOODEN BATTEN
FINE-GRADE SANDPAPER AND SANDING BLOCK
PRIMER

GETTING STARTED

Remove the loose plaster: chip away with a chisel until you reach a firm surface. Take great care not to harm the good plaster. Don't be tempted to put an implement into the hole and lever it off, as this can take good plaster with it.

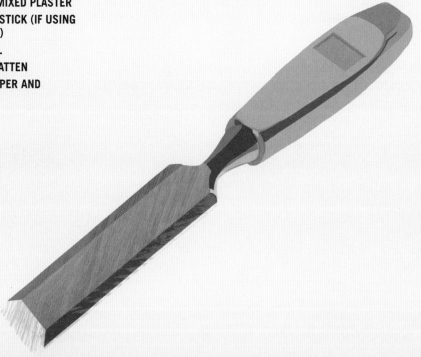

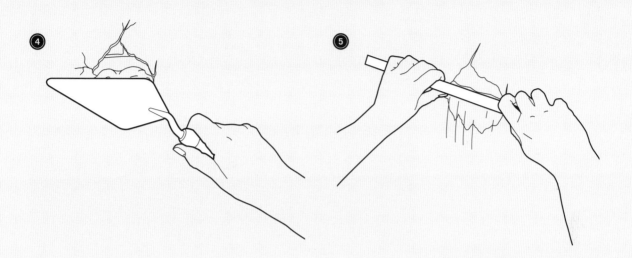

WHAT TO DO

1 Use a dry paintbrush to remove dust. Wipe down area with damp cloth.

2 Paint over hole and edges with PVA solution or water.

3 If using powdered plaster, mix in bucket using clean stick, according to packet instructions.

4 Use trowel to apply first coat of plaster to hole, pressing in firmly and taking care to fill up to join with old plaster.

5 Use wooden batten to wipe off excess plaster, ensuring batten runs over new plaster and onto old plaster on all sides, so hole will be filled to even height.

6 Build up deep areas in layers, allowing each layer to stiffen for two hours before applying next layer. Each layer should be no more than 50mm thick.

7 Leave to dry. Use fine-grade sandpaper lightly to sand over filled hole and surrounding area.

8 Apply primer before redecorating.

HOW TO NAIL IT!

- Some old plaster can sound hollow when tapped, but if it doesn't actually move then it is still good and you should leave it. Only loose plaster should be removed.

- Don't overlook the PVA stage to seal the old plaster, as it may be porous. If left unsealed, the two areas of plaster may never join properly and could develop into a new crack.

- If you don't have PVA, water alone will do the trick.

PAINT CEILINGS

69

Paint your ceiling before painting any walls (see page 150). Your best tool is a roller with an extension handle, although it can produce paint spray, so remove anything from the room you don't want to get speckled with paint, or cover it in a dustsheet.

▶ YOU'LL NEED

EMULSION PAINT, TO COVER AREA, PLUS EXTRA

STEEL TAPE MEASURE

DUSTSHEETS

STICKY TAPE AND MASKING TAPE

FEATHER DUSTER

OLD HAT AND SAFETY GOGGLES

STEPLADDER

CLEAN STICK

ROLLER TRAY

SMALL PAINTBRUSH, FOR EDGES

ROLLER, WITH EXTENSION HANDLE

GETTING STARTED

Choose paint to suit your job. See *Back to Basics* (page 24), for guide to different paint types.

Measure the area of the ceiling. You can do this by multiplying length by width of room to get a rough idea of size.

Check tins for guidance on coverage and remember to multiply by two if applying two coats. Round upwards in case of accidents or spillage.

Empty the room and cover up any furniture left with dustsheets. Protect your floors with plastic dustsheets. Tape sheets together with regular sticky tape, but fasten to floor edges/skirting board with masking tape.

Use duster to get rid of cobwebs and dust. Mask off any areas you don't want to get paint on.

Dress in old clothes and hat and goggles to keep the paint out of your hair and eyes. Open windows for ventilation.

Make sure your stepladder is positioned safely on an even surface before starting the job.

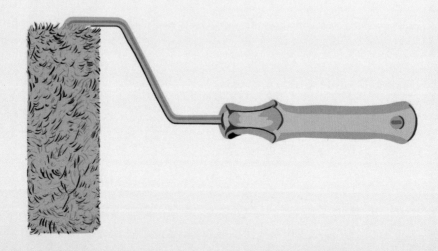

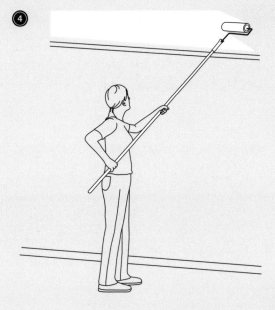

WHAT TO DO

1 Stir paint with clean stick or brush and pour into roller tray reservoir, until one-third full. Take tray up ladder with you and rest it carefully at the top. Position yourself as safely as you can and as close to the ceiling as possible.

2 'Cut in' edges of ceiling with small brush: paint overlapping strokes at right angles to the edge, then paint parallel to edge in a long, sweeping motion. Place brush a few millimetres from edge and allow bristles to splay out as you go. See also *Paint Walls*, step 2 (page 151).

3 Move ladder to side of room and attach extension handle to roller. Dip roller into reservoir – don't overload it – and roll it up and down tray a few times to get an even spread.

4 Paint ceiling with roller at an angle of around 45 degrees, using light, even strokes in random directions.

5 Start each reloaded roller in an unpainted area and work back towards last painted area.

6 Once dry, apply second coat, if desired.

HOW TO NAIL IT!

- Experiment until you get the right amount of paint on the roller – too much will send splatters everywhere, but too little will make the job go slowly. You need to think about your aching arms!

- When painting edges, you could also decant paint into a small container that you can hold easily at the top of the ladder.

- For more painting tips, see *Back to Basics* (pages 24–27).

PAINT WALLS

This DIY job can transform a room in hours but the key is in the preparation. As with all decorating jobs, protect clothes with overalls or wear old clothes.

▶ YOU'LL NEED

PAINT, TO COVER AREA, PLUS EXTRA

PRIMER, IF NEEDED

STEEL TAPE MEASURE

MATERIALS FOR PREPARING WALLS (SEE *GETTING STARTED*)

SOFT CLOTH OR SPONGE

⚠ **SUGAR SOAP OR WASHING-UP LIQUID**

STICKY TAPE AND MASKING TAPE

PLASTIC DUSTSHEETS

STEPLADDER, IF NEEDED

CLEAN STICK

SMALL PAINTBRUSH, FOR EDGES

MEDIUM/LARGE PAINTBRUSH OR ROLLER AND TRAY

GETTING STARTED

Choose paint to suit your job. See *Back to Basics* (page 24), for guide to paint types. Remember to prime bare plaster first (see *How to Nail it!*, opposite).

Calculate the area to be painted by multiplying height by width of each wall and adding together. Check tins for guidance on coverage and remember to multiply by two if applying two coats. Round upwards in case of accidents or spillage.

If you will be painting the ceiling, too, paint it first as as rollers can send paint spray down onto walls. See *Paint Ceilings* (page 148). If you will also be painting woodwork, paint that last. See *Paint Interior Woodwork* (page 168).

Prepare walls by filling any cracks or holes. Sand down to a smooth finish. If doing a large wall, a power sander will save you a lot of time (see pages 143-147).

Using soft cloth or sponge, clean walls with sugar soap or warm water and a little washing-up liquid. Leave to dry. Do this even if you think walls are clean, as grease from handprints can be invisible.

Protect your floors by taping plastic dustsheets to the floor. Tape sheets together with regular sticky tape, but fasten to floor edges/skirting board with masking tape. Mask off any areas you don't want to get paint on. Open windows for ventilation.

Make sure your stepladder is positioned safely on an even surface before using.

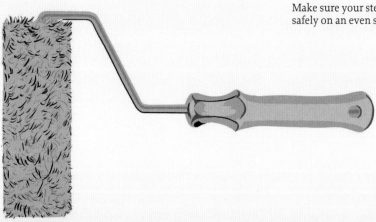

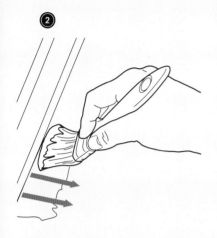

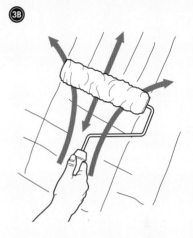

WHAT TO DO

1 Stir paint with clean stick or brush. If using roller, pour paint into tray until one-third full.

2 To 'cut in' edges: use small brush to paint overlapping strokes at right angles to the edge, then paint parallel to edge in a long, sweeping motion. Place brush a few millimetres from edge and allow bristles to splay out as you go. You can paint edges before or after the main painting, but you will get a less noticeable 'join' if you paint edges first.

3 Paint main wall areas in sections starting at the window or light source and moving away in parallel bands.

A Using a brush: work in panels of around one square metre, blending each panel together while paint still wet.

B Using a roller: dip roller into reservoir of tray – don't overload it – and roll up and down tray to get even spread. With light, even pressure, hold roller at an angle of 45 degrees and paint in random directions. Don't go too fast. Start each reloaded roller in an unpainted area and work back towards last painted area.

4 Continue until all walls painted. Try to finish a complete wall before taking a break so there's no difference in tone.

5 Leave to dry and apply second coat, as before.

HOW TO NAIL IT!

- Wrap paintbrushes and rollers in clingfilm or a plastic bag if you take a break – there's no need to wash them. Squeeze out as much air as possible.

- To store unused paint, make sure the lid is on tightly, then turn the tin upside down for a few seconds before turning upright again for storing. This will help seal the lid with paint, so air won't penetrate and cause a skin to form on the paint.

- If painting bare plaster, dilute your first coat of emulsion to one part water and four parts paint and use as a seal for the porous new plaster. Follow with at least two coats of undiluted emulsion.

PAINT DOORS

Doors see such heavy use that they can quickly get damaged, dented and dirty. Repairing and repainting can bring them back to life. As with all woodwork, you need to paint in the same direction as the wood grain.

▶ YOU'LL NEED

PRIMER, IF NEEDED

KNOTTING SOLUTION OR RESIN-BLOCKING PRIMER, IF NEEDED

UNDERCOAT, TO COVER AREA, PLUS EXTRA

TOPCOAT (GLOSS OR SATIN), TO COVER AREA, PLUS EXTRA

TRESTLES OR WORKBENCH, IF NEEDED

DUSTSHEET

MASKING TAPE, IF NEEDED

DOOR WEDGE, IF NEEDED

SCREWDRIVER

MATERIALS FOR PREPARING WOOD (SEE *WHAT TO DO*)

CLEAN STICK

SMALL PAINTBRUSHES

FINE- AND MEDIUM-GRADE SANDPAPER

TOOL UP POWER SANDER

TOOL DOWN SANDING BLOCK

GETTING STARTED

Choose the right primer and paint for your woodwork. See *Back to Basics* (page 24), for guide to paint types.

Gloss, or other paint with a durable shine, will be the most hardwearing. Never use a flat emulsion – it will get dirty far too quickly. Check tin for guidance on coverage and buy enough for two coats, if necessary.

You can paint doors in situ, or you can remove them from hinges and lay flat on a covered floor or on trestles. See *Cut Down Interior Door* (page 70), for removing and re-hanging a door.

Slide dustsheet under door to catch any drips.

If you're painting a glazed door, mask off the glass panels first.

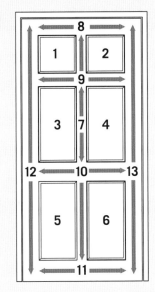

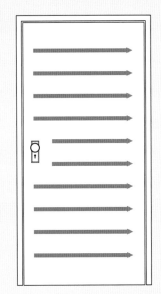

WHAT TO DO

1 If painting door in situ, use wedge to hold it open. Using a screwdriver, remove door handles. Leave wedge under door and keep a handle in your pocket, just in case you accidentally get shut inside.

2 Refer to *Paint Interior Woodwork* (page 168) for instructions on preparing and priming new wood, painted wood in good condition and painted wood where paint is loose or crumbling.

3 Paint undercoat first, over entire primed surface.

4 Stir paint for topcoat with clean stick or brush.

5 Paint along the wood grain, holding brush perpendicular to wood. When brush begins to drag, dip it in paint to reload it. As you coat each small area, run the tips of the same 'unloaded' brush over whole stretch in one long motion to 'tip', or smooth out, the brush strokes on the paint. 'Tip' the paint within one minute of it being painted on.

6 Paint hinge-side edge of door first, then outside and inside faces, as follows:

A For a panelled door: start with edges (mouldings) of any panels, then panel faces, then central vertical section, followed by top, middle and bottom cross rails and finishing with two side vertical sections.

B For a flush door: paint in sections from top left, working in same way as you would read a book (left to right, then down, left to right).

7 Finish by painting three exposed edges.

8 For best results, always apply a second topcoat. Sand lightly between coats.

9 When paint is dry, rehang the door, if necessary. See *Cut Down Interior Door* (page 70).

HOW TO NAIL IT!

- Paint both along and across the wood grain to work the paint in, but always finish a section by painting with the grain. When brush begins to drag, dip it in paint to reload it.

- When painting exterior or front doors, it's best to choose a specific front door paint that's extremely durable – but if the colour you want is not available, choose the most durable, high-gloss you can find.

- For more painting tips, see *Back to Basics* (pages 24-27).

PAINT STAIRWELL OR HALL

If you have mastered painting walls and ceilings, painting a stairwell or hall is only a little more difficult because some areas can be hard to reach. A roller with an extension pole is essential. Treat each area as if painting a separate room, completing one before starting the next. You'll need a helper to set up scaffolding, if not using a stair ladder.

▶ YOU'LL NEED

PRIMER AND PAINT FOR WALLS AND WOODWORK, TO COVER AREA, PLUS EXTRA

STEEL TAPE MEASURE

MATERIALS FOR PREPARING WALLS (SEE *GETTING STARTED*)

SOFT CLOTH OR SPONGE

⚠ SUGAR SOAP OR WASHING-UP LIQUID

STICKY TAPE AND MASKING TAPE

DUSTSHEETS

FEATHER DUSTER

↕ **TOOL UP** STAIR LADDER OR SCAFFOLDING

↕ **TOOL DOWN** STEPLADDER, LADDER AND SCAFFOLD BOARD, PLUS RAG OR TEATOWEL

CLEAN STICK

SMALL PAINTBRUSH, FOR MOULDINGS/CORNERS/ BALUSTRADES/EDGES

ROLLER TRAY

ROLLER, WITH EXTENSION HANDLE

GETTING STARTED

Choose the right primer and paint for your walls and woodwork. See *Back to Basics* (page 24), for guide to paint types. For high walls and ceilings, you won't have much control, so it's better to use the same colour so mistakes won't show. Remember to prime bare plaster first (see *How To Nail It!*, opposite). For steps, handrail and balustrades, choose a durable, high-sheen paint. These areas need to withstand a lot of traffic.

For walls, calculate the area to be painted by multiplying height by width of each wall and adding together. Check paint tin for coverage and remember to multiply by two if applying two coats. Round upwards in case of accidents or spillage.

Prepare walls by filling any holes or cracks. Sand down to a smooth finish. If doing a large wall, a power sander will save you a lot of time (see pages 143-147).

Using soft cloth or sponge, clean walls with sugar soap or warm water and a little washing-up liquid. Leave to dry. Do this even if you think walls are clean, as grease from handprints can be invisible.

Protect floors and stairs by taping dustsheets to the floor. Tape sheets together with regular sticky tape, but fasten to floor edges with masking tape. Be extremely careful not to create a trip hazard on stairs.

Protect woodwork, trims and anything you don't want to get paint on, with masking tape. Drape dustsheets over balustrades.

Use duster in high corners to get rid of cobwebs and dust. Open windows for ventilation.

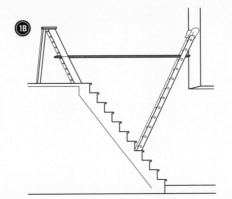

WHAT TO DO

1 Unless you are using scaffolding, or stair ladder to set ladder on stairs (**A**) you can construct a platform using a stepladder, ladder and a scaffold board, to reach head wall and well wall above stairway (**B**):

- Position stepladder on top landing safely back from top step.

- Wrap rag or teatowel around top of ladder so it doesn't mark walls and lean it against head wall, with feet resting against riser of step some way down the stairs.

- Lie a scaffold board horizontally between rungs of the two ladders. Have a friend on hand to help and ensure you're safe.

2 Stir paint with clean stick or brush and pour into roller tray reservoir, until one-third full.

3 Paint high ceilings around stairwell opening, using small paintbrush for 'cutting-in' edges, and roller with extension handle for main ceiling. See also *Paint Ceilings* (page 148).

4 Cut in edges for wall area you're working on first. See *Paint Walls*, *step 2* (page 151). If the top of the walls is really hard to reach, you can try taping a brush to the extension handle.

5 Paint main wall areas in sections starting at the window or light source and moving away in parallel bands.

6 To paint wall alongside staircase: start at bottom with roller parallel to angled staircase skirting board and roll upwards in a slight curving motion until roller is travelling vertically. Paint up to middle height of wall. Use roller extension pole to work from top down and blend into wet paint on lower section.

7 To paint steps, handrails and balustrades: see *Paint Interior Woodwork* (page 168). Use a small paintbrush and remember to mask off surrounding areas.

HOW TO NAIL IT!

- If your hallways don't have much natural light, don't paint them a dark colour. Choose one that complements the colour of the rooms leading off the hallway. Painting walls and ceiling the same colour will increase the sense of space.

- When laying protective coverings over stairs be very careful not to make it slippery. Tape down the covering along every stair so there's no chance it will slip off. You will be looking up more than down while painting and so won't be concentrating fully on what your feet are doing.

- If painting bare plaster, dilute first coat of emulsion to one part water and four parts paint and use as a seal for the porous new plaster. Follow with at least two coats of undiluted emulsion. For more painting tips, see *Back to Basics* (page 24).

PAINT FLOORS

A few thin coats wear less quickly than a thick coat, so go in sparingly with the paint. Painted wooden floorboards look great, but paint is also a good way to add interest to plyboard or concrete flooring without having to lay a different surface.

▶ YOU'LL NEED

PRIMER, TO SUIT FLOOR TYPE

FLOOR PAINT, TO COVER AREA, PLUS EXTRA

STEEL TAPE MEASURE

MASKING TAPE

CLEAN STICK

SMALL PAINTBRUSH, FOR EDGES

LARGE, NATURAL-BRISTLE BRUSH

ROLLER TRAY

ROLLER (OPTIONAL)

FINE-GRADE SANDPAPER

⚡ **TOOL UP** POWER SANDER

⚡ **TOOL DOWN** SANDING BLOCK

PAINT SEALER, IF NEEDED

FOR WOODEN FLOORBOARDS:

DUSTSHEETS

RAG OR LINT-FREE CLOTH

⚠ **WHITE SPIRIT**

FOR OTHER SURFACES:

BROOM AND MOP OR SPONGE, AS NEEDED

⚠ **SUGAR SOAP OR FLOOR CLEANER**

GETTING STARTED

Choose a primer to suit your floor type and a specialist floor paint, which will be much more durable than a standard paint.

Calculate the area to be primed and painted by multiplying length of room by its width. Check tins for guidance on coverage and don't forget to allow for at least two coats, ideally three. Round upwards.

Remove all furniture and pictures from room and open windows for ventilation.

If you will be sanding wooden floorboards, put dustsheets over any remaining items in room, such as built-in cupboards. Wear old clothes!

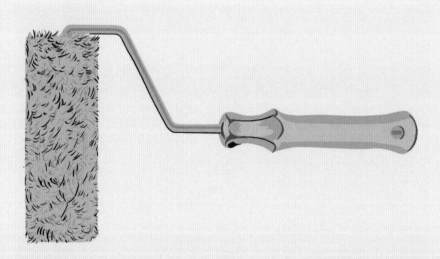

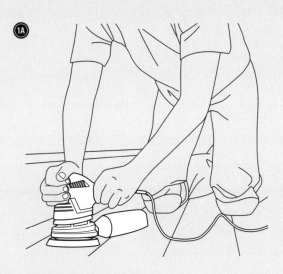

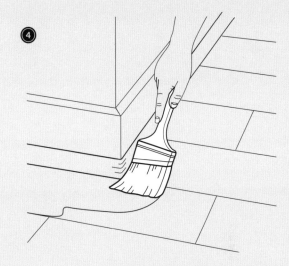

WHAT TO DO

① **A** If you are painting wooden floorboards, you will need to sand them first. Use fine-grade sandpaper and a power sander or block to sand floor lightly. For a large area, or a floor with lots of imperfections, consider using a larger, hired sander. See *Sand Floorboards* (page 122). Remove fine dust using soft cloth dampened with white spirit.

B For other surfaces, sweep, then clean floor with sugar soap or floor cleaner, and mop or sponge.

② Protect skirting boards with masking tape and apply primer, depending on floor type (a concrete floor will require a different primer from a wooden floor). Leave to dry overnight.

③ Stir paint with clean stick or brush and pour into reservoir of roller tray, until one-third full.

④ Cut in edges first. Use small brush to paint overlapping strokes at right angles to the edge, then paint parallel to edge in long sweeping motion. Place brush a few millimetres from edge and allow bristles to splay out as you go.

⑤ Start at the farthest corner of the room, so you can paint your way out. Apply the first, thin coat of paint with a natural-bristle brush – this creates a smooth finish. A roller will create a stippled finish. If painting floorboards, follow the grain of the wood.

⑥ Leave to dry for 24 hours.

⑦ Apply two more thin coats, allowing 24 hours before applying the next coat. Give the floor a light sand between coats.

⑧ Depending on the paint type, you may need to apply a paint sealer.

HOW TO NAIL IT!

- If it's not a warm day, keep the heating on while painting, to help the paint dry without it wrinkling.

- After the final coat of paint, it's acceptable to walk on the surface in socks after 24 hours. Leave your floor a few days longer before dragging furniture back into place, and no high heels for a month!

- If you want a white stain on floorboards, apply a thin coat of white emulsion, thinned with water. Allow to dry, then apply three coats of water-based varnish. Alternatively, mix a small amount of white emulsion (around two teaspoons) with about 250ml water-based varnish to make a tint. After the first coat, either apply two coats of untinted varnish or another tinted layer, depending on the colour you want.

PAINT RADIATOR

Unless your radiators are very rusty you should be able to paint them in situ. Depending on the type of radiator you have, you may want to choose a long, angled brush to help you get into awkward spaces. Spray paint can give you a really good finish.

▶ YOU'LL NEED

- **RADIATOR PAINT (TIN OR SPRAY)**
- **MASKING TAPE**
- **DUSTSHEET**
- **FINE-GRADE SANDPAPER**
- ⬆ **TOOL UP** POWER SANDER
- ⬇ **TOOL DOWN** SANDING BLOCK
- **SOFT CLOTH OR SPONGE**
- ⚠ **SUGAR SOAP OR WASHING-UP LIQUID**
- **ANTI-CORROSIVE METAL PRIMER OR OIL-BASED UNDERCOAT, IF NEEDED**
- ⬆ **TOOL UP** RADIATOR ROLLER OR LONG, ANGLED PAINTBRUSH
- ⬇ **TOOL DOWN** PAINTBRUSH
- **SCRAP CARDBOARD, GOGGLES AND MASK, IF USING SPRAY PAINT**

GETTING STARTED

Choose your paint – it should be heat-resistant and specifically for painting metal.

Turn heating off and let the radiator cool down before you begin.

Mask off areas not being painted and lay dustsheet to protect floor underneath.

Radiator rollers are actually made for painting the wall behind radiators, but the long handle and small head can also be useful for reaching the visible parts at the back of the radiator. If you have a radiator with deep ridges, an angled paintbrush is a good option.

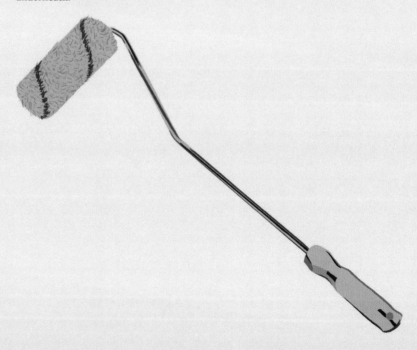

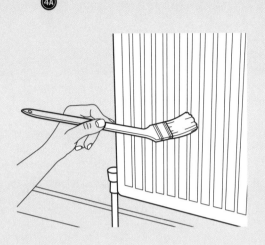

WHAT TO DO

1 Wearing mask, sand down radiator. You may find holding a piece of sandpaper easier. Make sure you sand any rusted areas really well.

2 Using soft cloth or sponge, clean radiator with sugar soap or warm water and a little washing-up liquid. Rinse with warm water and cloth and dry with soft cloth.

3 Paint metal primer or an oil-based undercoat over any bare metal or previously rusted areas.

4 Apply two coats of radiator paint, leaving four hours for drying between coats. Keep the coats as thin as possible to avoid drips.

A Use a medium-to-small brush, or an angled brush to get inside ridges.

B A radiator roller is also useful for painting visible areas behind the radiator.

C To spray-paint the radiator, cover all surrounding areas with dustsheets and make sure area is well-ventilated. Wear goggles and mask and read manufacturer's instructions. Put card between the radiator and the wall to stop the paint from going onto the wall.

5 Make sure paint is completely dry before turning radiator back on.

HOW TO NAIL IT!

- If your radiator has thick paint with drip marks, paint stripper will do a better job than sandpaper of getting down to a workable surface. Don't forget to wear protective gloves, goggles and a mask before using stripper, and read manufacturer's instructions.

- A standard undercoat or primer won't prevent cracking or discolouration. Make sure you use the appropriate paint and primer and take advice if you are unsure.

- Don't paint over bolts or moving parts or you could seal them shut.

STRIP WALLPAPER

75

Dont be tempted to put new wallpaper on top of old, unless the finish is excellent. Not only will it make your job harder later but the imperfections in the paper underneath can affect your lovely new job. When stripping wallpaper, patience is the key. Soak and wait, soak and wait, soak and wait again!

▶ YOU'LL NEED

CRAFT KNIFE

▲ **TOOL UP** WALLPAPER SCORER

▼ **TOOL DOWN** CRAFT KNIFE

↕ **TOOL UP** STEAM STRIPPER (BUY OR HIRE), PLUS PROTECTIVE GLOVES

↕ **TOOL DOWN** WARM WATER, WASHING-UP LIQUID AND SPONGE

WIDE SCRAPER

GETTING STARTED

If using a steam stripper, wear long sleeves and gloves to protect yourself.

Test ease of stripping by prising up a corner of wallpaper with craft knife. Pull paper up with even, moderate pressure, keeping it close to the wall. If it comes away easily, continue. If it doesn't come away, follow steps opposite.

Some walls may be easier than others, particularly in kitchens and bathrooms where the air is generally more moist. In addition, some papers are designed to be easier to peel off than others.

Be especially careful with plasterboard walls. You can easily damage the paper and gypsum layers and end up having to re-plaster!

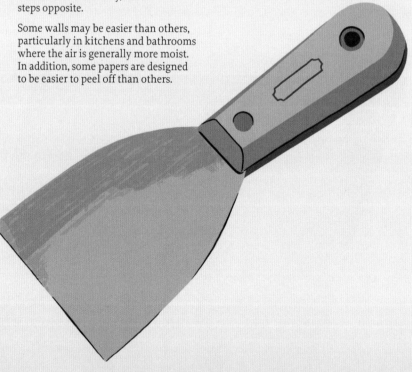

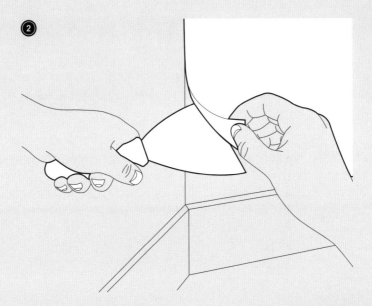

WHAT TO DO

Score wallpaper by making a series of shallow, criss-cross cuts with wallpaper scorer or craft knife. Be careful not to score the wall underneath. The more holes there are in the paper, the wetter it can get and the softer it will be.

Strip wallpaper using one of the following methods:

Sponge

1. Working from bottom of wall, soften scored wallpaper with soapy sponge and leave for about five minutes. Slide scraper under edge of paper to see if it's ready to strip. If not, sponge down again.

2. Try to pull away first strip. If it needs help, slide scraper under paper and push it up underneath, holding it at a 30-degree angle. If paper tears, re-wet it and try again.

3. Clean up glue residue by wiping down with sponge and warm, soapy water.

4. Leave to dry for at least two days before redecorating.

Steam stripper

1. Fill tank with water and switch on. Once light comes on and steam appears from plate, it's ready to use.

2. Working across from bottom of wall, place steamer plate on top of wallpaper for about 30 seconds to one minute. Hold the plate in one hand and use the other to scrape the area you have just softened. If paper tears, re-wet with steam stripper and try again.

3. Clean up glue residue by wiping down with sponge and warm, soapy water.

4. Leave to dry for at least two days before redecorating.

HOW TO NAIL IT!

- If using water and sponge on hard-to-remove wallpaper, make your own stripping solution. Mix fabric conditioner with water at a ratio of one part conditioner to two parts water. Alternatively, mix one part vinegar to three parts water. You could also add a handful of wallpaper paste to your bucket of soapy water to help hold the water on the wall.

- Clean off the scraper regularly. As the glue builds up, the scraper has to work harder.

- You could use a spray bottle instead of a sponge for a quick way of dampening the entire area.

HANG WALLPAPER

Wallpapering is the easiest way to bring pattern to a living space and can create dramatic effects. You should hang wallpaper as the final decoration stage, after you've painted ceilings and woodwork. Remember that walls are rarely straight, so align your paper to a plumb line (a piece of string with a weight at the end) rather than a corner.

▶ YOU'LL NEED

- STEEL TAPE MEASURE
- WALLPAPER, TO COVER AREA, PLUS EXTRA
- DUSTSHEETS
- MATERIALS FOR PREPARING WALLS (SEE *GETTING STARTED*)
- SOFT CLOTH OR SPONGE
- ⚠ SUGAR SOAP OR WASHING-UP LIQUID
- WALLPAPER PASTE, TO SUIT YOUR WALLPAPER TYPE
- SCREWDRIVER
- STRING, DRAWING PIN AND WEIGHT
- PENCIL
- RULER OR LONG SPIRIT LEVEL
- WALLPAPER SCISSORS
- MATERIALS FOR PASTING WALLPAPER (SEE PAGE 164)
- STEPLADDER
- PLASTIC SMOOTHER OR PAPERHANGING BRUSH
- WET SPONGE AND CLEAN RAG
- WIDE SCRAPER
- CRAFT KNIFE
- SEAM ROLLER

GETTING STARTED

Measure room area to calculate how much wallpaper you'll need. Include spaces for windows and doors as you will need extra for wastage.

Move as much furniture out of the room as possible and cover anything left with dustsheets.

Prepare walls by filling any holes or cracks. Sand down to a smooth finish. If doing a large area, a power sander will save you a lot of time (see pages 143-147).

Using soft cloth or sponge, clean walls with sugar soap or warm water and a little washing-up liquid. Leave to dry.

If walls are bare, apply a coat of diluted wallpaper paste to the entire area to prevent it absorbing too much paste.

Turn off electricity to the room at your switchboard or mains. Using screwdriver, remove light switch and socket covers (only do this AFTER you've washed the walls and once they are dry). See also *Wallpaper Around Obstacles* (page 166).

Choose a corner of the room to start wallpapering. Work from left-to-right if you are right-handed and vice-versa if you are left-handed.

Measure height of your first wall. The easiest way is to secure a piece of string at top of wall with a drawing pin, run it taut down to the skirting board, mark length, remove and measure alongside tape measure. Keep the string and drawing pin to make your plumb line.

⚠ STAY SAFE!

If in any doubt about working with electricity, always consult a professional.

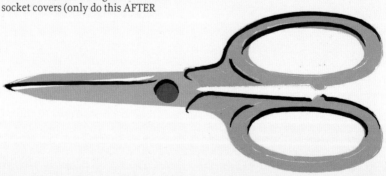

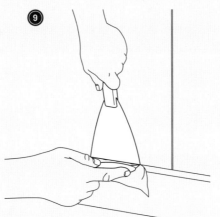

WHAT TO DO

1 If you are only papering one feature wall, start in the middle and work to sides. If you are papering an entire room, the key is to keep the paper vertical, even if corners are not.

2 To get your first vertical line, hang a plumb line – a weight attached to a piece of string – a little way out from your starting corner. Secure with drawing pin. Mark position of line down the wall, using plumb line as a guide. Join marks together using ruler or spirit level. This will give you a perfect vertical line as a guide for your wallpaper.

3 Unroll paper, pattern-side down, on pasting table. Measure, mark and cut 100mm longer than height of wall from ceiling to skirting, to allow for final trimming.

4 Apply wallpaper paste (see page 164). If using pre-pasted wallpaper you can skip this step, although professionals usually paste up even pre-pasted wallpaper.

5 Check which way up the pattern goes before bringing paper to the wall. On stepladder, align first sheet with the vertical line you drew, with approximately 100mm spare paper overhanging at skirting. Position it to the side of the line nearest starting point so that a small amount of paper goes around the corner.

6 Use smoother or paperhanging brush to smooth from middle outwards with medium pressure, taking care not to stretch paper.

7 To remove wrinkles and bubbles, gently pull edge of paper away from wall until they disappear. Smooth paper back to wall, from middle out.

8 Clean any excess adhesive using wet sponge. Wipe dry with clean rag.

9 Trim off excess paper at bottom by pressing wide scraper where paper meets skirting board, then running a craft knife along crease line.

10 Repeat steps 4-11 with second sheet, aligning it with first sheet and matching up any patterns. If patterned wallpaper doesn't seem to line up absolutely along whole length, prioritise matching it up at eye level.

11 Secure joints with seam roller (gently, without squeezing out adhesive) and repeat 10-15 minutes later.

12 When you reach a corner, remember to run around it, rather than butting sheets together at corners. If you have to, overlap sheets. Before pasting the first sheet of the next wall, always line up the paper with a new plumb line to make sure corners or uneven walls don't knock it out of line on your new wall.

13 Lap final sheet over first sheet. Clean any excess adhesive using wet sponge. Wipe dry with clean rag.

HANG WALLPAPER
APPLY PASTE

▶ YOU'LL NEED

**WALLPAPER PASTE,
TO SUIT YOUR WALLPAPER TYPE**

PASTE BUCKET

ROLLER TRAY (OPTIONAL)

LONG PASTING TABLE

PASTING BRUSH OR PAINT ROLLER

GETTING STARTED

Some wallpapers don't need pasting – they come pre-pasted, or are designed to be hung against a pasted wall. However, a professional will usually paste up even pre-pasted wallpaper.

The traditional method – and still the most common – is to apply wallpaper paste to the back of the paper. You can buy coloured wallpaper paste that dries clear, to help identify any areas that may have been missed.

It's important to let the paste soak into the paper before you hang it – the paper will expand slightly with the paste and if you hang it too soon, air bubbles may appear. Keep your workspace clean between sheets, but don't worry too much about spills as the paste is water-soluble.

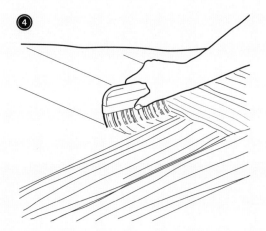

WHAT TO DO

❶ Mix up paste in a paste bucket according to manufacturer's instructions. Pour into roller tray, if you prefer.

❷ Lay cut length of wallpaper face-down on pasting table, with one end overhanging table.

❸ Load up brush or roller with paste, wiping off excess by dragging across edge of bucket or tray. Paste along centre of whole length on table, leaving overhanging piece unpasted. If paper is shorter than the pasting table, weigh down one end to stop it rolling back on itself.

❹ Work paste out towards edges from centre in herringbone pattern.

❺ If paper is longer than table, loosely concertina the pasted paper over itself – taking care not to crease it – and carefully move concertina to one end, bringing up unpasted paper onto the table.

❻ Repeat steps 2-4 until whole length of paper has been pasted.

❼ Leave pasted concertina of paper to soak up paste for as long as manufacturer recommends (usually five minutes). Hang the paper (see page 162).

❽ Wipe off any spilt paste from table using clean, wet sponge.

❾ Paste up more lengths and leave to soak before hanging.

HOW TO NAIL IT!

- When cutting damp wallpaper it can easily pull and tear. Ensure your blade is super-sharp.

- Don't let the roll of paper drop suddenly when you first position it at the top of the room, or its weight could tear or stretch the paper.

- Hanging lining paper first will give you a smoother surface for your wallpaper – a good way to disguise bumpy or uneven walls. Hang it horizontally or, if hanging it vertically, make sure the seams of two wallpaper layers don't fall in same place.

WALLPAPER AROUND OBSTACLES

The best way to wallpaper around obstacles – radiators, wall plugs, sockets, frames – is to remove them from the wall. This isn't always possible so there are tricks for working around them.

▶ YOU'LL NEED

VACUUM CLEANER OR BRUSH
PENCIL
WALLPAPER SCISSORS
RADIATOR ROLLER
MATCHSTICK
WIDE SCRAPER
CRAFT KNIFE
SCREWDRIVER
SMALL PAINTBRUSH

GETTING STARTED

Ensure electricity is switched off at switchboard or mains if you are going to be papering around electrical sockets and light switches.

⚠ STAY SAFE!

If in any doubt about working with electricity, always consult a professional.

WHAT TO DO

Paper around radiator

❶ Turn off heat and wait for radiator to cool. Clean dust and dirt behind radiator.

❷ Wallpaper up to the side of the radiator and tuck paper in behind radiator until you reach the supporting bracket. Hang the next sheet over the front of the radiator, flattening it as close to the radiator as possible. Mark position of the top point of bracket.

❸ Cut vertical line from bottom of paper up to top point of radiator bracket. Cut small rectangle at top of slit.

❹ Push paper behind radiator and into place around bracket using narrow radiator roller.

❺ Rejoin paper underneath radiator and trim at skirting as normal. See *Hang Wallpaper* (page 162).

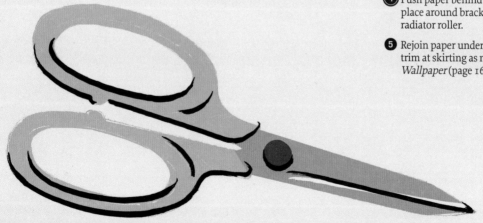

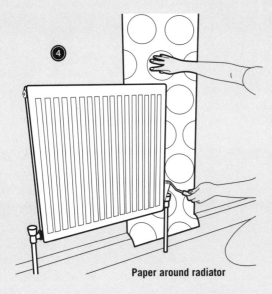

Paper around radiator

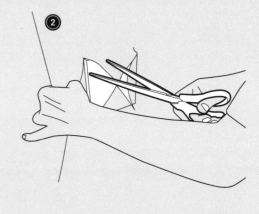

Paper around light sockets and switches

Paper over wall fixings

1 Remove fixings, such as picture hooks, from wall plugs.

2 Stick matchstick into wall plug so it stands proud of wall. Press stick through paper as you bring it over and smooth paper around hole. Remove matchstick and replace fixing.

Paper around door frame

1 Hang a full-length pasted strip so that one side of it overlaps door.

2 Make a diagonal cut from loose edge back to top corner of door frame.

3 Smooth down paper up to door frame. Trim off excess by pressing wide scraper where paper meets door frame then running a craft knife along crease. Alternatively, pull paper slightly away from wall and cut with scissors along crease line.

4 Repeat on other side in reverse, butting up to first strip.

Paper around light sockets and switches

1 Hang pasted paper over socket or switch and smooth gently so it makes impression on paper. Take care not to tear paper.

2 Pierce hole at centre with scissors and cut along lines to corners. Pull back flaps.

3 Trim flaps, leaving overlap of around 6mm of paper on socket or switch.

4 Double-check electricity is turned off at mains. Using screwdriver, partially unscrew faceplate and pull it 6mm away from wall.

5 Carefully ease paper overlap behind faceplate and use paintbrush to smooth away any air bubbles. Secure faceplate back in place.

6 Let paste dry before turning electricity back on.

HOW TO NAIL IT!

- An alternative way to wallpaper behind a radiator is to cut the sheet horizontally, all the way across, just above the top of the radiator bracket. Then, take a separate length of paper and paste it from the base of the skirting board to meet the bottom of the radiator bracket.

PAINT INTERIOR WOODWORK

Doorframes, window frames and skirting boards will be more durable and look better if painted properly. Good preparation is key, so make sure you prepare your surfaces well before even opening the paint tins.

▶ YOU'LL NEED

UNDERCOAT, TO COVER AREA, PLUS EXTRA

TOPCOAT (GLOSS OR SATIN), TO COVER AREA, PLUS EXTRA

STICKY TAPE AND MASKING TAPE

PLASTIC DUSTSHEETS

FINE- AND MEDIUM-GRADE SANDPAPER

⚡ **TOOL UP** POWER SANDER

▼ **TOOL DOWN** SANDING BLOCK

CLOTH OR SPONGE

PAINTBRUSHES

PLUS, AS NEEDED:

PRIMER

KNOTTING SOLUTION, OR RESIN-BLOCKING PRIMER

SCRAPER

⚠ SUGAR SOAP OR WASHING-UP LIQUID

WOOD FILLER

FLEXIBLE PUTTY KNIFE OR FILLING KNIFE

DECORATOR'S CAULK AND APPLICATOR GUN

GETTING STARTED

Choose the right primer and paint for your woodwork. See *Back to Basics* (page 24), for guide to paint types and painting tips. Remember that ordinary wall and ceiling paint will not last long on woodwork; something with a high sheen like gloss is the most hardwearing. You may need to apply knotting solution plus primer, or resin-blocking primer, for new or bare wood.

Protect your floors by taping down plastic dustsheets. Tape sheets together with regular sticky tape, but fasten to floor edges/skirting board with masking tape. In each case, mask off areas not to be painted.

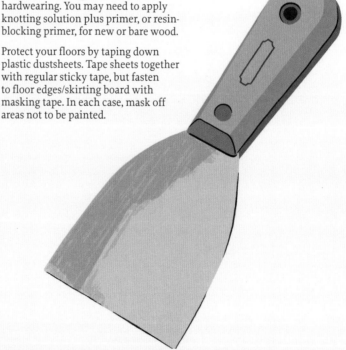

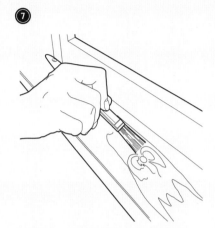

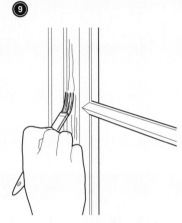

Wood where paint is loose or crumbling

WHAT TO DO

New wood

1 Sand down area to be painted with fine-grade sandpaper, using either power sander or sanding block. Wipe down with damp cloth.

2 Mask off areas not to be painted and paint wood with knotting solution and primer, or resin-blocking primer. This stops resin seeping through and staining the surface over time.

3 Sand lightly with fine- or medium-grade sandpaper, as above. Wipe down with damp cloth.

4 Paint on undercoat.

5 Finish with topcoat. Paint along the wood grain with chosen paint, holding brush perpendicular to wood. When brush begins to drag, dip it in paint to reload it. As you coat each small area, run the tips of the same 'unloaded' brush over whole stretch in one long motion to 'tip', or smooth out, the brush strokes on the paint. 'Tip' the paint within one minute of it being painted on.

6 If the paint looks a little streaky or if the coverage isn't good enough once dry, sand lightly again, and apply second coat. This will also give the most hardwearing finish.

Painted wood in good condition

If the previous paint is in good condition or you simply want to freshen things up, sand, as for new wood. Wipe down with a damp cloth and paint on a new topcoat. Add a further coat if required.

Wood where paint is loose or crumbling

1 Remove loose paint with scraper.

2 Using cloth or sponge, clean area with sugar soap or warm water and a little washing-up liquid. Wipe down with a damp cloth.

3 Fill any cracks, holes, chips and dips in the wood with wood filler. Apply with flexible putty knife or filling knife. Refer to *Repair Rotten Window Frame* (see page 82), if you are painting a window frame and find any soft areas of wood. Scrape off excess filler and leave to dry.

4 Sand entire area with medium-grade sandpaper, following with fine-grade, if necessary. Make sure filled areas are smooth. Wipe down with damp cloth.

5 If you need to replace putty, see *Replace Broken Pane of Glass* (page 84).

6 Fill any gaps between woodwork and wall/floor, or at joints, with decorator's caulk (see page 133).

7 Paint knotting solution and primer, or resin-blocking primer, over any exposed knots or bare wood. Once dry, sand with fine- or medium-grade sandpaper.

8 Follow with undercoat. For best results, use two coats, especially if you are covering a strong colour.

9 Finish with topcoat, applying it as for new wood (see step 5). If the paint looks a little streaky or if the coverage isn't good enough once dry, sand lightly again and apply second coat.

HOW TO NAIL IT!

- Don't overlook the sanding stage. This will 'key' the surface so new paint can adhere properly. If you paint straight onto gloss, the paint will soon come away.

- To find all the imperfections in the wood, which will need filling, shine a torch over the area and mark your findings in pencil.

- If painting window frames, paint early in the day to maximise the time you can keep the window open for drying.

PAINT EXTERIOR WOODWORK

Exterior woodwork is likely to need a good clean before you can do anything with it – nobody can paint over cobwebs. Good preparation will not only make the woodwork look better, but is essential for protecting and prolonging its life. If your woodwork rots it will be expensive to repair or replace.

YOU'LL NEED

UNDERCOAT, TO COVER AREA, PLUS EXTRA

EXTERIOR TOPCOAT (GLOSS OR SATIN), TO COVER AREA, PLUS EXTRA

FINE-, MEDIUM- AND COARSE- GRADE SANDPAPER

TOOL UP POWER SANDER

TOOL DOWN SANDING BLOCK

CLOTH OR SPONGE

PAINTBRUSHES

PLUS, AS NEEDED:

EXTERIOR PRIMER

KNOTTING SOLUTION OR RESIN-BLOCKING PRIMER

SCRAPER

SUGAR SOAP OR WASHING-UP LIQUID

SCRUBBING BRUSH

WOOD FILLER

FLEXIBLE PUTTY KNIFE OR FILLING KNIFE

MASKING TAPE

GETTING STARTED

Choose a dry, still day and never paint wet wood – check the forecast first. See *Back to Basics* (page 24) to help you choose right primer and paint for your woodwork. Select a weatherproof exterior wood paint – ordinary wall and ceiling paint is not suitable for woodwork, especially outdoors.

WHAT TO DO

Bare wood

Sand, prime and paint wood following instructions for *Paint Interior Woodwork* (page 169).

Painted wood in good condition

If the previous paint is in good condition or to freshen things up, sand lightly, wipe down with a damp cloth and paint with two coats of exterior topcoat.

Wood where paint is loose or crumbling

1 Remove loose paint with scraper.

2 Using a cloth or sponge, clean area with sugar soap or warm water and washing-up liquid. Use a scrubbing brush for droppings or hard deposits. Wipe with damp cloth.

3 Fill any cracks, holes, chips and dips as for *Paint Interior Woodwork* (page 169). Sand area using coarse-, medium- or fine-grade sandpaper, depending on roughness of surface. Finish with fine-grade. Wipe with damp cloth.

4 Coat any exposed bare wood with knotting solution and primer, or resin-blocking primer. Sand down with fine-grade sandpaper.

5 Follow with one coat of exterior undercoat.

6 Finish with exterior topcoat, as for *Paint Interior Woodwork* (see *New wood*, step 5, page 169). For the best finish and durability, use two coats, sanding in between once fully dry.

HOW TO NAIL IT!

- If you're painting all the exterior woodwork at your home, start at the top and work down, planning realistic amounts each day.

- Refer to *Repair Rotten Window Frame* (see page 82) if you are painting a window frame and find any areas of soft wood. To replace putty, see *Replace Broken Pane of Glass* (page 84).

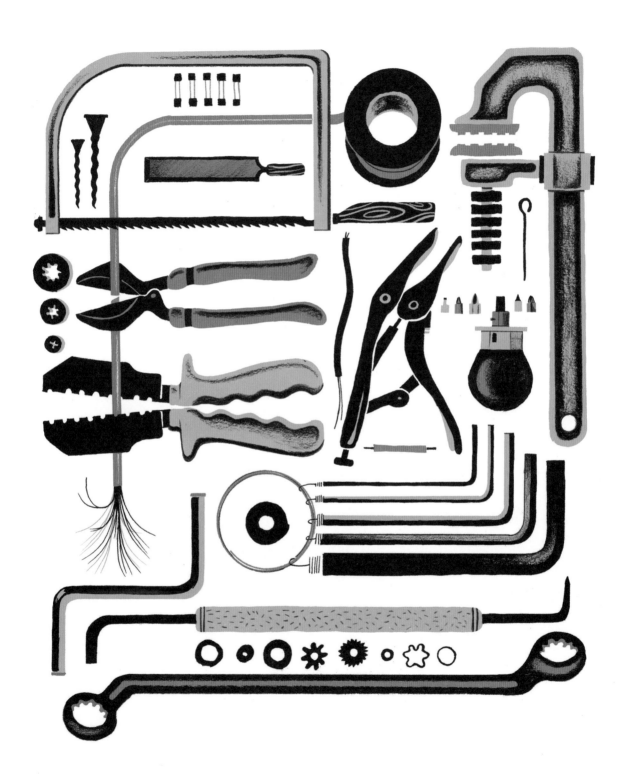

STORAGE AND FURNITURE

EVERYTHING YOU NEED TO GET THE JOB DONE

FIT FLOATING SHELVES

If you don't like being able to see shelf brackets, a more attractive option is to fit floating or hidden-fixture shelving. Thick, floating shelves look great and seem strong, but can only support light or medium weights. If you want to have stronger floating shelves, the method is more complex.

▶ YOU'LL NEED

MULTI-PURPOSE DETECTOR

FLOATING SHELF SET

SPIRIT LEVEL

BRADAWL OR NAIL

⚠ POWER DRILL, WITH BIT SUITABLE FOR WALL TYPE

SCREWS AND WALL PLUGS, AS NEEDED

SCREWS

SCREWDRIVER

GETTING STARTED

Choose a stretch of flat wall for your shelves and use a multi-purpose detector to check there are no hidden pipes or cables. On a stud wall, use the detector to locate the studs. Use these as fixing points.

❶ Hold metal strip in position on wall, using a spirit level to check it's horizontal. Mark fixing holes on wall using bradawl or nail.

❷ Drill holes with suitable bit to the depth of wall plug, if using, and push in. If fixing to studs, drill pilot hole. Screw metal strip in place.

❸ Fit the shelf onto the bars and secure with screws, if provided.

HOW TO NAIL IT!

• For more help on finding and fixing to studs, see *Back to Basics* (page 21).

FIT SIMPLE SHELVES

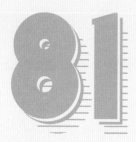

The simplest way to fit shelves is with brackets. These come in a variety of styles, from basic adjustable brackets to more ornate looking ones, with a number of different materials and finishes. Buy ready-cut shelves and brackets to match. Some shelves may come with predrilled holes.

YOU'LL NEED

- SHELF/SHELVES
- MULTI-PURPOSE DETECTOR
- PENCIL
- STEEL TAPE MEASURE
- 2 BRACKETS PER SHELF (MORE IF REQUIRED, DEPENDING ON LENGTH)
- SPIRIT LEVEL
- BRADAWL OR NAIL
- ⚠ POWER DRILL, WITH SMALL TWIST BIT AND BIT SUITABLE FOR WALL TYPE
- WALL PLUGS, IF NEEDED
- LONG SCREWS, TO GO 25MM INTO WALL
- SHORTER SCREWS, FOR SHELVES
- SCREWDRIVER

GETTING STARTED

Choose shelves to suit room style and load they will hold. The different materials, listed below, vary in strength and cost.

Chipboard: chips of wood glued together. The cheapest material and easy to cut to size and fix. Available with melamine or wood veneers.

MDF: medium-density fibreboard. Wood fibres stuck together under pressure. Can be painted, stained or varnished.

Blockboard: layers of soft wood between two layers of veneer. Still cheaper than solid wood and very strong.

Plywood: thin sheets of wood glued together with grain in alternating directions.

Solid wood: seal your preferred wood with wax or varnish to protect from dirt and for a natural finish.

Glass: should be at least 6mm thick. Requires medium- or heavy-weight brackets. Use toughened glass.

Choose from fixed or adjustable brackets and make sure they suit the size of the shelves and the weight they will bear. Check brackets don't extend past the depth of the shelf.

Fixed: simple supports best suited to single shelves.

Adjustable: tracks fix to the wall to take a series of brackets at suitable intervals. Fully adjustable but as the tracks and brackets are visible to the eye, less pretty to look at.

Screws should go into wall by 25mm, at the very least, with shorter ones needed for the shelf. If screws come with the brackets check they are the right size and type for your wall.

See *Back to Basics* (pages 18–21) for more advice on choosing screws, wall plugs and drill bits to suit your wall, and for tips on drilling.

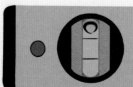

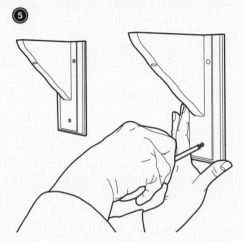

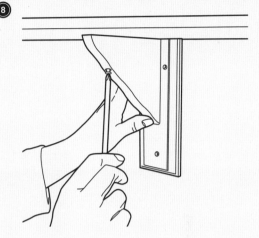

WHAT TO DO

1. Choose position for shelf. If fixing to a stud wall, ensure screw positions align with studs. Use a multi-purpose detector to locate studs and also to ensure you're not drilling into any cables or pipes. Generally, it's never a good idea to drill directly above or below light fittings or power sockets.

2. Hold shelf in place and mark position of bottom edge on wall in pencil. Use tape measure to mark position of both brackets, making sure they are evenly spaced.

3. Use spirit level to check shelf line and bracket marks are level.

4. Hold brackets in position and mark position of fixing holes on wall with bradawl or nail.

5. Drill holes at markings to depth of wall plugs, if using, and push into hole. For long screws, drill pilot holes. Screw brackets into place.

6. Lay shelf on brackets and mark fixing holes with bradawl or nail through bracket on underside of shelf.

7. Remove shelf, change drill bit and drill pilot holes in shelf for screws, if not already predrilled. Don't go all the way through the board.

8. Put shelf back and screw fixings into place.

HOW TO NAIL IT!

- Check the orientation of your bracket: longest arm goes against the wall and the shortest under the shelf.

- If shelves sag, it means the load is too heavy or the shelf is too thin. Move brackets closer together, or turn sagging shelf upside down and add bracket.

BUILD ALCOVE SHELVES

Alcoves are a good place for fitting shelves because you get built-in stops and you can achieve a really neat, practical finish without too much effort.

YOU'LL NEED

STEEL TAPE MEASURE

PENCIL

TOOL UP JIGSAW OR CIRCULAR SAW

TOOL DOWN HAND SAW

WORKBENCH OR OTHER SUITABLE CUTTING SURFACE (SEE PAGE 22)

50MM X 25MM WOODEN BATTENS, LENGTH AS REQUIRED

TIMBER OR 18MM MDF, FOR SHELVES

MULTI-PURPOSE DETECTOR

SPIRIT LEVEL

⚠ POWER DRILL, WITH COUNTERSINK, TWIST OR WOOD BIT AND MASONRY BIT

BRADAWL OR NAIL

WALL PLUGS, IF NEEDED

LONG SCREWS, TO GO THROUGH BATTENS AND 25MM INTO WALL

SHORT SCREWS, FOR SHELVES

WOOD FILLER

DECORATOR'S CAULK AND APPLICATOR GUN

PRIMER, PAINT AND PAINTBRUSH

GETTING STARTED

Measure width and depth of the alcoves. Using saw, cut a batten to fit back wall and two side battens to fit the depth. Remember to subtract the width of the back batten when cutting the two side battens.

Measure width of alcove at back and front and use narrowest measurement to saw timber or MDF for shelves.

Use a detector to note positions of hidden pipes and cables and avoid fixing there. If not fixing to masonry, locate studs using a detector and fix to these, if possible.

See *Back to Basics* (pages 18-23) for more advice on choosing screws, wall plugs and drill bits to suit your wall, and for tips on sawing and drilling.

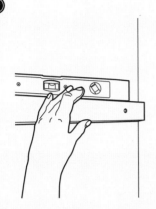

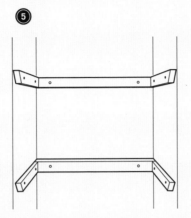

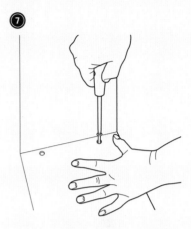

WHAT TO DO

1 Hold spirit level against wall and draw pencil line around alcove, where base of each shelf will sit.

2 Drill and countersink holes through centre line of each batten (see page 18). Space holes roughly 300mm apart, at most.

3 Hold rear batten in position with upper edge against pencil line (check again with spirit level). Using bradawl or nail, mark wall through all batten screw holes.

4 Remove batten. Switch to masonry or other suitable bit. Drill holes to depth of wall plug, if using, and insert. If fixing to studs, drill pilot holes. Line up batten and fix screws.

5 Position side battens with upper edge against pencil line and in line with rear batten. Fix side battens in same way, ensuring they are level. Follow same method for further shelves. Tighten all screw fixings.

6 Drill and countersink screw holes at each corner of shelf where it meets battens.

7 Fix shelf to battens with wood screws. Fill holes with wood filler.

8 Most alcoves will not be 'true' (i.e. straight), so hide any gaps at sides with decorator's caulk (see page 133). Alternatively, template the shape with a piece of card first.

9 Prime and paint as required. See *Paint Interior Woodwork* (page 168).

HOW TO NAIL IT!

• Bear in mind the height of the items you want to store on your shelves before marking out height of each shelf – and don't forget to take into account thickness of shelving material.

• For a neat finish, cut the visible ends of the side battens at an angle rather than square, with the longest edge supporting the shelf, so the battens appear to recede.

• For an even better appearance you can add battens along the front edge and a thin sheet of timber or plyboard on the underside, to cover the batten. This will give it the appearance of a floating shelf.

BUILD SIMPLE ALCOVE CUPBOARDS

Complement your alcove shelving with a cupboard in the lower part of the alcove – a great way of maximising storage space and tidying things away. This is a straightforward method which you should follow if you are building alcove cupboards for the first time, but not necessarily one an experienced joiner would use!

YOU'LL NEED

TIMBER OR 18MM MDF

MULTI-PURPOSE DETECTOR

SPIRIT LEVEL, PENCIL

SCRAPER PLUS PRYING BAR OR CROW BAR, IF REMOVING SKIRTING

STEEL TAPE MEASURE

TOOL UP JIGSAW OR CIRCULAR SAW

TOOL DOWN HAND SAW

WORKBENCH OR OTHER SUITABLE CUTTING SURFACE (SEE PAGE 22)

50 X 25MM WOODEN BATTENS, LENGTH AS REQUIRED

POWER DRILL, WITH COUNTERSINK, WOOD AND MASONRY BIT

BRADAWL OR NAIL

WALL PLUGS, IF NEEDED

LONG SCREWS, TO GO THROUGH BATTENS AND 25MM INTO WALL

SHORT SCREWS, FOR SHELVES AND CUPBOARD TOP

SCREWDRIVER, MALLET

6 FLAT METAL ANGLE CORNER BRACKETS, WITH SCREWS

4 HINGES, WITH SCREWS

DECORATOR'S CAULK, WOOD FILLER

PRIMER, PAINT AND PAINTBRUSHES

HANDLES, CATCHES AND FIXINGS

GETTING STARTED

See *Fit Simple Shelves* (page 174), for help on which timber to use.

Choose the height of your cupboard. A reasonable guide is just above hip level.

Use a detector to note positions of hidden pipes and cables and avoid fixing there. If not fixing to masonry, locate studs using a detector and fix to these, if possible.

See Back to Basics (pages 18-23) for more advice on choosing screws, wall plugs and drill bits to suit your wall, and for tips on sawing and drilling.

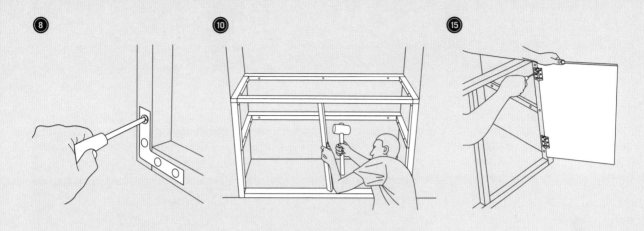

WHAT TO DO

1 Use pencil and spirit level to draw a line around alcove 70mm below chosen height (to allow for batten and shelf).

2 Remove skirting board. Gently tap scraper down the back of the top of the boards to break the bond with the paint or any filler. Insert prying bar or crow bar and prise carefully along length of skirting.

3 Begin by building a frame. Measure from floor to pencil line at both front edges of alcove. Saw two vertical battens to length.

4 Attach two vertical battens flush to front of alcove, at either side, with widest part (measuring 50mm) flat to wall, following method for *Build Alcove Shelves* (page 176).

5 Measure, cut and attach top rear horizontal batten and two smaller side battens, as if building a shelf. Align bottom edge of battens with pencil line. Ensure side battens fix firmly to top of vertical battens just fixed.

6 Cut and attach battens for any additional shelving inside cupboard, following method for *Build Alcove Shelves* (page 176).

7 Measure distance between two front vertical battens and cut two horizontal battens to fit snugly between them, one at the top and one at the bottom, running along the floor. Tap gently in place with mallet and check with spirit level.

8 Secure front horizontal battens to vertical battens by screwing in four metal angle corner brackets at back of battens, inside cupboard. These screw straight in without predrilling. Drill pilot holes, if easier.

9 Measure height from bottom horizontal batten to top. Cut one vertical batten to fit snugly between them.

10 Measure centre point of front horizontal battens and tap vertical batten into place with mallet. Secure with two metal angle corner brackets, as before.

11 Cut and attach any shelves to their battens following method for *Build Alcove Shelves* (page 176). Work from lower shelves upwards.

12 Cut cupboard top to size (make it slightly deeper if you want a small lip). Slip cupboard top onto battens. Drill, countersink and attach screws at each corner, where it meets battens. If you feel confident, drill from the inside so you won't get any visible holes.

13 Measure area for doors, allowing at least 10mm gap all the way round at each side to allow for doors to open easily. Cut timber or MDF to size.

14 Hold doors in position and mark hinge positions on frame and door in pencil. Measure carefully to ensure the same positioning on each door.

15 Screw hinges to door inside or outside as preferred; hold in position and screw other half of hinges to frame. Repeat for second door.

16 Hide any gaps at sides with decorator's caulk (see page 132) and fill all countersunk screw holes with wood filler.

17 Sand, prime and paint cupboard. See *Paint Interior Woodwork* (page 168).

18 Add handles and cupboard catches, following manufacturer's instructions.

HOW TO NAIL IT!

- If you feel confident, you can try building the front 'frame' of the cupboards flat on the floor, adding the doors, then lifting and securing the whole thing onto the wall in one go.

- If it's not appropriate to take off the skirting, use slightly wider battens on the front vertical side of the frame and use a jigsaw to cut the shape of the skirting out of the batten so it fits snugly.

- Stick a frame of thin MDF strips to the cupboard doors, to create a shaker-style look.

BUILD FLATPACK FURNITURE

Whether you come from the school of thought that believes in following instructions to the letter, or whether you prefer to dive straight in, building flatpack furniture can be very frustrating indeed. Follow a few simple guidelines and you'll find putting together any type of flatpack furniture a little easier.

▶ YOU'LL NEED

FLATPACK
(THIS SHOULD CONTAIN EVERYTHING YOU NEED, INCLUDING TOOLS)

BOWLS OR CONTAINERS, FOR SMALL PARTS

A HELPER, IF ASSEMBLING LARGE ITEM

⚠ **POWER DRILL, SCREWDRIVER AND ALLEN KEY, IF NEEDED**

GETTING STARTED

Clear a large space near where you would like your furniture to be positioned. Unpack the box carefully and lay out all components, including any fixings. Use small pot or bowls for each bag of small parts or screws.

WHAT TO DO

1. Lay panels on soft surface to prevent scratches.

2. Identify all parts, using instructions. Make sure you have the right number of everything, checking in box that nothing has been overlooked. If something is missing, return the complete pack and get a replacement.

3. Build tall pieces on their back to make assembly easier. If the unit has wheels or castors, fit these last.

4. In general, you will begin with the base panel, then connect side panels. Simple units have pre-drilled holes and fixings that screw in easily.

5. If your unit has glued dowels and cam fixings, place dowels and screwed pegs in base, add glue then push on side panel and tighten cam fixings. Continue with all panels.

6. Cover discs are sometimes supplied. Use these to cover screw heads and neaten the finish.

7. If you need to add doors, they will be hung on hinges. These hinges fit into pre-drilled holes on doors and cabinet sides. Fit hinge body to door and mounting plate to cabinet side. Attach with screws provided and adjust until doors hang squarely.

8. Add any shelves and door handles. Make sure all fittings and fixings are tight.

9. Fit wheels or castors if these are part of kit.

HOW TO NAIL IT!

- Try to be calm and methodical. Estimate the time you think the job will take, then double it. Don't put yourself under time pressure.

- If the unit comes with a hexaganol key (allen key), tape this and the instructions to the back of the furniture when complete. This way you can easily dismantle it for moving or selling at a later date.

- Have a basic toolbox at the ready – sometimes the tools provided can be a little flimsy, and you may need to use a power drill, screwdriver or sturdier allen key.

STRIP PAINTED FURNITURE

85

If you have a piece of wooden furniture covered in paint or varnish that you've grown tired of, strip it down and rekindle your love for it.

▶ YOU'LL NEED

DUSTSHEET, NEWSPAPER OR OLD CLOTH

SCREWDRIVER, IF NEEDED

PROTECTIVE GLOVES, SAFETY GOGGLES AND MASK

PAINTBRUSH

⚠ **PAINT STRIPPER**

SCRAPER, OLD SPATULA OR PUTTY KNIFE

OLD TOOTHBRUSH OR COTTON BUDS

CLEAN RAGS

⚠ **WHITE SPIRIT**

GETTING STARTED

First check there's no chance that this is an antique that you might be about to devalue with your improvements.

Work outside if you can. Otherwise, find a well-ventilated place to do your work, with no naked flames nearby.

NB: this method will only work if the bottom coat of paint is oil-based; in other words, old gloss paint. For furniture painted with emulsion, try either sanding or repainting and ageing (see page 182).

⚠ STAY SAFE!

Don't attempt this without wearing protective gloves, goggles and a mask – paint stripper really will hurt if it gets on your skin. It can even melt through plastic. If paint stripper does get on your skin, wash off immediately with soap and warm water.

WHAT TO DO

1. Lay down dustsheet, newspaper or old cloth. Set furniture on top.

2. Using a screwdriver, if necessary, remove any handles or non-wood pieces.

3. Wearing gloves, safety goggles and mask, paint thick layer of stripper all over furniture. Leave for 5-10 minutes to work.

4. Using a scraper, carefully remove the bubbled paint. Don't gouge too deeply.

5. Use old toothbrush or cotton buds to work into thin crevices.

6. Repeat steps 3-5 if the paint is thick or stubborn.

7. Use clean rags and white spirit to wipe down the whole piece. Check manufacturer's advice for guidance on disposal of brushes and chemicals.

HOW TO NAIL IT!

- Pastes and gels can be useful on vertical surfaces as they'll be less likely to run and drip.

- Don't skimp on the white spirit at the final stage.

- Read manufacturer's instructions carefully before using stripper.

PAINT AND AGE FURNITURE

You can give painted furniture an aged or shabby-chic look with a few simple techniques that don't involve leaving it out in the rain overnight. These methods are also a good way of covering up scratches or damage without forking out for expensive refinishing.

YOU'LL NEED

- DUSTSHEET, NEWSPAPER OR OLD CLOTH
- SCREWDRIVER, IF NEEDED
- MASK
- VERY FINE-GRADE SANDPAPER
- **TOOL UP** POWER SANDER
- **TOOL DOWN** SANDING BLOCK
- ALL-PURPOSE CLEANER; OR 200ML WARM WATER, PLUS 100ML VINEGAR, PLUS ¼ TSP WASHING-UP LIQUID
- SPONGE OR SOFT CLOTH
- MATT EMULSION PAINT
- GOOD-QUALITY PAINTBRUSHES

FOR DISTRESSED/AGED FINISH:
FINE-GRADE SANDPAPER

FOR CRACKLE GLAZE:
CRACKLE GLAZE
MATT EMULSION PAINT IN TWO COLOURS (NOT NON-DRIP)

GETTING STARTED

Choose how you would like to age your furniture.

Distressed/aged finish: repainting and sanding off the exposed areas that would most likely be worn with age is a simple and effective way to age furniture.

Crackle glaze: a paint-on glaze that causes the top coat to open in cracks to reveal the paint layer or wood underneath, mimicking old, cracked, porcelain glaze. Choose matt emulsion paint colours for bottom and top coat. The top coat will be the main colour of the piece and the bottom coat will show through any distressed areas. Generally, it is a good idea to choose contrasting paint colours.

Work outside if you can. Otherwise, find a well-ventilated place to do your work, with no naked flames nearby.

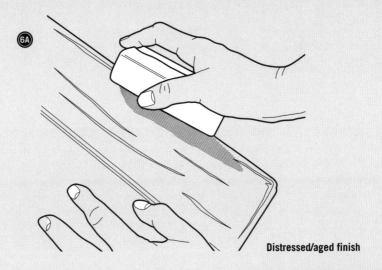

Distressed/aged finish

WHAT TO DO

1 Lay down dustsheet, newspaper or old cloth. Set furniture on top.

2 Remove any handles or hardware.

3 Wearing a dust mask, prepare all surfaces of furniture by sanding with medium- or fine-grade sandpaper, using power tool or sanding block.

4 Wash down all surfaces with an all-purpose cleaner, or solution of vinegar and detergent.

5 Paint bottom coat of emulsion all over furniture.

6 A Distressed/aged finish

Paint second coat if needed. Once dry, sand off the piece with fine-grade sandpaper, concentrating on exposed areas – corners, edges, details – rather than large, flat areas.

B Crackle glaze

Paint crackle glaze all over furniture. Apply against grain of wood.

Allow to dry. Paint top coat in contrasting colour over all surfaces, in different direction from glaze. Check top coat is of same consistency as single cream. Add water, if needed.

HOW TO NAIL IT!

- For crackle glaze, use a hairdryer to speed up drying and cracking of top coat of paint.

- Use crackle glaze randomly over large areas to give a more authentic look.

- When distressing furniture, try not to sand off the edges in a uniform line – leave areas where you don't sand so heavily and apply contrasting pressure.

STAIN AND VARNISH FURNITURE

Varnish gives protection against water, dirt and grease while allowing the natural colour of the wood to shine through. If the piece of furniture you're working with is in good condition, staining and varnishing is a great way of showing it off. If the wood's in bad condition, painting may be a better option. See *Paint Interior Woodwork* (page 168), and *Paint and Age Furniture* (page 182).

▶ YOU'LL NEED

- STAIN
- VARNISH
- DUSTSHEET, NEWSPAPER OR OLD CLOTH
- SCREWDRIVER, IF NEEDED
- ⚠ WOOD STRIPPER, IF NEEDED
- PROTECTIVE GLOVES, SAFETY GOGGLES AND MASK, IF USING STRIPPER
- PAINTBRUSHES
- FINE- AND VERY FINE-GRADE SANDPAPER
- ⬥ **TOOL UP** POWER SANDER
- ⬥ **TOOL DOWN** SANDING BLOCK
- DAMP CLOTH
- RUBBER GLOVES
- SEVERAL CLEAN, LINT-FREE CLOTHS AND RAGS
- CLEAN CONTAINER
- ⚠ WHITE SPIRIT

GETTING STARTED

You can varnish your woodwork without staining it first if you like its natural colour, but if you wish to enhance the colour with stain you will need to finish with varnish to give it a protective coat.

Choose stain colour and varnish finish. Some varnishes tend to yellow with age, so do your research carefully. See also pages 57 and 58.

Check tins for guidance on coverage when deciding how much to buy.

Before you begin, make sure the room is well ventilated and warm. If the weather is fine and not windy, you can work outside.

⚠ STAY SAFE!

Check manufacturer's instructions before disposing of used rags as they can be combustible.

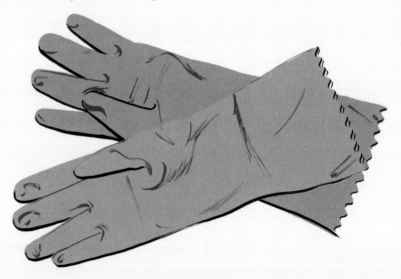

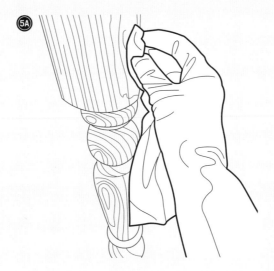

(5A)

WHAT TO DO

1 Lay down dustsheet, newspaper or old cloth. Set furniture on top.

2 Using a screwdriver, if necessary, remove any handles or non-wood pieces.

3 If your wood was previously varnished, remove it with wood stripper. Follow manufacturer's instructions and wear protective gloves, goggles and mask. See *Strip Painted Furniture* (page 181).

4 Sand down with fine-grade sandpaper, using power sander or sanding block. Wipe down with damp cloth.

5 **Stain wood**

A Dampen wood first with clean paintbrush. This helps it absorb stain – important for dark colours. Wearing rubber gloves, shake tin gently, dip cloth into stain and apply liberally to wood, along the grain.

B Wipe with a dry cloth to remove excess and get even distribution. Don't leave stain on wood too long. Wipe in direction stain was applied. If stain gets tacky before you wipe it off, apply more stain to 'wet' it again, then wipe.

C Leave for one to two hours to dry.

6 **Varnish wood**

A Wearing rubber gloves, mix a diluted varnish in separate, clean container: one part varnish to one part white spirit.

B Paint coat of diluted varnish evenly along the grain of wood to seal it. Leave to dry overnight.

C Sand down dry surface with very fine-grade sandpaper, using power sander or sanding block. Wipe down with damp cloth.

D Repeat steps B and C.

E Apply coat of undiluted varnish and leave overnight to dry.

HOW TO NAIL IT!

- A handheld power sander or sanding block and sandpaper work well for most wood, but it's easier to get inside small areas and cracks with folded-up sheets of sandpaper.

- Use 100 per cent cotton rags for applying stain. Synthetic fibres may not absorb the stain properly or may leave dyes behind on wood.

- Ideally, use a new brush for applying varnish – or, at least, a very clean one. Also, always pour varnish into a new container; dipping your brush into the tin can contaminate it.

HEATING
AND
INSULATION

EVERYTHING
YOU NEED
TO GET THE
JOB DONE

BLEED RADIATOR

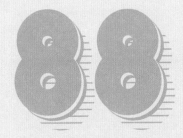

If the top of your radiator is cold while the bottom is warm, it's working inefficiently because there is air in the system. You will need to take the air out of the radiator. This is called bleeding. If you can't find your radiator key, you can buy a replacement from a DIY shop, or try using a flat-head screwdriver instead.

▶ YOU'LL NEED

TOOL UP RADIATOR KEY

TOOL DOWN FLAT-HEAD SCREWDRIVER OR ADJUSTABLE SPANNER

RAG OR SMALL BOWL

CLOTH

GETTING STARTED

First, turn off the central heating.

Start with the highest radiators in your house and work down.

Locate your radiator key and the bleed valve, which will be in one of the top corners of the radiator. Some radiators may have a valve that can be turned on with an adjustable spanner.

WHAT TO DO

1. Place a rag or small bowl on the floor underneath valve to protect floor from water spills.

2. Wrap your hands in a cloth.

3. Insert radiator key into valve and turn anticlockwise by a quarter- or half-turn. Do not unscrew by more than one full turn.

4. Listen as the air hisses and escapes. As soon as the water starts to appear, turn the key clockwise to shut off the valve.

HOW TO NAIL IT!

- Protect your hands if you are bleeding warm or recently-warm radiators, as the water splashes could be very hot.

- If you find your radiators regularly need bleeding, call out a heating engineer as there could be a fault in the system.

- If boiler pressure drops below 1½ bars, follow manufacturer's instructions for filling system.

INSULATE WATER TANKS

All hot water cylinders now come pre-insulated, but if you have an old one that isn't, make insulating it a priority. Cold water tanks also benefit from insulation. Never insulate directly under them, though, as the heat that rises through the ceiling helps to prevent freezing.

▶ YOU'LL NEED

CRAWL BOARD, IF NEEDED
PLUS, AS NEEDED:
HOT OR COLD WATER TANK JACKET
BLANKET INSULATION, PLUS STRING
PROTECTIVE GLOVES AND MASK,
IF USING FIBREGLASS
POLYSTYRENE SHEETS
CRAFT KNIFE
DUCT TAPE AND INSULATING TAPE

GETTING STARTED

Make sure you can get to the water tank safely. If it's in your loft and the floor has not been boarded, use a crawl board to work in the area safely.

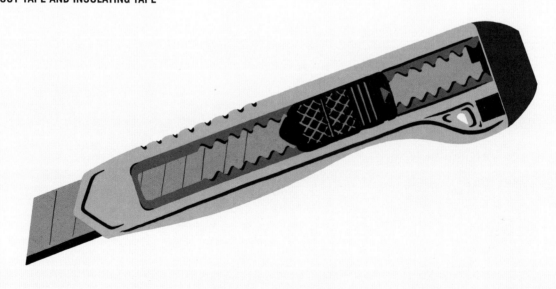

Cold water tank

WHAT TO DO

Cold water tank

1 *Purpose-made jacket:* measure the tank height and width and buy appropriate size. It doesn't matter if it's slightly large, as sections can be overlapped. Refer to manufacturer's instructions.

2 *Blanket insulation:* wear protective gloves and mask, if using fibreglass. Run insulation up four sides of the tank and secure with string. Insulate top with a polystyrene sheet, cut to size. Remember not to insulate directly under the tank.

3 *Polystyrene sheets:* cut to size using craft knife so one sheet lies on top of tank and four run down the sides, extending all the way to the floor. Cut notches from vertical sheets, if needed, for pipes to run through. Secure sheets with duct tape. Seal gaps with insulating tape.

Hot water cylinder

1 To fit purpose-made jacket, unwrap compressed segments so they can expand to full thickness. Loosely tie one strap around cylinder, just below curved top.

2 Working one insulation segment at a time, pull segment up through strap (loosening if necessary) until all are roughly in place.

3 Gather tops of all segments together and thread cord through eyelets. Secure around water outlet pipe. Secure remaining straps around cylinder.

HOW TO NAIL IT!

- If you're going to be insulating your loft floor (see *Insulate Loft*, page 197), plan to insulate your cold water tank at the same time, using the same materials (see *Cold water tank*, step 2).

- It won't be as effective, but if you have old duvets, insulating cylinders and tanks with these is better than nothing!

INSULATE PIPES

Insulating pipes isn't only a matter of saving heat and money. It will also prevent water freezing in them over winter, which can end in burst pipes and untold damage. It's important to insulate pipes anywhere they run through unheated spaces, such as a cold loft.

▶ YOU'LL NEED

CRAWL BOARD, IF NEEDED

CRAFT KNIFE

PIPE LAGGING, FOR LENGTH AND SIZE OF EXPOSED PIPES

CABLE TIES

DUCT TAPE

⚠ **JUNIOR HACKSAW**

WORKBENCH OR OTHER SUITABLE CUTTING SURFACE (SEE PAGE 22)

GETTING STARTED

Make sure you can access the pipes safely. If they are in your loft and the floor has not been boarded, use a crawl board to get to them safely.

Cut away any old or degraded lagging with a craft knife and dispose of it.

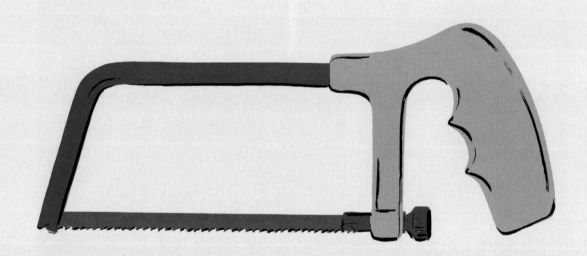

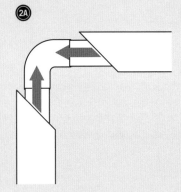

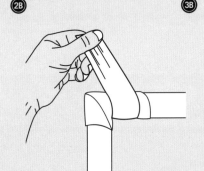

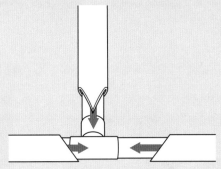

Lag right-angled joints

Lag T-joints

WHAT TO DO

❶ Open pipe lagging along slit and slip onto pipe. Secure with cable ties and duct tape around joints.

❷ Lag right-angled joints

A Cut 45-degree angles with junior hacksaw. You can do this by sight. Since the lagging is soft and joints are taped together, angles can be approximate.

B Push cut edges together and secure with duct tape.

❸ Lag T-joints

A Cut the ends of the lagging for the two 'arms' of the joint with opposite mitres, so that when slotted on to the pipe they leave an arrow shape between them.

B Cut a corresponding arrow shape out of the lagging for the third pipe, which should fit snugly between. Secure with duct tape.

❹ Lag obstructions

To fit around taps, stopcocks and other obstructions, slit along centre of lagging opposite pre-made slit, so lagging forms two flaps to wrap around obstruction. Secure with duct tape.

HOW TO NAIL IT!

- Buy the most expensive lagging you can afford and do not be tempted to use pipe tapes, which will degrade.

- If using tie wraps to secure your lagging, don't tie them so tightly that they press into it.

- You could use a mitre block and saw if you'd like to make really precise angles.

FIX NOISY PIPES

Pipes can make a noise when water flows through them for a number of reasons. The first step is identifying the cause. After that, the remedies are simple.

YOU'LL NEED

SCREWDRIVER

BUFFERS, SUCH AS FOAM INSULATION, RUBBER, KITCHEN SPONGE OFFCUTS OR OLD GARDEN HOSE

SCREWS AND WALL PLUGS, IF NEEDED

TOOL UP PLUMBER'S AUGER

TOOL DOWN WIRE COAT HANGER

GETTING STARTED

First, find the location of the noisy pipes, then follow the checks, below, to help you find the source of the noise.

• To check for loose pipes, turn on cold water and see if the pipe(s) are moving at the site of the noise. The pipe may be moving within its clasp, against a wall, or two pipes may be banging together.

• If there is no movement, turn on hot water only. If knocking happens, it could be steam from water that's too hot running through system.

• If pipe makes noise from hot and cold water, but is securely fixed, the pipe could be too small to cope with water supply, or be compromised (partly blocked) by mineral deposits.

• If you hear a hammering sound when you turn off a running tap, the air chambers in the plumbing system may have become waterlogged.

• If drainpipes make a sucking noise, the overflow vent could be blocked.

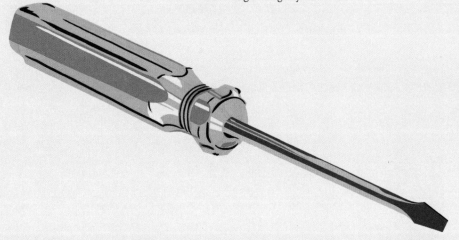

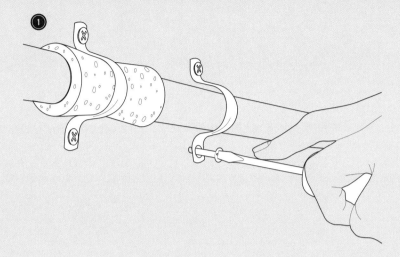

WHAT TO DO

1 Fix loose pipes: if the clasps attaching the pipes to the wall have become loose, fasten screws, or cushion pipe movement by filling clasp space with foam insulation, rubber, sponge or old hose. If two pipes are banging together put insulation between them. You may need to replace screws with longer ones, or replace wall plugs.

2 Fix steam knocking: turn down water heat level on boiler. Also refer to manufacturer's instructions to try reducing water pressure in system.

3 Fix compromised pipes: replace pipe. This is a job best left to a plumber or, for a temporary fix, insulate pipe (see page 190) to dampen noise.

4 Fix hammering water pipes: turn off mains water supply. Turn on the highest tap in your home, or the first in system. Then, turn off the lowest tap, or the last in system. If in doubt turn on all taps. Wait until water has drained from system. Turn off taps and re-open main valve.

5 Unblock drain vent: insert auger or unravelled wire coat hanger through overflow vent to unclog debris.

HOW TO NAIL IT!

- If the noises persist, call out a plumber who should be able to fix the problem easily.

- When tightening pipe fixings, be sure to leave some room for pipes to expand and contract with the temperature. Any cushioning you use should have some give.

DRAUGHTPROOF DOOR

Draughty doors are fine when you want to let in fresh air during the summer, but in colder months you are wasting heat by allowing it to escape through gaps. Simple adjustments can help keep the heat in and save you money.

YOU'LL NEED

BLU-TACK (RE-USABLE TACK)

DAMP CLOTH

STEEL TAPE MEASURE

SELF-ADHESIVE FOAM DRAUGHT-EXCLUDER STRIP, AT SIZE REQUIRED FOR GAPS

SCISSORS

PANEL PINS (OPTIONAL)

GETTING STARTED

Find out how big the gaps in the door frame are by opening the door, pushing blu-tack into the space between the frame and the door at one of the edges, then closing the door. Carefully remove the tack and measure the width it has squished to. Repeat for each frame edge, apart from door stop, in case gaps vary in size. Use these measurements as a guide for the size of foam strip needed.

WHAT TO DO

1 Clean dirt and loose paint from the doorframe with a damp cloth. Leave to dry.

2 Measure foam strip against doorframe and cut to size.

3 Remove backing paper and apply along the top and two sides of doorframe.

4 To hold foam strip in place more securely, use a small panel pin at each end.

HOW TO NAIL IT!

- Add keyhole and letterbox covers to your external doors to stop draughts through these holes, too.

- Screw a draught-excluding brush strip to the bottom edge of external doors.

DRAUGHTPROOF WINDOW

If you have draughty old windows, you may be fighting a losing battle to keep the warm air inside. Of course, curtains are a great draughtproofer but there is more you can do – try fitting foam draught excluders or brush seal.

▶ YOU'LL NEED

BLU-TACK (RE-USABLE TACK)

STEEL TAPE MEASURE

DAMP CLOTH

SELF-ADHESIVE FOAM DRAUGHT-EXCLUDER STRIP, AT SIZE REQUIRED FOR GAPS

SCISSORS

FOR SASH WINDOWS:

STEEL TAPE MEASURE

BRUSH SEAL, TO FIT UPPER AND LOWER SLIDING EDGES

⚠ **JUNIOR HACKSAW**

WORKBENCH OR OTHER SUITABLE CUTTING SURFACE (SEE PAGE 22)

MASKING TAPE, IF NEEDED

HAMMER

PANEL PINS

GETTING STARTED

See instructions for *Draughtproof Door* (opposite) to measure gaps in frame edges using reusable tack.

WHAT TO DO

Casement windows

Fit foam draught-excluders to all edges of window frame following instructions for *Draughtproof Door* (opposite).

Sash windows

❶ Fit foam draught-excluders to the top and bottom (non-sliding) edges of window frame (see opposite).

❷ Measure length of each sash and cut brush seal at a 90-degree angle with hacksaw, to fit.

❸ Position brush seal on inside frame alongside length of lower sash, holding it in place with masking tape, if necessary. Hammer panel pins through predrilled holes to secure seal to frame. Repeat for other side of lower sash.

❹ Position brush seal on outside frame alongside length of upper sash, holding it in place with masking tape, if necessary. Hammer panel pins through predrilled holes to secure seal to frame. Repeat for other side of upper sash.

HOW TO NAIL IT!

- You could also fit a swing bar lock on casement window to keep window and frames securely pressed together. See *Fit Window Locks* (page 208).

BOARD LOFT

To use your loft for storage you'll need to board over the joists: do not place anything between the joists or you may find it falling through. If you have insulated the loft (see page 198), you'll need to make sure the boards don't compress the insulation too much or they will affect its efficiency.

(see page 198)

YOU'LL NEED

MASK, PROTECTIVE GLOVES AND CLOTHING

KNEE PADS (OPTIONAL)

CRAWL BOARD, BIG ENOUGH TO SPAN FOUR JOISTS

TIMBER AND LONG SCREWS FOR RAISING JOIST HEIGHT, IF NEEDED

STEEL TAPE MEASURE

18MM CHIPBOARD PANELS

TOOL UP JIGSAW OR CIRCULAR SAW
TOOL DOWN HANDSAW

WORKBENCH OR OTHER SUITABLE CUTTING SURFACE (SEE PAGE 22)

⚠ POWER DRILL, WITH WOOD BITS

LONG SCREWS

SCREWDRIVER

LOFT CAPS, IF NEEDED

⚠ CHISEL AND MALLET, IF NEEDED

PENCIL

GETTING STARTED

Note that boarded loft floors are often only strong enough for storage – not, generally, for habitation. Be aware, too, that joists were only designed to hold up the ceiling below and may not be strong enough to hold lots of heavy storage. Once you have fitted boards, be sensitive to how much weight they can bear.

To board a loft floor for anything more than light storage, contact a structural engineer.

Make sure you buy loft boards that actually fit through your loft hatch.

You can't fix panels to joists if there are any wires or insulation across them. If this is the case, attach pieces of 75mm x 25mm timber across the joists at 90 degrees, so you are raising the joist height by 25mm. Raising joists stops insulation from being compressed and aids airflow.

⚠ STAY SAFE!

• Wear protective clothing, gloves and a face mask, particularly if working near fibreglass insulation.

• Stand or kneel on crawl board while doing any work in loft, to avoid slipping between joists and making a hole in your ceiling. Knee pads will make the job more comfortable.

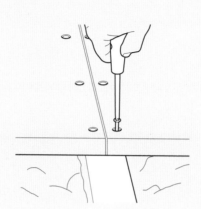

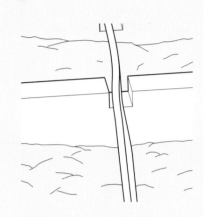

WHAT TO DO

❶ Measure area of boards needed by multiplying width by length of area to be covered. Add a little extra for wastage.

❷ Lay first row of boards out, end to end, at right-angles across joists. Make sure each is across at least three joists. Cut with handsaw, jigsaw or circular saw to ensure ends reach centre of joist.

❸ Butt second board up to first. Using wood bit, drill pilot hole through boards and into joists to depth of screw. If you don't want your screws to stand proud, drill countersink holes to sink them lower (see page 18). Secure boards to joist with screws.

❹ Work with one row of boards at a time and for subsequent rows, cut boards as needed so joins are staggered and don't line up.

❺ At light fittings, cut holes in board to enable access. Use loft caps to ensure halogen spotlights are kept away from insulation. See *Insulate Loft* (page 198).

❻ If wires have to run below the boards, you can chisel a notch in the joist for them to run through without being squashed. Mark positions on boards in pencil for future reference.

HOW TO NAIL IT!

• You can buy modern composite loft floorboards that come with insulating material bonded to them. It's worth doing some research to check if these may be suitable for your loft.

• Mark the top of board in pencil if there is anything you are covering over, so that you know which board to lift if you need it in the future.

INSULATE LOFT

95

Insulating the loft stops the heat that rises escaping from your house. You can insulate between, or on, rafters directly under your roof. Alternatively, you can insulate between, or on, joists directly above the ceiling of your top floor. If you insulate the rafters, you'll create a warm loft. If you insulate the loft floor, you'll create a cold loft but keep the heat in the house below.

▶ YOU'LL NEED

FOR FLOOR:
STEEL TAPE MEASURE
⚠ INSULATION, TO COVER FLOOR SPACE, PLUS EXTRA
LOFT CAPS, IF NEEDED
FACE MASK, PROTECTIVE GLOVES AND CLOTHING
KNEE PADS (OPTIONAL)
LAMP OR BATTERY-POWERED TORCHES, IF NEEDED
⚠ CHISEL OR CROW BAR
CRAWL BOARD, BIG ENOUGH TO SPAN FOUR JOISTS
2 PIECES OF SCRAP WOOD
CRAFT KNIFE
MATERIAL TO INSULATE TANKS, PIPES AND LOFT HATCH, IF NECESSARY
FOR RAFTERS:
⚠ INSULATION, TO COVER SPACE, PLUS EXTRA (SEE *GETTING STARTED*)
STAPLE GUN
JOINTING TAPE, IF USING SOFT INSULATION
TO EXTEND RAFTER DEPTH:
BATTENS, AS REQUIRED FOR HEIGHT NEEDED
⚠ POWER DRILL, WITH WOOD BITS
LONG SCREWS

⚠ STAY SAFE!

• Wear protective clothing, gloves and a face mask, particularly if working with fibreglass insulation.

• Laying insulation over electrical cables can be dangerous. Carefully lift them up to lie above the insulation, or tie them to the top of your joists.

• Keep insulation clear of recessed lights. Protect any halogen or spot light fittings with loft caps or loft covers – cylinder-shaped fire protectors (**A**). Insulation should be at least 75mm away from recessed light fittings and hot flues.

• If in any doubt about dealing with electrical wires and insulation, consult a qualified electrician.

• Stand or kneel on crawl board while doing any work in loft, to avoid slipping between joists and making a hole in your ceiling. Knee pads will make the job more comfortable.

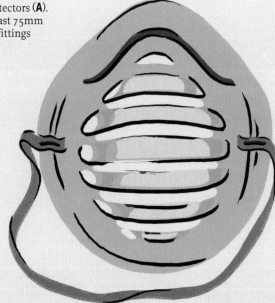

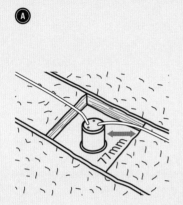

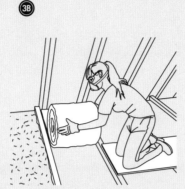

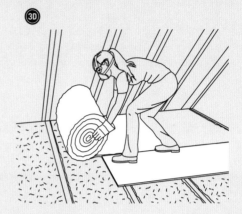

GETTING STARTED

First, choose the insulation material. For floors, the material should be a minimum of 270mm deep, according to UK government regulations. This can be made up from different layers. For roof insulation, it should be 200mm deep. Remember that cheap insulation is often less dense and less effective.

Blanket insulation: made from glass mineral wool. A skin irritant, so you must wear gloves, protective clothing and a face mask when installing it. It comes ready perforated to roll out in your joist spaces. It is by far the cheapest insulation.

Encapsulated insulation: this is glass mineral wool insulation 'encapsulated' in a thin plastic and metallic film so it's easier to handle – although protective gloves and clothing should still be worn.

Slab insulation: made from rock mineral wool, the slabs are semi-rigid so can easily be slotted into position between the rafters, without further fixing.

Recycled plastic bottle insulation: made from 85 per cent recycled plastic bottles. Non-irritant so can be laid without protective clothing. More expensive but a good way to reuse resources.

Sheep's wool insulation: made from 75-85 per cent wool, it's non-irritant and easy to install. It is the most expensive type but is an organic and renewable resource and, arguably, the most effective.

Measure space between joists. In older houses joists are usually spaced at 400mm; in modern houses, at 600mm.

To reach the ideal depth of 270mm you may have to insulate between joists, firstly at a depth of 100mm and then with a second, separate layer of 170mm. If space between joists is full, second layer will be laid over top of joists, at right angles to them. Check depth of joists before ordering insulation and consider whether you are planning to board your loft.

Calculate how many rolls of insulation you'll need for the first layer by multiplying the width of the loft by its length, subtracting 10 per cent (for space taken up by joists) and dividing by the area each roll provides. Repeat for top-up layer without taking away 10 per cent, as this layer sits on top of and covers joists.

For insulation between rafters, measure the area of roof and subtract 10 per cent for rafters.

Before you insulate, use the opportunity to have a good look at your loft space and check for any signs of damp or condensation. If you find any, contact a local roofer for professional advice.

WHAT TO DO

1 Clear your loft of any storage. Make sure you have enough light. Rig up a lamp or get good battery-powered torches where there is no permanent loft light.

2 Carry as much insulation as you can into loft before starting, to minimise trips up and down ladder.

3 Insulate loft floor

A Remove any loft boards to reveal joists, by prising up with chisel or crow bar. Place crawling board across timber near the eaves to work from. Move board across floor to support you as you go.

B Check manufacturer's instructions for right-side up. Starting at eaves, and leaving a 50mm gap for ventilation, unroll insulation along gap. It will be wider than gaps, so press down for snug fit. Avoid leaving gaps – the heat will find them.

C When length filled, compress insulation between pieces of scrap wood, then cut with knife. Cut insulation at cross beams, then unroll from opposite eaves towards beam.

D Roll out second, top-up layer at right angles to first layer until floor covered. Insulate cold water tank, if present (see page 188).

E Insulate exposed pipes (see page 190).

INSULATE LOFT

⑤

F Insulate the loft hatch using a special loft-hatch insulator (available from large hardware stores). Alternatively, fill a large bag with insulating material and staple it down, or glue a block of slab insulation in place.

❹ Insulate between rafters using slabs

A Check rafters will allow for 200mm insulation depth. Extend rafter depth, if necessary, by screwing on battens.

B Starting from top and working down, one rafter at a time, fit slabs between rafters. If they need cutting down, leave slightly oversize so they'll fit by friction. Leave at least 50mm between end of slab and loft floor for ventilation.

⑤ Insulate rafters using soft insulation

This is an alternative to insulating between rafters. Working horizontally, staple insulation to rafters, butting sheets together. Secure with jointing tape.

HOW TO NAIL IT!

• UK government regulations recommend that loft floor insulation be a minimum of 270mm thick. If you have old insulation that has compressed to less than this, top it up with other material to the minimum thickness. Any pre-existing insulation of less than 100mm is worth getting rid of so you can start again.

• Do not insulate directly underneath a water tank; it needs some heat to circulate underneath it to prevent freezing.

• In the UK, if you discover bats living in your loft, contact the Bat Conservation Trust before doing any loft work, as they and their roosts are protected by law.

HOME SAFETY
AND
SECURITY

EVERYTHING
YOU NEED
TO GET THE
JOB DONE

INSTALL FIRE ALARMS

Having working alarms in your home literally can be a lifesaver: you are twice as likely to die in a house fire if you have none. Fumes from a smouldering fire can build up overnight as you sleep, so a smoke alarm will be your first and only warning.

▶ YOU'LL NEED

- SMOKE, HEAT OR CARBON-MONOXIDE ALARMS, WITH FIXINGS
- MULTI-PURPOSE DETECTOR, IF NEEDED
- BATTERIES, IF NEEDED
- BRADAWL OR NAIL
- ⚠ POWER DRILL, WITH BITS NEEDED FOR WALL TYPE OR CEILING
- SUITABLE WALL PLUGS FOR WALL TYPE OR CEILING, IF NEEDED
- SCREWDRIVER

GETTING STARTED

Work out which type of alarms you need. Choose one that has the British Standard Kitemark.

Ionisation smoke alarm: the cheapest to buy. This will go off when it senses small smoke particles from flaming fires, such as from a chip pan or burning food.

Optical/photoelectric/'toast-proof' smoke alarms: more expensive to buy, but more sensitive to smoke from slow-burning fires, such as from sofas or wiring. Less sensitive to flaming fires.

Combined smoke alarm: sensitive to both types of fire.

Heat sensor: sensitive to temperatures of over 55°C and can work in humid rooms, so the only fire alarm suitable for kitchens and bathrooms.

Carbon-monoxide alarm: essential if you have any appliance that uses gas, oil, wood or coal. Even gas heaters and well-controlled open fires or log burners can be killers: if they aren't burning efficiently or the room isn't well ventilated, they can produce the lethal gas, carbon monoxide, which is undetectable until it's too late. You can buy combined smoke and carbon-monoxide alarms.

Work out where to position your alarms. Because steam can set off smoke alarms, there's no point in fitting them in the kitchen or bathroom. In those rooms, you should fit heat sensors that are activated by an increase in heat rather than smoke.

See *Back to Basics* (pages 18-21) for advice on choosing screws, wall plugs and drill bits to suit your wall, and for tips on drilling.

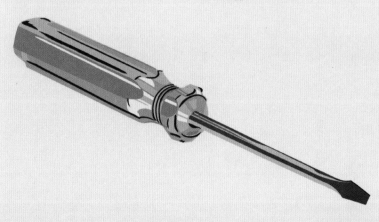

WHERE TO POSITION ALARMS

(A) Single-storey homes: in hallway, between sleeping and living areas. Ideally place on ceiling, at least 300mm away from wall or light fitting. On walls, place 150-300mm lower than ceiling height. Place heat sensors in kitchen and bathroom, if necessary.

(B) Large or multi-level homes: as above, plus at bottom of staircase and on each staircase landing. Also consider buying interconnected alarms so that smoke or heat detected on one level can trigger alarms all over the home.

(C) Homes with real fires or any gas supply: as above, with additional carbon-monoxide alarm. If you are using a combination smoke alarm, fit as smoke alarm. Otherwise, fit in same room as appliance or somewhere central (hallway, landing), at head height, at least one metre from boiler, fire, cooker or heater and not directly above anything that gives off steam.

WHAT TO DO

1 Locate best position for alarms (see *Getting Started*). Use a detector to note positions of hidden pipes and cables and avoid fixing there. Unless wall is masonry, locate studs using a detector and fix to these, if possible. If fixing to a ceiling, you'll most likely need plasterboard fixings, unless alarm comes with sticky pads. Ensure these are strong enough.

2 Remove cover of alarm and fit with batteries, if needed, following manufacturer's instructions.

3 Hold back plate to wall or ceiling and mark fixing points with bradawl or nail through holes. Drill holes to depth of wall plugs, if using, and push in. If fixing to studs, drill pilot holes.

4 Screw alarm in position. Replace cover and test.

HOW TO NAIL IT!

- Check your alarm batteries weekly and replace any dead batteries immediately (usually after 12 months). Recycle used batteries rather than throwing them away.

- Get a registered gas engineer to service all your gas appliances and flue once a year to check for carbon monoxide. In the UK, landlords have a duty to supply their tenants with an annual gas check certificate.

- If you are worried about losing battery power, you can find alarms that wire up to the mains (backed up by batteries) or that wire to light sockets, so they recharge every time the light is switched on.

FIT SPY HOLE

97

A spy hole is a simple device to fit and gives an added level of security by allowing you to see who is at the door before you decide whether to open it.

YOU'LL NEED

STEEL TAPE MEASURE
SPY HOLE, WITH FIXINGS
PENCIL, BRADAWL OR NAIL
⚠ POWER DRILL, WITH WOOD BITS
SCREWDRIVER

GETTING STARTED

Measure the thickness of your front door and buy a spy hole to fit – they come in varying sizes.

Choose a height for the spy hole that most members of the household will be able to look through comfortably.

WHAT TO DO

1 Measure the width of the door and find the midpoint, at chosen height. Mark position with pencil, bradawl or nail.

2 Drill hole in door. Most spy holes are 10mm wide, so use 10mm drill bit. Drill until bit almost emerges through door, then drill back in from the other side.

3 Push outside half of spy hole into door.

4 Screw in inside half on other side of door. Secure pieces together by tightening by hand and finishing with screwdriver.

HOW TO NAIL IT!

- Use a small drill bit to create a small pilot hole before you drill the main hole. This will help you to keep straight and give you confidence.

- To replace an old or damaged spy hole, use a screwdriver to remove it. Clean any dirt and debris from hole before fitting new spy hole, as above.

FIT DOOR CHAIN

Even if you have a spy hole in your front door, you should consider fitting a door chain as an extra level of security. If you have a UPVC front door, keep well clear of glass borders and use self-drilling screws which screw directly into the aluminium that's inside the door, and require no predrilling.

▶ YOU'LL NEED

SECURITY CHAIN, WITH FIXINGS
PENCIL, BRADAWL OR NAIL
SPIRIT LEVEL
⚠ **POWER DRILL, WITH WOOD BITS**
SCREWDRIVER
⚠ **CHISEL AND MALLET, IF NEEDED**

GETTING STARTED

Choose height for your chain and mark fixing holes for chain slider on inside of your front door with pencil, bradawl or nail. The usual position would be near the latch for ease of access. Check holes are level using spirit level.

WHAT TO DO

1 Drill pilot holes at marks using wood drill bit smaller than fixing screws. Screw on chain slider.

2 Mark position of chain holder on doorframe. This should align with chain slider.

3 Mark fixing holes for chain holder. Drill pilot holes and screw chain holder in place.

4 Test chain.

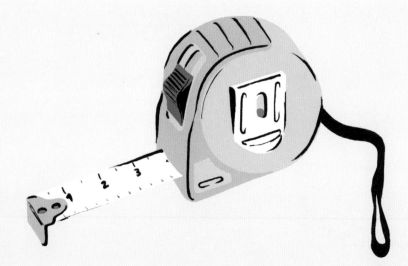

HOW TO NAIL IT!

• For a smart finish, recess the chain holder into the door frame. Before fixing it in place, hold chain holder in position and draw round it. Use a chisel and mallet to carve the recess out. Stand in a steady position when working with a chisel and watch your fingers: chisels can be extremely sharp.

FIT FRONT DOOR LOCKS

99

The more locks on your front door and the more levers, pins or discs a lock has, the more secure your home will be. That said, you don't need to go wild; a mortise deadlock and a night latch (cylinder rim lock) are usually fine. If you only want one lock on your door, choose something really secure that you can deadlock.

▶ YOU'LL NEED

STEEL TAPE MEASURE

MORTISE DEADLOCK OR NIGHT LATCH (CYLINDER RIM LOCK) KIT, WITH FIXINGS

PENCIL AND RULER

⚠ POWER DRILL, WITH WOOD AND SCREWDRIVER BITS, PLUS WIDE WOODCUTTING BIT FOR CYLINDER LOCK

MASKING TAPE

DOOR WEDGE

⚠ WIDE AND NARROW CHISELS

MALLET

⚠ PADSAW, FOR SHAPING MORTISE DEADLOCK KEY HOLE

BRADAWL OR NAIL

SCREWDRIVER

⚠ JUNIOR HACKSAW, IF NEEDED

WORKBENCH OR OTHER SUITABLE CUTTING SURFACE, IF NEEDED (SEE PAGE 22)

GETTING STARTED

Measure your door before you buy locks, to ensure they will fit. Household insurance stipulates that your door locks conform to British Standard (look for the kitemark).

Choose positions for your locks:

Mortise deadlock: about halfway up the door where – importantly – the timber is solid. If your door is panelled, avoid the joint of the horizontal rail or you could weaken the door's structure.

Night latch: also known as cylinder rim lock. Position one-third of way down door from the top.

Read manufacturer's instructions before starting.

WHAT TO DO

Fit mortise deadlock

❶ Open front door and mark midpoint in pencil on side edge of door at required height.

❷ Hold lock edge (deep recessed part) up to side edge of door and mark top and bottom edges. Draw vertical midpoint line with pencil and ruler.

❸ Select drill bit 2mm wider than lock body. Mark depth of lock on drill bit with masking tape.

❹ Hold door steady with door wedge. Drill out lock recess by making series of overlapping holes down along vertical pencil line.

❺ Use chisel and mallet to open up row of circular holes into rectangular shape to fit lock.

❻ Insert lock and draw around faceplate position with pencil.

❼ Using chisel and mallet, cut out recess for faceplate within markings. Start by making a series of cuts on pencil outline, then chisel out – a little at a time. Keep testing until you have a good fit.

❽ Hold lock body against face of door and mark location of keyhole. Repeat on other side of door.

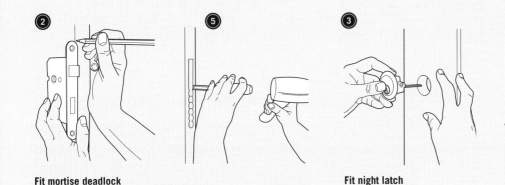

Fit mortise deadlock

Fit night latch

⑨ Cut out keyhole each side. Shape using wood drill bit slightly larger than keyhole. Use padsaw for lower part. Cut out bottom with narrow chisel.

⑩ Push in lock and test keys.

⑪ Hold faceplate in position, mark fixing positions with bradawl or nail and screw into place, drilling pilot holes first, if necessary.

⑫ Screw on keyhole covers, drilling pilot holes first, if necessary.

⑬ With bolt out and held against doorframe, mark strike plate position and depth of bolt box. Use marks to position strike plate on inside surface of doorframe. Use template if provided.

⑭ Use chisel and mallet to cut out wood for the hole receiving the bolt. Chisel a little at a time and keep testing for fit.

⑮ Check door closes properly. Chisel out recess for striking plate as above, testing until you have a good fit. Screw plate into place and test.

Fit night latch

❶ Mark position of hole for lock cylinder, at comfortable height, 60mm in from edge of door.

❷ Check instructions for diameter of hole you will need to drill, before selecting bit – usually 32mm. Drill hole. When drill bit begins to emerge from other side of door, change sides and complete hole from the other side.

❸ Fit cylinder parts together and insert into hole from outside. The cylinder should have enough room to turn.

❹ Secure mounting plate in position on inside of door using connecting screws so both plate and keyhole remain in correct upright position.

❺ Place lock case in position on mounting plate. The connecting bar may need shortening. If so, do this with junior hacksaw. If door edge needs cutting to fit lip of lock case, use chisel and mallet. Keep testing for fit as you work.

❻ Mark fixing positions and drill pilot holes, if necessary. Fasten lock case to door with screws.

❼ Line up striking plate with bolt and mark its position on door frame with pencil. Use chisel to create recess for striking plate, if required.

❽ Mark fixing positions with bradawl or nail and screw in securely.

HOW TO NAIL IT!

- For added security you can fit a bolt 150mm lower than the top door hinge and 150mm higher than the bottom hinge.

- Some locks come with templates for fitting. Using these will save any measurement errors!

FIT WINDOW LOCKS

100

Block a potentially easy access point for burglars by fitting window locks. Doing this may also mean you're able to reduce your home insurance quote. Different window types require different locks. Make sure you keep the keys in the same room and know where they are in case of emergencies.

YOU'LL NEED

- **SWING BAR LOCK AND FIXINGS, FOR CASEMENT WINDOW, OR CLAMP LOCK AND FIXINGS, FOR SASH WINDOW**
- **STEEL TAPE MEASURE**
- **PENCIL, BRADAWL OR NAIL**
- **SCREWDRIVER**
- ⚠ **POWER DRILL, WITH WOOD BITS, IF NEEDED**

GETTING STARTED

Choose the lock suitable for your windows.

There are a number of options for casement windows. Most locks are made up of two parts that fix to both frame and window and lock together. You can also buy locking handles, mortise locks and stay locks that can lock a window while slightly open, allowing for ventilation.

For sash windows, you can choose from various types of surface-fitted locks where a clasp is fixed to the upper sash and a receiver to the lower sash. Alternatively, you can fit a dual screw bolt that bolts through both sashes. Sash stops are easy to fit, but permanently limit the amount you can open the window. They screw into the upper sash so that the lower sash can only be opened as far as the stop.

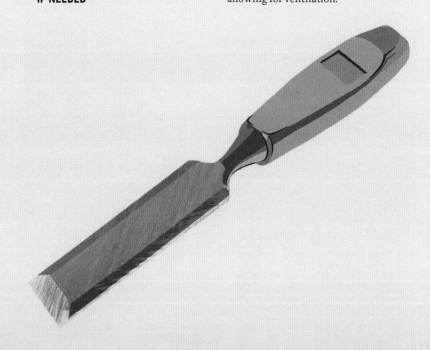

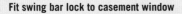

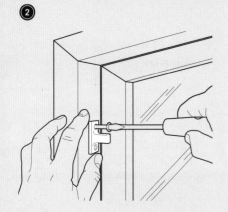

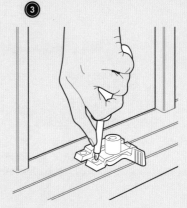

Fit swing bar lock to casement window

Fit clamp bar lock to sash windows

Fit swing bar lock to casement window

1. Open window and mark position of locking plate 1mm from edge of fixed frame.

2. Mark fixing holes with bradawl or nail. Screw on locking plate.

3. Close window, find correct position of lock body against plate and mark position of fixing holes with bradawl or nail.

4. Loosely fix lock body in position with one screw.

5. Check swing bar fits over plate and tweak if necessary.

6. Screw on lock body securely.

7. Close window, close lock and fasten with supplied key.

Fit clamp bar lock to sash windows

1. With sash windows in closed position, measure to find the centre of the rail furthest from you – this is the upper sash. Mark in pencil.

2. Place lock in position, centred over pencil mark, and mark fixing holes with bradawl or nail. Screw lock on.

3. Place the receiver part of the lock onto rail of sash closest to you and align with lock. Mark screw holes with bradawl or nail.

4. Loosely fix receiver part into position with one screw.

5. Check lock works properly and adjust if necessary.

6. Screw securely into place.

HOW TO NAIL IT!

- Even if your windows are locked, intruders could be able to smash glass to get into your home. Laminated glass and double glazing help security, but you should still check the putty and glazing beads aren't loose so the pane could be easily removed.

- UPVC windows usually come fitted with quality locks, but if not, contact the supplier to get them fitted, rather than attempting the job yourself.

- If you find screwing directly into the bradawl holes difficult, drill small pilot holes first.

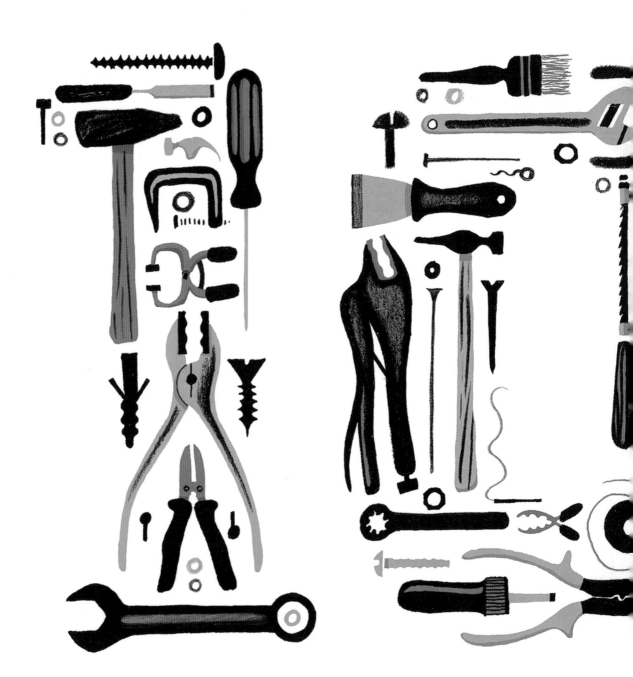

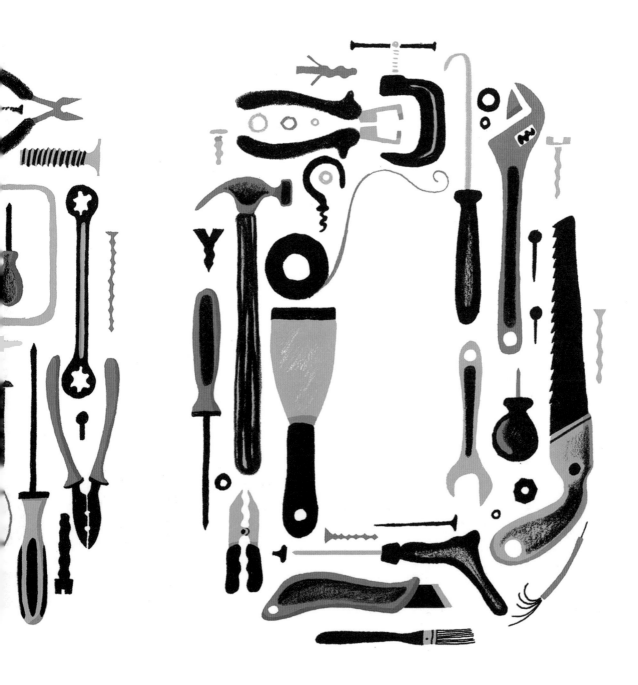

INDEX

FIND EVERYTHING YOU NEED HERE

GOOD LUCK

Author's acknowledgments

Thank you to all those at Quadrille Publishing and beyond; to those who helped research and shape the book and the wonderful designers and illustrators that have achieved the impossible – making a DIY book look utterly gorgeous!

I consider myself incredibly lucky. I'm surrounded by truly great people who, because they do the brilliant jobs they do, have given me the inspiration and the time to write this book.

Thank you to the wonderful team at Rise Hall. I can't tell you the difference you have made. Thank you to the brilliant team at Tepilo, for turning my online estate agency dream into a reality. Thank you to the fabulous MySingleFriend.com team; you are a ray of sunshine in a dark and lonely world! Thank you to Red House TV and Channel 4; you make my job a total joy. Thank you to Paul Stevens, my book agent, and Laura Hill, my agent, for the constant encouragement.

Last, but by no means least, thank you, Graham, for your sound judgment and unfaltering support.